The idea behind this volume—slice Mark into sections and introduce each via extracanonical Jewish materials—is splendid. Happily, so too is the execution. *Reading Mark in Context* will expand students' horizons and motivate them to go looking for more of the same.

DALE C. ALLISON JR., Princeton Theological Seminary

This work is brilliantly designed to provide a maximum benefit in a relatively concise space, with contributors highlighting various sample passages relevant to Mark's Gospel. Readers familiar with the New Testament are far more likely to remember elements of the New Testament's ancient milieu when they are pegged to New Testament material. This offers a brilliant introduction of the relevance of early Jewish context for readers of the New Testament, as well as windows into Mark.

CRAIG S. KEENER, F. M. and Ada Thompson Professor of Biblical Studies, Asbury Theological Seminary

Reading Mark in Context is consistently informative, respectful towards the primary texts, and eminently readable, written by scholars who have published on the Gospel of Mark, and thus a helpful guide for students and pastors who seek a better understanding of the most concise of the canonical Gospels.

ECKHARD J. SCHNABEL, Mary F. Rockefeller Distinguished Professor of New Testament, Gordon Conwell Theological Seminary

How does one best learn relevant historical background material to the Gospels? Traditionally, one reads a brief introduction to overall trends and then looks for where they might illuminate individual passages. More interesting, if done well, is to begin with the biblical text and then read portions of the Apocrypha, Pseudepigrapha, Dead Sea Scrolls, Josephus, or even the oldest of the rabbinic literature that allows close comparisons and contrasts with the biblical subject matter. This anthology takes the latter approach, makes excellent and relevant selections from the noncanonical material, and uses a broad range of good scholars who briefly make the relevant comparisons with selections from most all the major passages in the Gospel of Mark. The task *is* done well so that this volume has excellent textbook potential as well as satisfying the curiosity of many other readers.

CRAIG L. BLOMBERG, distinguished professor of New Testament, Denver Seminary

While the Judaic context of the Gospel of Mark has given rise to interminable speculations regarding sources, the fruitful task of comparative analysis is a rarity in scholarly discourse. Now, in *Reading Mark in Context* the novice reader is presented with the fruit of a comparative inquiry at its finest. The Jewish writings function like a light upon the narrative, making visible to the attentive reader the profundity of the Markan account of Jesus of Nazareth and illustrating the riches therein with contextual clarity. This is a unique and valuable collection that balances competent usage of the Jewish texts with judicious insights into the Gospel of Mark.

DANIEL M. GURTNER, Ernest and Mildred Hogan
Professor of New Testament Interpretation, The
Southern Baptist Theological Seminary

READING
MARK
IN CONTEXT

READING
MARK
IN CONTEXT

JESUS AND SECOND TEMPLE JUDAISM

BEN C. BLACKWELL, JOHN K. GOODRICH
& JASON MASTON, EDITORS

To our parents:
Mack and Brenda Blackwell,
John and Julie Goodrich,
and Mark and Debbie Maston

This book is more than Corban (Mark 7:11).
It is a token of our heartfelt appreciation
for your endless love and support.

Contents

Foreword

I n recent years I have often been asked, "How do we find out more about the first-century Jewish world?"

This question often comes after I have given a lecture or seminar paper, whether to a general audience or to scholars from other fields (say, systematic or philosophical theology). In such contexts, I frequently stress that, though the approaches taken by the church fathers in the fourth and fifth centuries and by the Reformers in the sixteenth and seventeenth centuries retain great importance, what really matters for understanding the New Testament is to learn to live within the world of Jesus and his first followers. Again and again people ask me, sometimes in surprise, how they might learn more, and—sometimes in alarm!—what might change if they did.

Examples of the problem are easy to find. Many Christians still suppose that when Jesus spoke about "the kingdom of God" he was talking about the ultimate postmortem destination of believers ("heaven," in popular imagination). A quick glance at the Psalms, Isaiah, or Daniel should have put paid to that, but looking at how the idea of God's kingdom was deployed in the first century should make it even clearer. Likewise I have heard Christian teachers explaining that "son of man" refers to Jesus's "humanity," or perhaps his "humility," as though we could understand the use of that phrase in the first century without reference to the Jewish literature in which the phrase is used, or, indeed, to the book of Daniel where it has a much richer meaning that people often suppose.

But it won't do simply to cite a few phrases, important though they are. What matters is *to learn to think like a first-century Jew*. We recognise, of course, that first-century Jews were at least as diverse as twenty-first century Americans, but there are several broad features of the culture to which we must pay attention. I have often said, when people ask me the usual question, that one excellent way is simply to read the works of Josephus as if they were a historical novel. Josephus has many faults, but *he was there* and knew personally most of the key players in the first-century Jerusalem world. But then, once you've read Josephus, you probably want to get hold of the Dead Sea Scrolls . . . and so on. And, in particular, you should become familiar with the "Apocrypha" and its cousin known as the "Pseudepigrapha."

These books are not enormous. You can get to know them quite well in a few weeks of sustained reading. Some parts are puzzling, even to specialists. But often they are extremely illuminating.

There are still deep prejudices against this proposal. The books in question in the Apocrypha are regarded as "canonical" by Roman Catholics (and other non-Protestant churches), while Protestantism has regarded them, at best, as secondary, not as authoritative. (There are other, darker, prejudices sometimes at work, since the books in question are Jewish, and tragically some Christians have thought it their business to de-Judaize early Christianity and even Jesus himself.) But the point of getting to know these books is not to use them to build up a body of authoritative Christian doctrine but to be sure that the texts we *do* regard as authoritative—the New Testament itself as well, of course, as the Old—are being understood as closely as possible in the way their first authors and readers would have understood them. In a sense, this is simply doing on a larger scale what we're doing every time we open a lexicon to look up a word in the Greek New Testament: we are checking up on what the word, and then the larger unit, would have meant at the time. It won't do simply to say, "Well, the church fathers and Reformers read the Bible too." We today have unprecedentedly good access to the first-century Jewish world, and it is part of Christian obedience to make the fullest use we can of such resources in going ever deeper into the roots of our faith. To put it more sharply: that great scholar John Calvin did his best with the tools available to him to understand the Bible in its original meaning. If he had had today's resources, he would have used them like a shot.

One excellent way of finding our feet in what initially may seem a strange environment is to look at particular New Testament texts in the light of various aspects of the Jewish world of the time. This procedure functions rather like an archaeological dig: the researcher sinks a spade cautiously into one particular spot to see what can be found. A book like this one consists of a sequence of such spot-checks. It can't pretend to do more than that: when you sink your spade into Jesus's controversies and line them up with what we find in Josephus (as is done in ch. 3), you will find vital illumination, but you shouldn't imagine that therefore Josephus has nothing else to say about the rest of Mark's Gospel, or that there aren't other ancient sources that would also illuminate the controversies. The chapters thus form a series of invitations that are both enlightening in themselves and pointers toward further possibilities.

The present volume serves a dual purpose. It introduces the reader to many of the most important Jewish texts of the period, but it does so by following through the sequence of Mark's Gospel, thus providing a kind of running commentary on the whole of this vital and early Christian text. The book will thus be of great value *both* to anyone wanting a text-based introduction to the first-century Jewish world *and* to anyone wanting to think their way through Mark's Gospel in its original setting.

It is encouraging to me (as I now approach retirement!) to see that most of the contributors here are from the younger generation of biblical specialists. These contributions show that the discipline is alive and well and capable of producing real and lasting fruit in the days to come, both in the academy and in the church. We live in exciting times in scholarship and church as well as in the wider world. These explorations will contribute to that ongoing sense of new possibilities in exegesis, theology, and mission.

TOM WRIGHT
Rt Revd Prof N T Wright DD FRSE
Research Professor of New Testament and Early Christianity,
University of St Andrews

Abbreviations

Old Testament, New Testament, Apocrypha

Gen	Genesis		
Exod	Exodus	Hag	Haggai
Lev	Leviticus	Zech	Zechariah
Num	Numbers	Mal	Malachi
Deut	Deuteronomy	Matt	Matthew
Judg	Judges	Rom	Romans
1–2 Sam	1–2 Samuel	1–2 Cor	1–2 Corinthians
1–2 Kgs	1–2 Kings	Gal	Galatians
1–2 Chr	1–2 Chronicles	Eph	Ephesians
Neh	Nehemiah	Col	Colossians
Esth	Esther	1–2 Tim	1–2 Timothy
Ps/Pss	Psalm/Psalms	Heb	Hebrews
Isa	Isaiah	1–2 Pet	1–2 Peter
Jer	Jeremiah	Tob	Tobit
Ezek	Ezekiel	Bar	Baruch
Dan	Daniel	1–2 Macc	1–2 Maccabees
Hos	Hosea	Sir	Sirach/Ecclesiasticus
Mic	Micah		

Dead Sea Scrolls

1QH[a]	Hodayot[a]/Thanksgiving Hymns[a]
1QM	Milḥamah/War Scroll
1QpHab	Pesher Habakkuk
1QS	Serek Hayaḥad/Rule of the Community (also Community Rule)
1QSa/1Q28a	Rule of the Congregation
1QSb/1Q28b	Rule of the Blessings
4Q161	Pesher Isaiah[a]
4Q162	Pesher Isaiah[b]
4Q169	Pesher Nahum
4Q171	Pesher Psalms[a]

4Q174	Florilegium
4Q176	Consolations/Tanḥumim
4Q177	Catena[a]
4Q252	Commentary on Genesis A
4Q262/4QS[h]	Rule of the Community
4Q274	Toḥorot A
4Q282	Unidentified Fragments B
4Q285	Sefer Hamilḥamah
4Q374	Moses Apocryphon A
4Q385	Pseudo-Ezekiel[a]
4Q386	Pseudo-Ezekiel[b]
4Q390	Apocryphon of Jeremiah E
4Q500	Benediction
4Q504	Dibre Hame'orot[a]/Words of the Luminaries[a]
4Q521	Messianic Apocalypse
11Q10	Targum of Job
11Q11	Apocryphal Psalms[a]
11Q13	Melchizedek
11Q19	Temple Scroll[a]
CD	Cairo Genizah copy of the Damascus Document

RABBINIC LITERATURE

b. 'Erub.	Tractate 'Erubin (Babylonian Talmud)
b. Giṭ.	Tractate Giṭṭin (Babylonian Talmud)
b. Ḥag.	Tractate Ḥagigah (Babylonian Talmud)
b. Pesaḥ.	Tractate Pesaḥim (Babylonian Talmud)
b. Sanh.	Tractate Sanhedrin (Babylonian Talmud)
b. Ta'an.	Tractate Ta'anit (Babylonian Talmud)
Deut. Rab.	Deuteronomy Rabbah
Gen. Rab.	Genesis Rabbah
Lam. Rab.	Lamentations Rabbah
Lev. Rab.	Leviticus Rabbah
Midr.	Midrash
m. 'Abot	Mishnah 'Abot
m. 'Arak.	Mishnah 'Arakin
m. Giṭ.	Mishnah Giṭṭin
m. Ḥag.	Mishnah Ḥagigah
m. Ḥul.	Mishnah Ḥullin

m. Kelim	Mishnah Kelim
m. Ketub.	Mishnah Ketubbot
m. 'Ohal.	Mishnah 'Ohalot
m. Roš Haš.	Mishnah Roš Haššanah
m. Soṭah	Mishnah Soṭah
m. Yebam.	Mishnah Yebamot
m. Yoma	Mishnah Yoma
Pesiq. Rab.	Pesiqta Rabbati
Tanḥ.	Tanḥuma
Tg. Isa.	Targum Isaiah
Tg. Ps.	Targum Psalms
Tg. Ps.-J.	Targum Pseudo-Jonathan
Tg. 1 Sam.	Targum 1 Samuel
t. Ber.	Tractate Berakot (Tosefta)
t. Me'il.	Tractate Me'ilah (Tosefta)
t. Menaḥ.	Tractate Menaḥot (Tosefta)
t. Sukkah	Tractate Sukkah (Tosefta)
y. Soṭah	Tractate Soṭah (Jerusalem Talmud)

Other Ancient Texts

1 En.	1 Enoch
2 Bar.	2 Baruch
Ag. Ap.	*Against Apion* (Josephus)
Ann.	*Annales* (Tacitus)
Ant.	*Jewish Antiquities* (Josephus)
Aug.	*Divus Augustus* (Suetonius)
Barn.	Barnabas
Cal.	*Gaius Caligula* (Suetonius)
Decl.	*Declamationes* (Ps.-Quintilian)
Dial.	*Dialogi* (Seneca)
Dig.	*Digesta* (Justinian)
Ep.	*Epistulae* (Horace)
Flacc.	*In Flaccum/Against Flaccus* (Philo)
Gen. an.	*Generation of Animals* (Aristotle)
Hist. Alex.	*History of Alexander* (Curtius Rufus)
Hist. eccl.	*Ecclesiastical History* (Eusebius)
Is. Os.	*Isis and Osiris* (Plutarch)
J.W.	*Jewish War* (Josephus)

Jub.	Jubilees
LAB	Liber antiquitatum biblicarum/Book of Biblical Antiquities (Pseudo-Philo)
Legat.	*Legatio ad Gaium/On the Embassy to Gaius* (Philo)
Life	*The Life* (Josephus)
Metam.	*Metamorphoses* (Ovid)
Migr.	*De migratione Abrahami/On the Migration of Abraham* (Philo)
Mor.	*Moralia* (Plutarch)
Moses	*De vita Mosis/On the Life of Moses* (Philo)
Mut.	*De mutatione nominum/On the Change of Names* (Philo)
Nat.	*Naturalis historia/Natural History* (Pliny the Elder)
Post.	*De posteritate Caini/On the Posterity of Cain* (Philo)
Prob.	*Quod omnis probus liber sit/That Every Good Person Is Free* (Philo)
PSI	Pubblicazioni della Società Italiana (*Papiri greci e latini*)
Pss. Sol.	Psalms of Solomon
P.Flor.	*Papiri greco-egizii, Papiri Fiorentini*
P.Lond.	Papyrus London (*Greek Papyri in the British Museum*)
P.Yadin	Papyrus Yadin (*The Documents from the Bar Kochba Period in the Cave of Letters*)
Sat.	*Satirae/Satires* (Juvenal)
SEG	Supplementum epigraphicum graecum
Spec.	*De specialibus legibus/On the Special Laws* (Philo)
T. 12 Patr.	Testaments of the Twelve Patriarchs
T. Ash.	Testament of Asher
T. Benj.	Testament of Benjamin
T. Dan	Testament of Dan
T. Jud.	Testament of Judah
T. Levi	Testament of Levi
T. Mos.	Testament of Moses
T. Reu.	Testament of Reuben
T. Sol.	Testament of Solomon
T. Zeb.	Testament of Zebulun
Verr.	*In Verrem* (Cicero)

JOURNALS, PERIODICALS, REFERENCE WORKS, SERIES

AB	Anchor Bible
ABRL	Anchor Bible Research Library
ACCS	Ancient Christian Commentary on Scripture

AGJU	Arbeiten zur Geschichte des antiken Judentums und des Urchristentums
AYBC	Anchor Yale Bible Commentary
BBR	*Bulletin of Biblical Research*
BCAW	Blackwell Companions to the Ancient World
BibInt	Biblical Interpretation Series
BSIH	Brill's Studies in Intellectual History
BTB	*Biblical Theology Bulletin*
BZNW	Beihefte zur Zeitschrift für die neutestamentliche Wissenschaft
CBQ	*Catholic Biblical Quarterly*
CCSL	Corpus Christianorum: Series Latina. Turnhout: Brepolis, 1953–
CEJL	Commentaries on Early Jewish Literature
ConBNT	Coniectanea Biblica: New Testament Series
CSCO	Corpus Scriptorum Christianorum Orientalium. Edited by Jean Baptiste Chabot et al. Paris, 1903
DCLS	Deuterocanonical and Cognate Literature Studies
DSD	*Dead Sea Discoveries*
DJD	Discoveries in the Judaean Desert
DJDJ	Discoveries in the Judaean Desert of Jordan
ESV	English Standard Version
ExpTim	*Expository Times*
FRLANT	Forschungen zur Religion und Literatur des Alten und Neuen Testaments
FSBP	Fontes et Subsidia ad Bibliam Pertinentes
GAP	Guides to the Apocrypha and Pseudepigrapha
HTR	*Harvard Theological Review*
HTS	Harvard Theological Studies
IEJ	*Israel Exploration Journal*
JBL	*Journal of Biblical Literature*
JCT	Jewish and Christian Texts
JETS	*Journal of the Evangelical Theological Society*
JGRChJ	*Journal of Greco-Roman Christianity and Judaism*
JJS	*Journal of Jewish Studies*
JSJSup	Supplements to the Journal for the Study of Judaism
JSNT	*Journal for the Study of the New Testament*
JSNTSup	Journal for the Study of the New Testament Supplement Series
JSOTSup	Journal for the Study of the Old Testament Supplement Series
JSP	*Journal for the Study of the Pseudepigrapha*

JTS	*Journal of Theological Studies*
LCL	Loeb Classical Library
LNTS	The Library of New Testament Studies
LSTS	The Library of Second Temple Studies
NAB	New American Bible, revised edition
NASB	New American Standard Bible
NCBC	New Cambridge Bible Commentary
NETS	*A New English Translation of the Septuagint*. Edited by Albert Pietersma and Benjamin G. Wright. New York: Oxford University Press, 2007
NIGTC	New International Greek Testament Commentary
NIV	New International Version
NovT	*Novum Testamentum*
NovTSup	Supplements to Novum Testamentum
NPNF²	*Nicene and Post-Nicene Fathers*, Series 2
NRSV	New Revised Standard Version
NTL	New Testament Library
NTS	*New Testament Studies*
PSI	*Papiri greci e latini*. Edited by G. Vitelli et al. Florence: Pubblicazioni della Società italiana per la ricerca dei papiri greci e latini in Egitto, 1912–2008
PTSDSSP	Princeton Theological Seminary Dead Sea Scrolls Project
ResQ	*Restoration Quarterly*
RevQ	*Revue de Qumran*
SBEC	Studies in the Bible and Early Christianity
SBLMS	Society of Biblical Literature Monograph Series
SJLA	Studies in Judaism in Late Antiquity
SNTSMS	Society for New Testament Studies Monograph Series
STDJ	Studies on the Texts of the Desert of Judah
SVTP	Studia in Veteris Testamenti Pseudepigraphica
TSAJ	Texte und Studien zum antiken Judentum
TUGAL	Texte und Untersuchungen zur Geschichte der altchristlichen Literatur
TynBul	*Tyndale Bulletin*
UPATS	University of Pennsylvania Armenian Texts and Studies
VTSup	Supplements to Vetus Testamentum
WBC	Word Biblical Commentary
WUNT	Wissenschaftliche Untersuchungen zum Neuen Testament

OTHER ABBREVIATIONS

AD	*anno Domini* (in the year of our Lord)
BC	before Christ
ca.	circa (approximately)
NT	New Testament
LXX	Septuagint
OT	Old Testament

Introduction

—∞∞∞—

Ben C. Blackwell, John K. Goodrich, and Jason Maston

The text lives only by coming into contact with another text (with context). Only at the point of this contact between texts does a light flash, illuminating both the posterior and anterior, joining a given text to a dialogue.

M. M. Bakhtin

The Gospel of Mark is widely considered the earliest and most influential narrative of the ministry and passion of Jesus Christ. Although undervalued for centuries because of its brevity and shortage of explicit teaching material, Mark's Gospel is now celebrated as a cleverly crafted ancient biography, emphasizing action, irony, and intrigue over more direct and discursive modes of theologizing. Indeed, what it lacks in "red letters" it more than makes up for in literary artistry. Mark stands out among the New Testament books for its compelling characters, fast-paced storytelling, and dramatic plot twists[1]—all of which the evangelist skillfully leverages to persuade his readers to become disciples of Jesus Christ. As famed commentator Henry Swete lauded long ago, "The briefest of the Gospels is in some respects the fullest and the most exacting; the simplest of the books of the New Testament brings us nearest to the feet of the Master."[2]

Writing sometime in the 60s or 70s AD, Mark[3] presents Jesus as the Son of God commissioned to announce and inaugurate the good news of God's approaching and long-awaited eschatological kingdom. The first-century

---

1. See, e.g., Kelly R. Iverson and Christopher W. Skinner, eds., *Mark as Story: Retrospect and Prospect* (Atlanta: Society of Biblical Literature, 2011); Matthew Ryan Hauge and Christopher W. Skinner, eds., *Character Studies and the Gospel of Mark*, LNTS 483 (London: T&T Clark, 2014).

2. Henry Barclay Swete, *The Gospel according to St. Mark: The Greek Text with Introduction Notes and Indices* (London: MacMillan, 1898), vi.

3. The authorship, date, and setting of Mark's Gospel remain disputed. For a recent survey of scholarly views, see Darrell L. Bock, *Mark*, NCBC (Cambridge: Cambridge University Press, 2015), 1–10.

people of Israel remain in a condition of exile under the rule of imperial and demonic powers. Thus, over the course of its sixteen chapters, the Gospel reveals Jesus to be Israel's promised redeemer and **Messiah**-king (Christ), even as his identity and authority remain contested by many of his fellow countrymen—not least the nation's most learned teachers and priestly leaders.

Jesus's mission, though, is neither to remove from office Israel's religious elite nor to incite rebellion against the Roman Empire. Rather, Jesus concerns himself almost entirely with teaching, healing, and recruiting throngs of faithful adherents who are invited to participate in an altogether different world order—God's in-breaking reign. From the villages of rural Galilee to the capital in Jerusalem, Jesus calls upon his disciples to pursue service over power, self-denial over self-gratification—an ethic Jesus himself embodies when he is ultimately arrested and tried by the Jewish leadership and subsequently sentenced and crucified by imperial authorities.

The death of Jesus, however, neither tarnishes his messianic status nor suspends God's impending rule. The Gospel climaxes, and Jesus's identity is authenticated, when three of his female followers journey to his tomb, only to find it inexplicably empty. Rather than the body of their teacher, they encounter a mysterious young man clothed in white who explains that Jesus, though crucified, is now risen—an announcement that leaves the women (and the reader) confounded as they contemplate the implications of this good news for their lives and beyond.

The pastoral objective of the Gospel is easily missed even by those familiar with the story of Jesus. Mark's narrative, moving as rapidly as it does, aims to stir the reader to ponder his or her existence in the light of Jesus's life, death, and resurrection. As Rhoads, Dewey, and Michie remark, "The story seeks to shatter the readers' way of seeing the world and invites them to embrace another."[4]

Not all readings of Mark, however, are equally illuminating or transformative. The Second Gospel, like the rest of the Bible, was written at a time and in a culture quite different from our own. Accordingly, reading the Gospels *wisely*, as most second-year biblical-studies students will know, requires careful consideration of a passage's historical-cultural context.[5] The study of Mark's Gospel is no different. And although it is true that some

---

4. David Rhoads, Joanna Dewey, and Donald Michie, *Mark as Story: An Introduction to the Narrative of a Gospel*, 2nd ed. (Minneapolis: Fortress, 1999), 1.

5. See Jonathan T. Pennington, *Reading the Gospels Wisely: A Narrative and Theological Introduction* (Grand Rapids: Baker Academic, 2012), 111–12.

contextual awareness is better than none, it is also true that failure to immerse oneself within the religious environment of the New Testament world will likely result in not only unconscious imposition of alien meaning onto the biblical text but also a poorer understanding of the person and work of Jesus Christ.

The eighteenth- and nineteenth-century First Quest for the historical Jesus is a case in point. Contributors to this scholarly movement produced *Lives*, or historical portraits, of Jesus through academic methods of inquiry.[6] Driven initially by post-Enlightenment rationalism and later by the psychologizing and moralizing tendencies of late nineteenth-century Romanticism, these biographies relied on the tools of historical criticism to separate the authentic *Jesus of history* (believed to be preserved most reliably in Mark) from the mythical *Christ of faith* (presumed to be manufactured by the evangelists and early church) in an effort to make the real Jesus of Nazareth relevant for a modern age.[7]

Yet subsequent scholarship has exposed both the uncritical subjectivity and contextual neglect plaguing most of these distorted profiles. Most notably, Albert Schweitzer decried how each of those modern biographers had simply "created Him [Jesus] in accordance with his own character."[8] Moreover, Schweitzer criticized these historical reconstructions for failing to situate Jesus properly within the milieu of ancient Jewish **apocalyptic**. "The eschatology of Jesus," Schweitzer maintained, "can therefore only be interpreted by the aid of the curiously intermittent Jewish apocalyptic literature of the period between Daniel and the Bar-Cochba rising. . . . Historically regarded, the Baptist, Jesus, and Paul are simply the culminating manifestations of Jewish apocalyptic thought."[9]

While Schweitzer's stinging critique of the First (Old) Quest led to a lengthy period void of serious historical Jesus research, some of his other contributions would fail to be accepted in his own day. For instance, many have criticized Schweitzer for portraying Jesus as a failed eschatological

---

6. For a readable introduction to the various Quests, see the fine survey in Helen K. Bond, *The Historical Jesus: A Guide for the Perplexed* (London: Bloomsbury, 2012), 1–36.

7. Eventually, even Mark was argued to be historically suspect since it too was shown to be theologically compromised; cf. William Wrede, *The Messianic Secret: Das Messiasgeheimnis in den Evangelien*, trans. J. C. G. Greig (London: James Clarke, 1971 [1901]).

8. Albert Schweitzer, *The Quest of the Historical Jesus*, trans. W. Montgomery (London: Adam and Charles Black, 1910), 4. The late nineteenth-century Irish Jesuit priest George Tyrrell also famously criticized the authors of the *Lives* (esp. Adolf von Harnack) for merely producing "the reflection of a Liberal Protestant face, seen at the bottom of a deep well" (*Christianity at the Cross-roads* [London: Longmans, Green and Co., 1909], 44).

9. Schweitzer, *Quest of the Historical Jesus*, 365–66.

prophet,[10] as well as for having exaggerated the separation of Judaism from Hellenism.[11] Nevertheless, later scholars identifying with the New Quest for the historical Jesus (1950s–1970s), such as Ernst Käsemann and Günther Bornkamm, and especially those identifying with the Third Quest (1980s and beyond), such as Ben Meyer, E. P. Sanders, John Meier, Dale Allison, and N. T. Wright, have stood on Schweitzer's shoulders by offering thorough readings of the Gospels and analyses of the life of Jesus in the light of their Jewish theological context.[12]

The impact of Sanders's *Jesus and Judaism* has been especially long-standing. Complaining of scholarship's inability to produce a plausible portrait of Jesus, Sanders has been influential in challenging students of the New Testament to read the Gospel accounts against a more reliable histori-cal backdrop—one that does more justice to the actual practices and beliefs of early Judaism and can account not only for the content of Jesus's teaching but for his actions as well. "[T]he enormous labour which for generations has been expended on the investigation of the teaching material in the Gospels," Sanders asserts, "has not yielded a convincing historical depiction of Jesus—one which sets him firmly in Jewish history, which explains his execution, and which explains why his followers formed a persecuted messianic sect. What is needed," Sanders continues, "is more secure evidence, evidence on which everyone can agree and which at least points toward an explanation of these historical puzzles."[13] The "more secure evidence" Sanders him-self draws upon are of three types: (1) certain "almost indisputable facts" about Jesus,[14] (2) "knowledge about the outcome of his life and teaching,"[15]

---

10. Cf. Schweitzer, *Quest of the Historical Jesus*, 368–69.

11. See, e.g., Martin Hengel, *Judaism and Hellenism: Studies in Their Encounter in Palestine during the Early Hellenistic Period*, trans. J. Bowden (Philadelphia: Fortress, 1974). Cf. Troels Engberg-Pedersen, ed., *Paul beyond the Judaism/Hellenism Divide* (Louisville: Westminster John Knox, 2001).

12. Ernst Käsemann, "The Problem of the Historical Jesus," in *Essays on New Testament Themes*, trans. W. J. Montague (London: SCM, 1964 [1960]), 15–47; Günther Bornkamm, *Jesus of Nazareth*, trans. Irene and Fraser McLuskey (London: Hodder and Stoughton, 1960 [1956]); Ben F. Meyer, *The Aims of Jesus* (London: SCM, 1979); E. P. Sanders, *Jesus and Judaism* (Minneapolis: Fortress, 1985); John P. Meier, *A Marginal Jew*, 5 vols. (New York: Doubleday, 1991–2016); Dale C. Allison, *Jesus of Nazareth: Millenarian Prophet* (Minneapolis: Fortress, 1991); idem, *Constructing Jesus: Memory, Imagination, and History* (Grand Rapids: Baker, 2010); N. T. Wright, *Jesus and the Victory of God*, Christian Origins and the Question of God 2 (Minneapolis: Fortress, 1996).

13. Sanders, *Jesus and Judaism*, 5.

14. Namely, that "Jesus was baptized by John the Baptist"; "Jesus was a Galilean who preached and healed"; "Jesus called disciples and spoke of there being twelve"; "Jesus confined his activity to Israel"; "Jesus engaged in a controversy about the temple"; and "Jesus was crucified outside Jerusalem by the Roman authorities" (ibid., 11 and 17).

15. Namely, that "[a]fter his death Jesus's followers continued as an identifiable movement," and "[a]t least some Jews persecuted at least parts of the new movement (Gal. 1.13, 22; Phil. 3.6),

and (3) "knowledge of first-century Judaism."[16] Sanders's book, in keeping with many of his other scholarly projects, significantly emphasizes this last source of evidence, "attempt[ing] to draw special attention to the significance of Jesus's deeds and words in [the context of] first-century Jewish Palestine."[17]

Sanders's own approach was therefore to examine Jesus's teaching and actions in the milieu of Jewish restoration eschatology, seeking to recover the authentic Jesus of history from canonical accounts colored by later Christian theology. Similar to Schweitzer's reconstruction, Sanders maintains that Jesus envisioned himself as an eschatological Jewish prophet who expected the imminent onset of a new world order in which God would build a new temple, reassemble Israel's twelve tribes, and welcome the wicked. In this sense, Sanders suggests that there was little unique about what Jesus believed and taught when compared to his Jewish contemporaries—Jesus did not protest temple abuses, he did not reject the Mosaic law, he did not offend the Pharisees, and he did not introduce anything remotely new when emphasizing love, grace, and forgiveness.

Unsurprisingly, not all of Sanders' proposals have been widely accepted. Nevertheless, as a result of Sanders's work, other Third Questers are more aware than ever of the importance of situating Jesus within his Second Temple Jewish context and interpreting the Gospels in close relation to contemporary Jewish literature.[18] As N. T. Wright remarks, "If we really believe in any sense in the incarnation of the Word, we are bound to take seriously the flesh that the Word became. And since that flesh was first-century Jewish flesh, we should rejoice in any and every advance in our understanding of first-century Judaism and seek to apply those insights to our reading of the Gospels."[19]

Even so, many readers of the Bible today, especially in the evangelical tradition, give little, if any, attention to early Jewish texts. For some, this is simply a matter of *familiarity*. Being generally unaware of the literature produced during the Second Temple period, many assume that the so-called

---

and it appears that this persecution endured at least to a time near the end of Paul's career (II Cor. 11.24; Gal. 5.11; 6.12; cf. Matt. 23.34; 10.17)" (ibid., 11 and 17).

16. Ibid., 17.

17. Ibid.

18. Most scholarly responses to Sanders have likewise offered comparisons of Jewish texts with the Gospels. See, e.g., Allison, *Jesus of Nazareth*, 95–171; Wright, *Jesus and the Victory of God*; cf. idem, *The New Testament and the People of God*, Christian Origins and the Question of God 1 (Minneapolis: Fortress, 1992).

19. N. T. Wright, *The Challenge of Jesus: Rediscovering Who Jesus Was and Is* (Downers Grove, IL: InterVarsity Press, 1999), 26.

"silent years" between the Testaments witnessed little to no development beyond the inherited traditions of the Hebrew Scriptures. Such readers therefore overlook early Jewish literature because they assume that the New Testament was written in a literary-theological vacuum.

For others, this avoidance is a matter of *canonicity*. Although aware of the existence of extrabiblical Jewish literature, these readers often consider ancient religious books lying outside of Scripture to be theologically irrelevant or even dangerous. Accordingly, they bar these works from hermeneutical consideration, basing such avoidance on their commitment to *sola Scriptura* or related post-Reformation doctrines on the clarity and sufficiency of Scripture.

For still other readers, the neglect of Second Temple literature is simply a matter of *utility*. Despite realizing that the Jewish people authored important religious works between the Testaments, many remain unsure how these noncanonical texts can be studied profitably alongside the Bible. They therefore disregard early Jewish literature, being either regretful they don't have the training to apply extrabiblical insights or anxious they might distort the New Testament message if they tried.

While we understand the above concerns, the rewards for even non-specialists studying Second Temple texts far outweigh the challenges and supposed risks of doing so. Indeed, there are many advantages to becoming familiar with early Judaism and the relevant literature. Bruce Metzger helpfully assessed the importance of these works (esp. the **Apocrypha**) for biblical studies over a half century ago:

> Though it would be altogether extravagant to call the Apocrypha the keystone of the two Testaments, it is not too much to regard these intertestamental books as an historical hyphen that serves a useful function in bridging what to most readers of the Bible is a blank of several hundred years. To neglect what the Apocrypha have to tell us about the development of Jewish life and thought during those critical times is as foolish as to imagine that one can understand the civilization and culture of America today by passing from colonial days to the twentieth century without taking into account the industrial and social revolution of the intervening centuries.[20]

---

20. Bruce M. Metzger, *An Introduction to the Apocrypha* (Oxford: Oxford University Press, 1957), 151–52. See also David A. deSilva, *The Jewish Teachers of Jesus, James, and Jude: What Earliest Christianity Learned from the Apocrypha and Pseudepigrapha* (Oxford: Oxford University Press, 2013), who argues that Jesus and his half-brothers "learned and adopted . . . traditions

Concerns about canonicity are also difficult to justify. We, too, embrace the evangelical and wider Protestant belief in the authority of inspired Scripture. Refusing to engage early Jewish literature on theological grounds, however, goes well beyond this commitment. Even Martin Luther famously insisted that the books of the Apocrypha "are not held as equal to the sacred Scriptures, and nevertheless are useful and good to read."[21] In fact, the Apocrypha was included in most early Protestant printings of the Bible (e.g., Luther's Bible and the King James Version), though now separated into its own section. It was only in the early nineteenth century when Bibles began to be printed without it. Obviously the mishandling of these texts remains a real concern to those in the church, just as it does to many within critical scholarship; over half a century ago Samuel Sandmel warned the academy of illegitimate uses of background material, calling it "parallelomania."[22] Yet the appropriate solution to the misuse of comparative literature is not its outright dismissal but its responsible handling by students of Scripture.

Many readers seem particularly anxious about the illegitimate *imposition* of external meaning onto the biblical text. That is a fair concern. What some fail to realize, however, is that comparative studies are (or should be) just as interested in exposing the theological *differences* between texts as observing their *similarities*. Indeed, it was even Sanders's contention that any "good hypothesis with regard to Jesus's intention and his relationship to Judaism should . . . situate Jesus believably in Judaism and yet explain why the movement initiated by him eventually broke with Judaism."[23] Wright cautions similarly: "Jesus cannot be separated from his Jewish context, but neither can he be collapsed into it so that he is left without a sharp critique of his contemporaries."[24] Thus, while one should avoid utilizing early Jewish

---

otherwise known only in particular extrabiblical texts" (10); "Jesus's teaching was certainly innovative, but much more of his teaching has a 'pedigree' than is often supposed" (9). A similar case is made by Matthias Henze, *Mind the Gap: How the Jewish Writings between the Old and New Testament Help Us Understand Jesus* (Minneapolis: Fortress, 2017), 4: "In order to understand Jesus and his message, we have to have a basic understanding of first-century Judaism. To gain that understanding, reading the Old Testament alone is not enough. Jesus did not emerge from the Old Testament, he emerged from the Judaism of his time."

21. Cited in *The Apocrypha: The Lutheran Edition with Notes* (St. Louis: Concordia, 2012), xviii. See also how Matthew Barrett defends the sufficiency of Scripture while also urging Protestants to recognize the value of extrabiblical data for the task of hermeneutics: "Such factors demonstrate the high importance of general revelation, even guarding us against certain biblicist caricatures of *sola Scriptura*" (*God's Word Alone—The Authority of Scripture: What the Reformers Taught . . . and Why It Still Matters* [Grand Rapids: Zondervan, 2016], 338–39).

22. Samuel Sandmel, "Parallelomania," *JBL* 81 (1962): 1–13.

23. Sanders, *Jesus and Judaism*, 18.

24. Wright, *Jesus and the Victory of God*, 98.

literature merely as a foil for the New Testament documents, their differences must be highlighted if their individual meanings are to be appreciated and a dialogue between them is to take place. To interpret the Gospels wisely, then, students must not *ignore* Second Temple Jewish literature but *engage* it with frequency, precision, and a willingness to acknowledge theological continuity *and* discontinuity.

Yet while monographs that situate Jesus within Judaism abound, there exist virtually no nontechnical resources for beginning and intermediate students to assist them in seeing firsthand how Jesus is similar to and yet different from his Jewish contemporaries. This volume seeks to investigate Jesus's relationship with Second Temple Judaism by bringing together a series of accessible essays that compare and contrast the perspectives and hermeneutical practices of Jesus and his various kinsmen. Going beyond an introduction that merely surveys historical events and theological themes, this book examines select passages in Second Temple Jewish literature in order to illuminate the context of Jesus's actions and the nuances of his teaching.

To provide focus, the volume concentrates on the Gospel of Mark, a suitable target text on numerous counts. As noted above, Mark is the earliest and most influential narrative account of Jesus, probably having served as a source for both Matthew and Luke, and possibly John.[25] Among the canonical Gospels, Mark is also the most economic in length and one of the easiest to divide into coherent units. A book whose contribution to the origin and thought world of the New Testament is highly disproportionate to its length, Mark has an importance for the study of Jesus and early Christianity that is impossible to exaggerate.

Following, then, the progression of Mark, each chapter in the volume (1) pairs a major unit of the Gospel with one or more sections of a thematically related Jewish text, (2) introduces and explores the theological nuances of the comparator, and (3) shows how the ideas in the comparator illuminate those expressed in Mark. The end of each chapter also contains a short list of other thematically relevant Second Temple Jewish texts recommended for additional study and a focused bibliography pointing students to critical editions and higher-level discussions in scholarly literature. Finally, at the end of the book is a glossary where readers will find definitions of important terms. Whether one reads the entire book or only a few essays, it is our hope that readers will gain a new appreciation for extrabiblical Jewish texts, begin

---

25. Bock, *Mark*, 11: "In Jesus research today, Mark is a starting point or a key source for most serious historical treatments of Jesus."

to see the many benefits of studying the New Testament alongside of its contemporary literature, and acquire a better understanding of Jesus as he is presented in the Gospel according to Mark.

Before proceeding to our comparisons, however, it is necessary to survey briefly the events of the **Second Temple Period** and the literature that it produced.

Introducing the Second Temple Period and Early Jewish Literature

FROM THE FIRST TEMPLE PERIOD TO THE SECOND

In the exodus, a pivotal event in the history of national Israel, Abraham's family was liberated from Pharaoh after nearly four centuries of forced labor. The Israelites were led by God into the desert and given the Mosaic law at Sinai to regulate Hebrew life and religion, with the sacrificial system at the center of their community (Exod 19:1–8). Separated from the nations through their distinctive way of life (Lev 20:22–26), the Israelites were to keep the commandments that God had given them lest they profane the holy **covenant** and be exiled from the land of promise (Lev 26:14–39; Deut 28:15–68; 30:15–20).

From the conquest of Canaan to the end of the united monarchy, the nation inhabited the land for almost five-hundred years. During that era, King Solomon built the first temple in the mid-tenth century, fulfilling David's original aspiration for the project (1 Kgs 6:1–8:66). After Solomon's death the kingdom divided, and, following a series of evil rulers, Israel's northern ten tribes (the kingdom of Israel/Samaria) were captured and exiled by Assyria in 722 BC (2 Kgs 17:1–23; 18:9–12). The southern two tribes (the kingdom of Judah) ultimately fared no better. By the beginning of the sixth century the Babylonians had waged war on Jerusalem, and in 586 BC King Nebuchadnezzar destroyed the city, including the first temple, and exiled many of its inhabitants (2 Kg 24:10–25:21; 2 Chr 36:17–21).

The Babylonian captivity marks a low point in Israel's history. The nation had faced the full brunt of the Deuteronomic curses as a result of their covenant disobedience. Consequently, the Israelites were without a homeland, just as Yahweh had promised would happen through Moses and the prophets.

Yet even before their captivity, God had also promised that he would return his scattered people to the land and fully restore the nation (Lev 26:40–45;

Deut 30:1–10; 32:34–43; Isa 40:1–66:24; Jer 30:1–31:40; Ezek 36:8–37:28). Israel was to experience the glory of its former days, and as it would turn out, they did not remain under Babylonian rule for long. In 539 BC Cyrus of Persia conquered Babylon and famously decreed that all exiles could return to their ancestral homelands (2 Chr 36:22–23; Ezra 1:1–4). Many Israelites therefore gradually returned to and rebuilt Jerusalem. Zerubbabel was instrumental in the rebuilding of the temple, while Nehemiah oversaw the construction of the city walls (Ezra 3:8–6:15; Neh 2:9–6:15). It is the building of this second temple in 516 BC that marks the beginning of the Second Temple period.

The newly renovated city, however, was not what was promised. When Israel's returnees gazed at the new temple's foundation, some celebrated while others cried over its unimpressive stature (Ezra 3:10–13; Hag 2:3). Israel's promised restoration had not arrived at the hands of Ezra and Nehemiah. As the centuries to follow would demonstrate, the peace and prosperity God swore to his people had yet to be realized in the period immediately following the Babylonian exile. Instead, generation after generation witnessed subjugation and suffering at the hands of still other foreign powers—namely, Medo-Persia, Greece, and Rome—and these experiences significantly colored the texts these Jews produced.

Israel survived under the rule of the Medo-Persian Empire from 539 to about 332 BC, when the Greek Empire led by Alexander the Great conquered the known world. Alexander's rule would not last long. Following his death in 323 BC, Alexander's territories were partitioned among his military generals, who established their own kingdoms (e.g., the Ptolemaic Kingdom in Egypt, the **Seleucid Kingdom** in Syria) and continued the former ruler's systematic spread of **Hellenism**, or Greek culture (1 Macc 1:1–9; 2 Macc 4:7–17). These kingdoms, which were often embroiled in war with one another, also created challenges for the Jews who were positioned geographically between them. The Seleucid Kingdom in particular, under the rule of **Antiochus IV Epiphanes** in 167 BC, raided Jerusalem (1 Macc 1:20–40), desecrated the temple (1:47, 54, 59), outlawed observance of the covenant (1:41–53), and prohibited possession of the Torah (1:56–57). In his pursuit of **Hellenization**, Antiochus banned the Jews' customs (1:41–44) and violently forced their assimilation (1:50, 57–58, 60–64). But Antiochus's persecution was not passively tolerated. The Jewish resistance that arose in response (the **Maccabean Revolt**, 167–160 BC) resulted in the Jews' repossession of the land, rededication of the temple, and institution of the festival of Hanukkah (1 Macc 4:36–59; Josephus, *Ant.* 12.316–25).

With the renewed national sovereignty of the **Hasmonean** Kingdom, various groups held differing opinions about how to manage the political and temple leadership of Israel. This infighting eventually led to the weakening of the Jewish national leadership, and Pompey, a Roman general contemporaneous with Julius Caesar, seized control of Israel in 63 BC, making it a territory of the Roman Republic. Although Rome largely tolerated Jewish religious practices, pressures leading toward political, cultural, and religious assimilation were ever present. Eventually the **Zealots** (a Jewish resistance group) fomented the hopes of another successful revolt. But the Romans, under the soon-to-be Emperor Titus, defeated the Jews and destroyed the Second Temple in AD 70 (Josephus, *J.W.* 6.220–70), thus bringing an end to the **Second Temple period**.

The Second Temple period (516 BC–AD 70) began with the Jews under the control of the Persians and ended with them under the control of the Romans. This was without question a time of crisis for the Jewish people, and devout men and women reflected on their experiences in a variety of ways. With the continuous pressures of consecutive foreign nations pushing the Jews toward assimilation, numerous Second Temple Jewish literary works preserve their thoughts and hopes about God and life in the covenant. These reflections survive in the numerous literary works produced during this period. We turn now to survey these texts.

OVERVIEW OF SECOND TEMPLE JEWISH LITERATURE

The Second Temple Jewish writings were composed by numerous authors in multiple languages over several hundred years. Moreover, they derive from geographical provenances extending over much of the **ancient Near East**. Thus, there is no easy way to characterize or categorize these texts. Still, scholarly surveys of ancient Judaism normally assign individual Second Temple Jewish texts to one of three main literary bodies—the Septuagint, the Apocrypha, and the Pseudepigrapha—collections that were unrecognized by the original authors, having been determined by later editors and scholars. Accordingly, these corpuses overlap in different places.

The **Septuagint** (abbreviated **LXX**) is a collection of Jewish texts in Greek that includes the Greek translation of the Old Testament as well as other Jewish writings. It was the most widely used Greek version in antiquity, though other Greek versions also existed. The Old Testament **Apocrypha** (also called the **deuterocanonical** books) are a subset of the texts found in the Septuagint (though not in the Hebrew Bible) that were accepted as authoritative by patristic (and medieval) Christians and included in the Vulgate (a Latin translation that became the authoritative version for the medieval church).[26] Different Christian groups have variations in their **canonical** lists related to the Apocrypha, but the primary collection includes the books of Tobit, Judith, Additions to Esther, the Wisdom of Solomon, Sirach (Ecclesiasticus), Baruch, the Epistle of Jeremiah, Additions to Daniel (the Prayer of Azariah, Song of the Three Young Men, Susanna, and Bel and the Dragon), and 1 and 2 Maccabees. Certain churches also afford special status to works such as 1 and 2 Esdras (= "Ezra" in Greek), the Prayer of Manasseh, and Psalm 151. In addition to the Greek translation of the Hebrew Bible and what later became known as the Apocrypha, the LXX also includes, in certain copies, the books of 3 Maccabees, 4 Maccabees, 1 Esdras, the Psalms of Solomon, and Odes of Solomon (including the Prayer of Manasseh).

The Old Testament **Pseudepigrapha** (meaning "falsely attributed writings") is a diverse body of ancient Jewish works, many of which claim to be authored by famous Old Testament persons although they did not write them. Some Septuagint works mentioned above are also falsely attributed. For example, neither the Wisdom of Solomon nor Psalms of Solomon were authored by Israel's third king, though they bear his name. In distinction to the Septuagint and the Apocrypha as fixed bodies of texts, all early Jewish religious literature not considered to be (deutero)canonical are commonly placed in the open category of pseudepigrapha—aside from **Philo**, **Josephus**, and the **Dead Sea Scrolls**.[27]

While these classifications (esp. Apocrypha) are widely used and indeed useful for classifying texts that may be considered authoritative in certain religious traditions, an alternative and more descriptive way to group these writings is according to genre. We survey the main early Jewish literary genres below.[28]

The first early Jewish literary genre to be familiar with is *history*. Several works fall into this category, including 1–2 Esdras and 1–2 Maccabees. The books of 1–2 Esdras (Vulgate) refer to the books of Ezra and Nehemiah

---

26. The canonical status of these texts for patristic Christians is unclear, but they did treat them as authoritative. These texts were later included in the Old Testament by Roman Catholic and Orthodox Christians because of their reception by the church in the patristic period.

27. Loren T. Stuckenbruck, "Apocrypha and Pseudepigrapha," in *Early Judaism: A Comprehensive Overview*, ed. J. J. Collins and D. C. Harlow (Grand Rapids: Eerdmans, 2012), 173–203, at 191–92.

28. Our overview generally follows the categories of James C. VanderKam, *An Introduction to Early Judaism* (Grand Rapids: Eerdmans, 2001), 53–173.

and thus report Israel's immediate postexilic history.[29] The books of 1–2 Maccabees chronicle important events between the biblical testaments, including the **Maccabean Revolt**. Together, the early Jewish histories are essential for understanding the events, influences, challenges, and commitments of the Second Temple Jewish people.

A second early Jewish literary genre is *tales*. According to James Vander-Kam, these are "stories with no serious claim to historicity but [which] aim to inculcate wise teachings through the stories and the speeches they narrate."[30] To this category belong such books as Tobit, Judith, Susanna, 3 Maccabees, and the Letter of Aristeas. These works normally cast important, sometimes heroic, men and women at the center of their narratives in order to model Jewish piety and inspire trust in God's promises.

Our third genre is *rewritten Scripture*. Often books belonging to this group also take a narrative form, since these works typically reproduce, paraphrase, and elaborate on the accounts of specific Old Testament events and characters. To this category belong such books as Jubilees (a retelling of the biblical events from creation to Mt. Sinai) and the Genesis Apocryphon (an expansion of select patriarchal narratives). Also considered by some scholars as rewritten Scripture are the Life of Adam and Eve (an account of the advent of death and restoration of life) and the Testaments of the Twelve Patriarchs (an elaboration on Jacob's final words to his twelve sons in Genesis 49). Works such as these are important for demonstrating how biblical literature was interpreted during the Second Temple period, when exegetical commentaries were quite rare.[31]

Fourth among the early Jewish literary genres is *apocalypse*, which normally consists of otherworldly visions given to a human recipient (seer) through the mediation of a supernatural, sometimes angelic, being. Most Jewish apocalypses were written in the second and third-centuries BC during times of great distress. They therefore seek to bring comfort to suffering Jewish communities by providing a heavenly perspective on past, present, and future events. Often coded in elaborate symbolism, these visions typically anticipate the eventual cessation of evil and political oppression. Early Jewish apocalypses include 4 Ezra, the Sibylline Oracles, the Testament of

---

29. The contents of 1–2 Esdras differ in the ancient Greek (LXX) and Latin (Vulgate) corpuses in which they were transmitted. The title 2 Esdras, for instance, can refer to the apocalyptic work also known as 4 Ezra; in other cases, it refers to the book of Nehemiah (Vulgate) or to the books of Ezra and Nehemiah combined (LXX).

30. VanderKam, *Introduction to Early Judaism*, 69.

31. Cf. Molly M. Zahn, "Rewritten Scripture," in *The Oxford Handbook of the Dead Sea Scrolls*, ed. T. H. Lim and J. J. Collins (Oxford: Oxford University Press, 2010), 323–36.

Moses, and several portions of 1 Enoch: the Book of Watchers (1 Enoch 1–36); the Similitudes/Parables of Enoch (1 Enoch 37–71); the Astronomical Book (1 Enoch 72–82); the Book of Dreams (1 Enoch 83–90); and the Apocalypse of Weeks (1 Enoch 91:11–17; 93:1–10).

The fifth and sixth genres, *poetry* and *wisdom literature,* are similar in both content and style to their antecedent biblical literature (Job, Psalms, Proverbs, Ecclesiastes). Hebrew poems are normally songs of praise and lament utilizing meter and structural parallelism. The songs written during this period of Jewish history commonly entreat the Lord for deliverance from pain and oppression. Examples include the Psalms of Solomon, the Prayer of Manasseh, and the Prayer of Azariah and Song of the Three Young Men. Wisdom literature appeals to common experience in order to instruct people how to live virtuously. Examples include Sirach (Ecclesiasticus), the Wisdom of Solomon, and perhaps Baruch and the Epistle of Enoch (1 En. 91–108).[32]

Four additional collections deserve special mention, the origins of which we know far more about than the various works previously surveyed. First are the works of Philo (ca. 20 BC–AD 50). A diaspora Jew influenced by Platonism from Alexandria, Egypt, Philo authored numerous philosophical treatises and exegetical studies on the Pentateuch. Second are the books of the historian Josephus (AD 37–ca. 100). Once a Jewish Pharisee and military leader, Josephus was taken captive during the war against Rome and eventually made a Roman citizen and dependent of Emperor Vespasian. Josephus's four extant works include: a history of the Jewish people (*Jewish Antiquities*), an account of the Jerusalem War (*Jewish War*), a work in defense of Judaism and the Jewish way of life (*Against Apion*), and an autobiography (*The Life*).

Third are the **Dead Sea Scrolls**. Although the majority of the scrolls discovered near **Qumran** are ancient copies of the Old Testament or versions of apocryphal and pseudepigraphal texts (e.g., Tobit, 1 Enoch, Jubilees), many are **sectarian** documents—works that describe how the Dead Sea community originated and was organized and how members of the community should live and worship. These works are labeled by the Qumran cave number in which they were found (1Q, 4Q, etc.) and a cataloging number, though many have other shortened names describing their content (e.g., 1QS = Community Rule; CD = Damascus Document; 4Q176 = Consolations). The fourth collection is the rabbinic literature. This literature is extensive and consists of the Mishnah, the Jerusalem Talmud, the Babylonian Talmud, the Targumim, and a variety of other writings. The Mishnah and Talmuds come

---

32. VanderKam, *Introduction to Early Judaism,* 115–24.

from after the NT period, while some of the Targumim and other writings may stem from the NT period. While one must be careful about imposing later traditions on the earlier period, when used properly the rabbinic writings can shed much light on the practices and beliefs of Judaism in the first century.

Our goal here has been only to provide a concise overview of certain foundational elements for understanding early Jewish history and literature. For a full account, the reader should consult the resources listed below. Having oriented ourselves to Jesus's Jewish context, we now turn to read Mark's Gospel in conversation with some of these Second Temple Jewish texts.

FOR FURTHER READING

For the most comprehensive overview of early Jewish literature, see Craig A. Evans, *Ancient Texts for New Testament Studies: A Guide to the Background Literature* (Peabody, MA: Hendrickson, 2005), which summarizes the literature and provides the bibliographic details for critical texts, research tools, and key scholarly works. The volume's appendixes also show how Jewish literature can illuminate the New Testament. See also David W. Chapman and Andreas J. Köstenberger, "Jewish Intertestamental and Early Rabbinic Literature: An Annotated Bibliographic Resource Updated (Part 1)," *JETS* 55 (2012): 235–72, and David W. Chapman and Andreas J. Köstenberger, "Jewish Intertestamental and Early Rabbinic Literature: An Annotated Bibliographic Resource Updated (Part 2)," *JETS* 55 (2012): 457–88.

Standard Translations of Early Jewish Literature

Bauckham, Richard, James R. Davila, and Alexander Panayotov, eds. *Old Testament Pseudepigrapha: More Noncanonical Scriptures*. Grand Rapids: Eerdmans, 2013.

Charlesworth, James H., ed. *The Old Testament Pseudepigrapha*. 2 vols. New York: Doubleday, 1983–85.

Coogan, Michael D., Marc Z. Brettler, Carol Ann Newsom, and Pheme Perkins, eds. *The New Oxford Annotated Apocrypha: New Revised Standard Version*. Rev. 4th ed. Oxford: Oxford University Press, 2010.

García Martínez, Florentino, and Eibert J. C. Tigchelaar, eds. *The Dead Sea Scrolls Study Edition*. 2 vols. Leiden: Brill, 1997–98.

Pietersma, Albert, and Benjamin G. Wright, eds. *A New English Translation of the Septuagint*. Oxford: Oxford University Press, 2007.

Introductions to Early Jewish Literature

Chapman, Honora Howell, and Zuleika Rodgers, eds. *A Companion to Josephus*. BCAW. Chichester: Wiley-Blackwell, 2016.

Collins, John J. *The Apocalyptic Imagination: An Introduction to Jewish Apocalyptic Literature*. 3rd ed. Grand Rapids: Eerdmans, 2016.

Collins, John J., and Daniel C. Harlow, eds. *Early Judaism: A Comprehensive Overview*. Grand Rapids: Eerdmans, 2012.

deSilva, David A. *Introducing the Apocrypha: Message, Context, and Significance*. Grand Rapids: Baker, 2002.

Helyer, Larry R. *Exploring Jewish Literature of the Second Temple Period: A Guide for New Testament Students*. Downers Grove, IL: InterVarsity Press, 2002.

Kamesar, Adam, ed. *The Cambridge Companion to Philo*. Cambridge: Cambridge University Press, 2009.

Mason, Steve. *Josephus and the New Testament*. 2nd ed. Peabody, MA: Hendrickson, 2002.

Nickelsburg, George W. E. *Jewish Literature between the Bible and the Mishnah: A Historical and Literary Introduction*. 2nd ed. Minneapolis: Fortress, 2011.

Strack, H. L., and G. Stemberger. *Introduction to the Talmud and Midrash*. Edinburgh: T&T Clark, 1991.

VanderKam, James C. *An Introduction to Early Judaism*. Grand Rapids: Eerdmans, 2001.

VanderKam, James C., and Peter Flint. *The Meaning of the Dead Sea Scrolls: Their Significance for Understanding the Bible, Judaism, Jesus, and Christianity*. San Francisco: HarperCollins, 2002.

CHAPTER 1

Rule of the Community and Mark 1:1–13: Preparing the Way in the Wilderness

RIKK WATTS

Probably written in the mid to late 60s, Mark is widely regarded as the earliest Gospel. It is also unique among them in immediately presenting its account as the fulfillment of a cluster of scriptural texts (1:2–3): Malachi 3:1, with echoes of Exodus 23:20, and Isaiah 40:3. Because Mark strikingly attributed the cluster only to Isaiah (1:2), Jerome later gently chided Mark for making a mistake (CCSL 78.452). More likely this either reflects the ancient practice of citing only the most important author, is an example of Mark's well-recognized "sandwich" structure (**intercalation**)—the Malachi/Exodus text (1:2b) is sandwiched between the Isaiah attribution (1:2a) and the actual citation (1:3)—or is a combination of both.

Mark's emphasis on Isaiah is unsurprising. Isaiah is by far the most frequently cited prophet in the **Dead Sea Scrolls** and the NT. In reconstructions of first-century triennial synagogue readings of Torah, a massive two-thirds of the accompanying prophetic readings come from Isaiah.[1] The reason for this popularity is evident. No other scriptural book offered such an extended presentation of Israel's future hope of Yahweh's personal coming "in power" to rescue his oppressed people from exile, leading his "blind" people home, and dwelling among them in a restored Zion to which all nations would come.[2]

---

1. Cf. Charles Perrot, "The Reading of the Bible in the Ancient Synagogue," in *Mikra: Text, Translation, Reading, and Interpretation of the Hebrew Bible in Ancient Judaism and Early Christianity*, ed. M. J. Mulder and Harry Sysling (Assen: Van Gorcum; Philadelphia: Fortress, 1988), 137–59, at 141–43.

2. B. W. Anderson, "Exodus Typology in Second Isaiah," in *Israel's Prophetic Heritage*, ed. B. W. Anderson and W. Harrelson (New York: Harper, 1962), 177–95; R. E. Watts, "Exodus

Isaiah 40:3's comforting call to prepare for Yahweh's coming was equally influential. Malachi 3:1's "who will *prepare the way* before *me*" is itself a deliberate echo of Isaiah (cf. *"prepare the way* for the LORD"), which is perhaps why Mark includes it. Imagery from the larger unit (Isa 40:1–11) appears in such a wide range of Jewish texts that it could fairly be described as a *locus classicus* of Israel's eschatological salvation.[3]

Mark is therefore in good company in appealing to Isaiah, and particularly Isaiah 40:3. Where he diverges is in his understanding of what it means to "prepare" and what this "way" looks like. To illustrate, we will first examine how Isaiah 40:3 was used in the Rule of the Community and then compare this to what Mark does.

Rule of the Community

"THEY SHALL SEPARATE FROM THE HABITATION OF THE MEN OF INIQUITY TO GO TO THE WILDERNESS"

Our copies of the Rule of the Community (1QS) date from around 100–50 BC when members of the **Essene** sect are thought to have lived at Khirbet-**Qumran** in the Judean desert. The twelve extant manuscripts (some fragmentary and differing in content) distributed across three caves testify to its importance. Cited in two key places, Isaiah 40:3's central role is clear.[4] The first constitutes the group's manifesto (1QS 8:1–9:2), which lays out their theological purpose:

> [13] . . . conforming to these teachings, they shall separate from the habitation of the men of iniquity to go to the wilderness, there to prepare the way of truth, [14] as it is written, "In the wilderness prepare the way of the LORD, make straight in the desert a highway for our God" [Isa 40:3]. [15] This means the study of the Law, decreed by God through the hand of Moses for obedience, so as to act in

---

Imagery," in *Dictionary of the Old Testament Prophets*, ed. M. J. Boda and J. G. McConville (Downers Grove, IL: InterVarsity Press, 2012), 205–14.

3. E.g., 1QS 8:12b–16a; 9:17b–20a; 4Q176; Bar 5:5–7; Sir 48:24–25; 1 En. 1:6; Pss. Sol. 11; T. Mos. 10:1–5; and later Pesiq. Rab. 29/30A, 29/30B, 30 and 33; cf. Tanḥ on Deut 1:1.1; Gen. Rab. 100.9; Lev. Rab. 1.14; 10.2; 21.7; Lam. Rab. 1.2.23, 1.22.57; Midr. Pss. 4.8; 22.27; 23.7; Deut. Rab. 4.11. Cf. Klyne Snodgrass, "Streams of Tradition Emerging from Isaiah 40:1–5 and Their Adaptation in the New Testament," *JSNT* 8 (1980): 24–45.

4. James H. Charlesworth, "Intertextuality: Isaiah 40:3 and the Serek Ha-Yahad," in *The Quest for Context and Meaning: Studies in Biblical Intertextuality in Honor of James A. Sanders*, ed. C. A. Evans and S. Talmon, BibInt 28 (Leiden: Brill, 1997), 197–224, at 223.

keeping with what has been revealed from age to age, [16] and by what the prophets have revealed by His holy spirit. (1QS 8:13–16)[5]

The second describes the role of the Instructor who is to educate the community in this purpose:

> [19] . . . the men of the community [*Yaḥad*], each will walk perfectly with his fellow, guided by all that has been disclosed to them. This is the time to "prepare the way [20] in the desert" [Isa 40:3]. He shall teach them in all that has been revealed to direct their works in that time, and instruct them to separate from every man who does not turn his way [21] from all evil. These are the regulations of the Way for the Instructor in these times, as to his loving and hating. . . . (9:19–21)

Preparing the Way in the Desert. Several related points emerge. First, it is important to understand these citations in the context of the group's self-designation. Their being a part of the *Yaḥad* ("unity," 1:1, 12, 16) and their divisions into thousands, hundreds, fifties, and tens (2:21–22) symbolically echo the wilderness community in the exodus (Exod 18:21–25). This, along with their council of twelve men and three priests (1QS 8:1–16a), which signify the twelve tribes and three priestly families, suggest they saw themselves as true Israel. Second, while in keeping with Isaiah they are in the literal wilderness, what matters is their location's theological significance. The desert in Isaiah 40–55 is the place of hope where true Israel is reconstituted. Third, although Isaiah is often read as envisaging a literal highway, in context the image speaks less to physical construction than to repentance, trust, and obedience.[6] This suggests that Isaiah's "preparing the way" was primarily a spiritual metaphor, which is how 1QS takes it.

Walking in Faithful Obedience. Over against the cursed men of iniquity who "walk in the ways of wickedness" (5:10), the group's fundamental concern was to "walk in perfection" (1:8) in all God's decrees and "ways" (CD 2:16) so as "to effect truth, righteousness, justice, loving-kindness, and humility toward one another . . . in order to atone for sin by doing justice and enduring trials, and to walk with all by the specification of the truth" (8:2–4; cf. 9:4–5). Only in this way would they see their vindication, the defeat of Belial (Satan) and his congregation, and the establishment of a suitable priesthood in Jerusalem.

---

5. Translations of the Dead Sea Scrolls are mine.

6. Rikki E. Watts, "Consolation or Confrontation? Isaiah 40–55 and the Delay of the New Exodus," *TynBul* 41 (1990): 31–59.

But what precisely did this obedience entail? In the first instance, it meant walking in the Way (9:18, 21; 10:21) of the particular Torah interpretation of the as-yet-unidentified "Teacher of Righteousness" (CD 1:10–11). God had made known to him the mysteries of the prophets in the last days (1QpHab 7:1–5) and through him smoothed "the way" for the truth (4Q171 3:16–17). With their blind eyes opened (CD 1:9; 2:14), his followers became a faithful "new temple" in Israel (1QS 8:5–6; 9:3–6). Having been invited into God's new "covenant of mercy" (1QS 1:7–9), they were to remain faithful during the present time of Belial's dominion (1:16–20).

This faithfulness included special diligence in observing the right calendar of feasts (1:13–15; cf. Jub. 6:23–38), eschewing wealth by holding everything in common (1QS 6:19–22), and maintaining strict purity. One could be defiled by Belial (1:23–24; CD 4:12–19), by outsiders—with whom they could neither discuss their teachings nor from whom accept food, drink, or anything (1QS 5:15–17)—and even by lesser members of the community (cf. Josephus, *J.W.* 2.150). Holiness meant not only regular ablutions (1QS 3:9; 5:13) but the near total segregation from the wicked in Israel, including the **Pharisees** whom they disparaged as "seekers of smooth things" (CD 1:14–2:1; 4Q177 2:12–13), who "walk" according to their deceitful teaching (4Q169 2:2, 8). Membership thus required a long preparation (1QS 6:13–23), and the Instructor hid his teachings, neither reproaching nor arguing with "the men of the pit" (9:16).

In sum, far from all Israel being saved, the nation by and large was under God's judgment, the current regime in Jerusalem was apostate, and the *Yaḥad* alone constituted the faithful remnant. Apparently, Isaiah's promise of Yahweh's return and the end of Israel's exile had for them not been fully realized. Accepting that holiness was a matter of Torah obedience, they were considerably stricter than the Pharisees. This meant—in this time of **eschatological** separation, and as the prophet Isaiah commanded through the holy spirit (cf. Isa 11:16b)—that a literal withdrawal to a pure life in the desert was necessary to prepare for Yahweh's return. With this in view, we turn to Mark.

Mark 1:1–13

"PREPARE THE WAY FOR THE LORD, MAKE STRAIGHT PATHS FOR HIM"

Mark, too, is a foundational document aimed at establishing the identity of faithful Israel. However, whereas 1QS was still awaiting the Lord's return, for Mark he has already come in Jesus. Consequently, in keeping with ancient practice, Mark's explicit opening appeal to Isaiah (1:1–3) provides the context not only for his preparatory prologue (1:4–13) but even more importantly for his far more extensive account of what the Lord's coming looked like (1:14–16:8, with 1:14–15 providing a transitional introductory summary). Mark, like 1QS, apparently believed that Isaiah's promises of the return from exile had not previously been fully realized. Unlike 1QS, he asserts that Isaiah's "good news" of God's victory (Isa 40:9; 41:27; 52:7) has now been "fulfilled" in Jesus (Mark 1:1, 14–15).

In terms of his prologue, Mark's preparation also begins "in the wilderness" and is similarly spiritual. But his preparatory teacher is instead John the Baptist. Whereas Qumran stipulated repeated washings, John required a single baptism. Unlike Qumran's teacher, his preaching and baptizing was accessible to all and occasioned a far greater response: "The whole Judean countryside and all the people of Jerusalem went out to him. Confessing their sins, they were baptized by him in the Jordan River" (Mark 1:5). In stark contrast to 1QS, almost nothing is said of John's teaching. Mark has but two concerns: first, the surpassing power of the coming one, and second, that this one will "baptize . . . with the Holy Spirit" (Mark 1:7–8). Traditionally attributes of Yahweh alone, the Lord who comes is, astonishingly, Jesus (1:2–3, 9). For Mark, the human Jesus, however mysteriously, embodies the very presence of Yahweh (cf. 2:10, 28; 6:47–51).

At the same time and in contrast to 1QS's community, Jesus alone is true Israel. He is also God's beloved messianic son (Ps 2:7), for whom both Israel and the *Yaḥad* hoped, and his servant (Isa 42:1; Mark 1:10–11; strikingly, unlike 1QS, Mark has no explicit interest in a renewed priesthood). Jesus alone is driven by the Spirit into the wilderness, not to observe Torah or to perfect purity but to defeat Satan (Mark 1:12–13)—again something only Yahweh can do. As for the rest of Mark's Gospel, Jesus does not remain in holy isolation but returns to Galilee (1:14–15). Through him, Satan's (Belial's) kingdom is now at an end (3:23–27), and all manner of people are purified not through Torah observance but trust in him (1:23–27, 40–42; 3:7–11; 5:25–34; 6:54–56). In Jesus the mystery of the "last-days" kingdom is revealed, and the word of the prophets fulfilled (1:15; 4:10).

There is similarly a division in Israel (3:6, 22) and the Pharisees too are denounced (3:5; 7:6–13). For Mark, Jesus's interpretation of Torah is unquestionably the norm. Even so, what truly separates insiders from outsiders (3:31–35; 4:10–11) is no longer primarily Torah interpretation, calendar observance (entirely absent from Mark), nor ritual purity (7:14–22) but one's response to the Spirit-empowered Jesus (1:34; 2:7, 27–28; 4:41; 8:27–30; 9:7; 14:61–62; 15:39; cf. 1:10; 3:28–30) around whom Israel is reconstituted (3:13) and God's true family gathered (3:31–35).

In contrast to the strictures of 1QS, Jesus eats with sinners (Mark 2:15–17), rewards even a cup of cold water given in his name (9:41), requires only the rich man to sell everything (10:21), openly proclaims his message to all (1:39; 4:1)—as much as they were able to understand (4:33)—and publicly engages with and denounces Israel's hard-hearted leadership (2:1–3:5, 22–30; 7:1–13; 11:15–17; 11:27–12:40).

Mark too has a "way" upon which true Israel is to walk (8:22–10:52; see 8:27; 9:33–34; 10:32, 52) and to which their blind eyes must be opened (8:22–30; 10:46–52). But it is the way of the crucified Son of Man (8:34), characterized not by Torah obedience or ritual purity but by cross-bearing loyalty to Jesus and care of others (9:42–50; 10:1–14, 21; cf. 12:28–34). Whereas the *Yahad* hoped for the glory of God's kingdom coming in power, Jesus's inner circle actually saw it (9:1–8). And although Mark is not explicit, there are indications that Jesus saw himself as the beginning of God's newly rebuilt temple (12:10–11). It is not the community who atones for sin through its obedience, but it is Jesus who establishes the covenant through his death (10:45; 14:23–24). Finally, whereas by the time of Mark's writing 1QS's teacher had long died, Mark concludes with the incredible claim that Jesus had been raised from the dead and, in the same breath, almost pedestrianly, that he would go before his disciples not into the desert but Galilee (16:6–7).

It is clear that 1QS and Mark inhabit the same uniquely Jewish thought world with similar interests and the same intense focus on Israel's future hope. But 1QS is in Hebrew and addresses a select Jewish group. Mark, like the **LXX**'s earlier translation of Israel's narrative, is in Greek, and his much broader audience includes gentiles (cf. Mark 7:3–4). More significantly, whereas both the LXX and 1QS saw Torah as the cornerstone of Israel's faithfulness to Yahweh, Mark breathtakingly gives that place to Jesus. While Jesus holds his opponents to Torah obedience (Mark 7:6–13), he not only asserts that he fulfills its offer of life (3:4–6; cf. Deut 32:39) but speaks with greater authority (Mark 7:19)—so much so that he reworks Israel's historic Passover around himself (14:22–25). The document 1QS hoped for Yahweh's return. Mark claims that Isaiah 40's prophecy was fulfilled in the person of Jesus, whose calm, Yahweh-like authority, evident in healing compassion and searing judgment, dominates both his Judean landscape and everything beyond.

FOR FURTHER READING

Additional Ancient Texts

In addition to the numerous texts cited in the opening section (see note 3 above), the later Tg. Isa. 40:3, under the influence of 40:10–11, has the way being prepared for God's people to return to restored Jerusalem. New exodus themes are evident in 4Q176 Consolations. In a wider frame, texts such as 1 Enoch 46, Psalms of Solomon 17, and 4 Ezra 13 witness to Jewish messianic expectations.

English Translations and Critical Editions

Garcia Martínez, Florentino, and Eibert J. C. Tigchelaar, eds. *The Dead Sea Scrolls: Study Edition*. 2 vols. Leiden: Brill, 1997–98.

Secondary Literature

Hays, Richard B. *Echoes of Scripture in the Gospels*. Waco: Baylor University Press, 2016.

Marcus, Joel. *The Way of the Lord: Christological Exegesis of the Old Testament in the Gospel of Mark*. Louisville: Westminster John Knox, 1992.

Mauser, Ulrich W. *Christ in the Wilderness: The Wilderness Theme in the Second Gospel and Its Basis in the Biblical Tradition*. Studies in Biblical Theology 39. London: SCM, 1963.

Schofield, Allison. "The Wilderness Motif in the Dead Sea Scrolls." Pages 37–53 in *Israel in the Wilderness: Interpretations of the Biblical Narratives in Jewish and Christian Traditions*. Themes in Biblical Narrative 10. Edited by Kenneth Pomykala. Leiden: Brill, 2008.

Watts, Rikki E. *Isaiah's New Exodus in Mark*. WUNT 2/88. Tübingen: Mohr Siebeck, 1997; Grand Rapids: Baker, 2001.

———. "Mark." Pages 111–249 in *Commentary on the New Testament Use of the Old Testament*. Edited by G. K. Beale and D. A. Carson. Grand Rapids: Baker Academic; Nottingham: Apollos, 2007.

CHAPTER 2

The Parables of Enoch and Mark 1:14–2:12: The Authoritative Son of Man

KRISTIAN A. BENDORAITIS

In the first verses of Mark, the preparatory activities of John the Baptist are chronicled (1:4–8), Jesus is baptized (1:9–11), Jesus is tested in the wilderness (1:12–13), and the message of Jesus is announced: "The time has come. . . . The kingdom of God has come near. Repent and believe the good news!" (1:14–15). In a way unique to this Gospel, Mark moves quickly into the ministry of Jesus, omitting a genealogy, birth narrative, and backstory like we find in Matthew and Luke. Thus the passages that immediately follow are key to helping shape the tone, cadence, and first impressions of Jesus and his ministry.

Who, then, is Jesus according to the opening sequences of Mark? Of course, the Gospel's prescript discloses his identity upfront: Jesus is "the Messiah, the Son of God" (1:1). The narrative in 1:16–2:12, however, answers that question by way of a different method, demonstrating through a series of incidences that Jesus possesses exceptional authority. Indeed, in rapid succession we see Jesus calling his disciples, teaching in the synagogue, casting out demons, and healing the sick (see figure 2.1).

Moreover, in this passage we find the first time in Mark that the term "Son of Man" is applied to Jesus (2:10).[1] What, then, do Jesus's actions, together with this title, tell us about his identity? In this essay we will compare Mark's Son of Man with the figure known as the Son of Man in the Parables of Enoch (1 En. 37–71) in order to demonstrate that Mark portrays Jesus having a *divine identity* and exercising *divine authority* as he teaches, heals, and forgives sins.

---

1. See also Mark 2:28; 8:31, 38; 9:9, 12, 31; 10:33, 45; 13:26; 14:21, 41, 62.

Figure 2.1: Jesus's Demonstration of His Authority

Markan Pericope	Jesus's Demonstration of His Authority
1:16–20	Jesus calls the first disciples
1:21–28	Jesus teaches with authority and exorcises an unclean spirit
1:29–31	Jesus heals Peter's mother-in-law
1:32–34	Jesus heals at evening time
1:35–39	Jesus preaches in surrounding areas
1:40–45	Jesus heals a leper
2:1–12	Jesus (the Son of Man) heals a paralytic and forgives sins

The Parables of Enoch

"AND THE SUM OF JUDGMENT WAS GIVEN UNTO THE SON OF MAN"

The Danielic Son of Man. The term Son of Man is both striking and somewhat enigmatic. While it is frequently found on the lips of Jesus, it is rarely seen in the rest of the New Testament. In fact, Jesus and the Gospel writers may have used the term Son of Man, but they did not coin it. The term "son of man" or "sons of man" is found in the Old Testament and often refers to one's humanness.[2] Yet in the book of Daniel the language concerning the Son of Man seems to take on a different aspect. Here the text presents a human-like figure who approaches the heavenly throne and is given power and authority by God. In a vision, Daniel sees

> one like a son of man, coming with the clouds of heaven. He approached the Ancient of Days and was led into his presence. He was given authority, glory and sovereign power; all nations and peoples of every language worshiped him. His dominion is an everlasting dominion that will not pass away, and his kingdom is one that will never be destroyed. (Dan 7:13–14)

---

2. For example, see Num 23:19; Job 35:8; Ps 80:17; Ezek 2:1; 3:1; 11:15; 38:2; 47:6.

Mark 1:14–2:12

"THE SON OF MAN HAS AUTHORITY ON EARTH TO FORGIVE SINS"

The Authoritative Son of Man. In Mark 2:1–12, a paralyzed man is lowered through the roof of the house in which Jesus is teaching (2:4). Jesus responds by saying, "Son, your sins are forgiven" (2:5). Yet the scribes and teachers of the law accuse Jesus of blasphemy, questioning, "Who can forgive sins but God alone?" (2:7). Jesus replies with a question of his own: "Which is easier: to say to this paralyzed man, 'Your sins are forgiven,' or to say, 'Get up, take your mat and walk'?" (2:9). Rather than wait for an answer, Jesus responds to the scribes, "I want you to know that the Son of Man has authority on earth to forgive sins" (2:10). He then turns to the paralytic and says, "I tell you, get up, take your mat and go home," which the man does immediately (2:11–12).

In this initial reference to the Son of Man, Jesus uses the title to refer to himself. Indeed, he uses it to support the notion that he possesses "authority on earth to forgive sins" (2:10), authority Jesus must disclose to explain his preceding and seemingly preposterous announcement concerning the forgiveness of the paralyzed man's sins. Forgiveness of sins was part of a larger expectation of the prophets relating to eschatological hope (Isa 33:24; Jer 31:34; Jub. 22:14).[4] Similarly, healing and the restoration of wholeness was part of the hope of salvation that was to arrive in the new age. The manifestation of Jesus's authority on earth through healing and forgiveness therefore suggests that Mark is narrating the in-breaking of God's eschatological activity into the world.[5] Furthermore, through his acts of healing and forgiveness Jesus demonstrates that he is exercising divine authority, an attribute usually reserved for God alone. Thus, for Jesus to declare that he possesses this authority is considered blasphemy to the scribes (Mark 2:7).

While this is the first time in Mark that Jesus's authority creates conflict with the Jewish leaders, the demonstration of Jesus's authority in his healing and teaching has already been a common element in the Gospel. Jesus is endowed with divine presence through the Spirit at his baptism (1:9–11); he exorcises an unclean spirit and is recognized by it as "the Holy One of God" (1:24); and Jesus authoritatively purifies a man from leprosy, a serious disease marked by ritual uncleanliness and ostracization (1:40–45). Additionally, Mark notes Jesus teaching with a "new" authority, much to the amazement

---

4. James D. G. Dunn, "The Son of Man in Mark," in *Parables of Enoch: A Paradigm Shift*, ed. D. L. Bock and J. H. Charlesworth, JCT 11 (London: T&T Clark, 2013), 18–34, at 20.

5. Robert A. Guelich, *Mark 1–8:26*, WBC 34A (Dallas: Word, 1989), 86.

of the crowds (1:22, 27). Whoever Jesus is, he is not just another one of "the teachers of the law" (1:22).

Slightly Contrasting Portraits. Like Mark's portrait of Jesus in these first few chapters of his Gospel, the Parables paint a picture of a Son of Man with divine authority given to him by God. However, this figure is portrayed distinctively in the two texts. This may suggest a similar theological understanding of the Son of Man that pervades the use of the term, while also reflecting the way the term has developed differently in separate contexts. For example, the Parables present the Son of Man in a *heavenly* context, seated on a throne of divine glory and administering eschatological judgment. Mark, on the other hand, explicitly notes the Son of Man's authority "on earth" (2:10), suggesting the immanence of Jesus's authority and its ability to reach into the lives of those who encounter him.

Mark and the Parables also differ in how they narrate the Son of Man relating to humanity. The Parables's Son of Man is a champion for the righteous at the heavenly final judgment, yet Mark's earthly Son of Man is also a hope for the unrighteous: "It is not the healthy who need a doctor, but the sick. I have not come to call the righteous, but sinners" (2:17). Mark connects Jesus as the Son of Man to the forgiveness of sins (2:5–10), yet the Son of Man never explicitly forgives sins in the Parables of Enoch, nor is the declaration of forgiveness attributed to him. Indeed, the setting of the Parables at the final judgment suggests the opportunity for mercy may have passed (cf. 1 En. 62:9).

In conclusion, Mark seems to present Jesus, as the Son of Man, exercising God's authority on earth. In this way, the interpretation of the Son of Man in the Parables can give a context, or framework, in which to view Mark's presentation of the Son of Man. While the Enochic (and Danielic) tradition presents the Son of Man as a final eschatological judge in heaven, Jesus as the Son of Man in Mark is one who presently forgives sins "on earth." If the Son of Man is the one to judge at the end of age, then it is shocking that this figure in Mark has arrived in the present to offer an earthly pardon. God's forgiveness manifests itself in Jesus, the authoritative Son of Man, who, counterintuitively, has come "to give his life as a ransom for many" (10:45).

FOR FURTHER READING

Additional Ancient Texts

Other texts that might give insight into the esoteric term Son of Man and suggest evidence of its development include 4 Ezra and 2 Baruch, both dated to near the end of the first-century AD. In particular, 4 Ezra 13 has imagery similar to Daniel 7 and continues to give dimension to the figure of the one like a son of man as an individual. For similar reasons, 2 Baruch can be of interest as it shows another interpretation of the Danielic son of man. Like 4 Ezra, 2 Baruch makes reference to this figure issuing judgment (2 Bar. 40:1–2; 72:2–3; 4 Ezra 13:10–11, 37–38) and sitting on a throne (2 Bar. 73:1).

English Translations and Critical Editions

Isaac, E. "1 (Ethiopic Apocalypse of) Enoch: A New Translation and Introduction." Pages 5–89 in vol. 1 of *The Old Testament Pseudepigrapha*. Ed. James H. Charlesworth. New York: Doubleday, 1983.

Knibb, Michael A. *The Ethiopic Book of Enoch*. 2 vols. Oxford: Clarendon, 1978.

Nickelsburg, George W. E., and James C. VanderKam. *1 Enoch: The Hermeneia Translation*. Minneapolis: Fortress, 2012.

Secondary Literature

Boccaccini, Gabriele, ed. *Enoch and the Messiah Son of Man: Revisiting the Book of Parables*. Grand Rapids: Eerdmans, 2007.

Hooker, Morna D. *The Son of Man in Mark: A Study of the Background of the Term "Son of Man" and Its Use in St Mark's Gospel*. Montreal: McGill University Press, 1967.

Hurtado, Larry W., and Paul L. Owen, eds. *'Who Is This Son of Man?': The Latest Scholarship on a Puzzling Expression of the Historical Jesus*. LNTS 390. London: T&T Clark, 2011.

Nickelsburg, George W. E., and James C. VanderKam, *1 Enoch 2: A Commentary on the Book of 1 Enoch, Chapters 37–82*. Hermeneia. Minneapolis: Fortress, 2012.

Snow, Robert S. *Daniel's Son of Man in Mark: A Redefinition of the Jerusalem Temple and the Formation of a New Covenant Community*. Eugene, OR: Pickwick, 2016.

Stuckenbruck, Loren T., and Gabriele Boccaccini, eds. *Enoch and the Synoptic Gospels: Reminiscences, Allusions, Intertextuality*. Atlanta: SBL Press, 2016.

Walck, Leslie W. *Son of Man in the Parables of Enoch and in Matthew*. JCT 9. London: T&T Clark, 2011.

CHAPTER 3

Josephus and Mark 2:13–3:6: Controversies with the Scribes and Pharisees

MARY MARSHALL

In 2:1–3:6 Mark outlines five challenges to the behavior of Jesus and his disciples by representatives of the Jewish leadership: (1) Jesus's authority to forgive sins is questioned by the scribes (2:1–12); (2) the scribes of the **Pharisees**[1] ask the disciples why Jesus eats with tax collectors and sinners (2:13–17); (3) Jesus is asked (by an anonymous group) why his disciples, unlike those of John the Baptist and those of the Pharisees, do not fast (2:18–22); (4) the Pharisees accuse Jesus's disciples of transgressing the Sabbath law by picking heads of grain (2:23–28); and (5) the Pharisees and others look for a reason to accuse Jesus of transgressing the Sabbath law when he heals a man with a shriveled hand (3:1–6). Mark thus introduces the opposition to Jesus that will dog his ministry and culminate in his crucifixion. Indeed, 3:6 concludes the section with a dark foreshadowing of Jesus's eventual fate: "Then the Pharisees went out and began to plot with the Herodians how they might kill Jesus."

This study will focus on Mark's construal of the four controversies involving Pharisees, in which my reading of the Gospel will be informed by **Josephus**'s comments on the Pharisees in his *Jewish Antiquities* (or *Antiquities of the Jews*). Alongside certain books in the New Testament, Josephus is one of very few surviving witnesses to the Pharisees and is

---

1. My translation in 2:16 departs from the NIV, which prefers "teachers of the law who were Pharisees." Indeed, the identity of these "scribes of the Pharisees" is a matter of considerable debate among scholars. We might best think of a scribe of the Pharisees as an individual occupied with writing or documents (*possibly* performing some legal function) who is affiliated with, or otherwise a supporter or follower of, the Pharisees.

our most detailed source of information about them. If this observation alone does not encourage comparison between Josephus's depiction of the Pharisees and our Markan text, it is also worth noting that, from Josephus's generally positive description of them as a popular and highly regarded group, we might be surprised to find Mark portraying them in contrast to Jesus and even in active opposition to him.

Josephus

"The Excellence of the Pharisees"

The Jewish historian Josephus is thought to have been born in AD 37 and is known today solely from his extant writings, which comprise an unparalleled source of information about Jews and Judaism in the first century. Yet Josephus was no impartial chronicler; indeed, it is Josephus's prejudices and pursuit of sometimes incompatible agendas that make reading his work so interesting (and entertaining). Born into a Jerusalem family with sufficient wealth and leisure for education, Josephus later became a revolutionary general in the war against Rome. Having met with defeat, Josephus surrendered to the Roman forces and later lived under the patronage of the imperial family, writing books for a gentile, Greek-speaking audience. Josephus is frequently torn between loyalty to his Jewish origins and cause on the one hand, and his obligations to the Roman emperor on the other. Although he is probably best known for his seven-volume account of the Jewish War (*Jewish War*), this study is concerned with a later project in twenty volumes: the *Antiquities of the Jews*, which relates the history of the Jewish people from the creation of the world to the twelfth year of the reign of Emperor Nero (AD 66).

In the eighteenth volume of that work, Josephus embarks on his account of events dated to AD 6, particularly the uprising of two Jews, Judas the Gaulanite and Saddok the Pharisee, who were against the proposals of Quirinius (a Roman governor) to make an assessment of Jewish property. In Josephus's opinion, the actions of these two men "sowed the seed" of trouble that led to Judea's rebellion against Rome sixty years later. Josephus criticizes Judas and Saddok for creating a new and "intrusive" school of philosophy. They demonstrate, Josephus says, that "innovation and reform in ancestral traditions weighs heavily in the scale in leading to the destruction of the congregation of the people" (*Ant.* 18.9).[2]

---

2. Translations of Josephus are from LCL (*Josephus*, trans. H. St. J. Thackeray et al., 13 vols, LCL [Cambridge: Harvard University Press, 1926–65]).

The Reputation of the Pharisees. It is at this point that Josephus launches into an excursus on the three ancient philosophies of the Jews—**Essenes**, **Sadducees**, and Pharisees (*Ant.* 18.11–25)—against which the so-called "fourth philosophy" of Judas and Saddok may be seen as illegitimate. Josephus's description of the Pharisees is brief but conveys a good deal of information. Josephus states:

> [The Pharisees] follow the guidance of that which their doctrine has selected and transmitted as good, attaching the chief importance to the observance of those commandments which it has seen fit to dictate to them. They show respect and deference to their elders, nor do they rashly presume to contradict their proposals. (*Ant.* 18.12)

Here the Pharisees are associated with following teachings and observing commandments. Elsewhere, Josephus will refer to the Pharisees' reputation for "unrivalled expertise" in their country's laws.[3] In *Antiquities* 18, however, Josephus makes no particular or direct reference to Jewish law or legal interpretation; instead, he makes a point of explaining the Pharisees' attitude toward their elders. In this context, respect and deference amount to more than courtesy. Remember that Josephus disapproves of innovation and rash reform, but might be supposed to approve of the Pharisees, who do not innovate but uphold the proposals of their elders.[4]

The Influence of the Pharisees. The next several lines of *Antiquities* 18 explain the Pharisees' positions regarding fate, free will, and the afterlife, which will not concern us here.[5] The final point to emerge concerning the Pharisees from *Antiquities* 18 is their influence.

> Because of these views they are, as a matter of fact, extremely influential among the townsfolk; and all prayers and sacred rites of divine worship are performed according to their exposition. This is the great tribute that the inhabitants of the cities, by practicing the highest ideals both in their way of living and in their discourse, have paid to the excellence of the Pharisees. (*Ant.* 18.15)

---

3. *Life* 19; see also *J.W.* 2.162. This reputation for accuracy (the Greek word is also associated with strictness and thoroughness) is also prevalent in the New Testament portrayals of the Pharisees; see, e.g., Acts 22:3 and 26:5.

4. Adherence to ancestral tradition is something associated with the Pharisees elsewhere in the *Antiquities*; see 13.298 and 17.41.

5. Some of these ideas are taken up in Jason Maston's chapter 22 on Mark 12.

The Pharisees are presented, therefore, as a highly regarded group, to whom the people defer and imitate their "highest ideals," although they may not be Pharisees themselves. Such is the extent of this general approval that Josephus adds that the Sadducees, who are certainly not Pharisees and do not agree with the Pharisees' teachings, are nevertheless forced to toe the Pharisaic line, in order to be tolerated by the masses (*Ant.* 18.17; cf. 13.298). It is perhaps no surprise, then, to read in the *Jewish War* that the Pharisees "cultivate harmonious relations with the community" (*J.W.* 2.166).

The picture of the Pharisees to emerge from *Antiquities*, then, is of a well-respected group with a reputation for excellence and high ideals. They are not innovators but uphold the proposals of their elders. They are influential and popular and accustomed to prevailing in matters of practice. As we return to the passage in Mark, we shall see how these characteristics of the Pharisees found in Josephus might illuminate the controversies with Jesus.

Mark 2:13–3:6

"POUR NEW WINE INTO NEW WINESKINS"

In four out of five of the controversies in Mark 2:1–3:6, Jesus and his disciples are shown in opposition, either directly or indirectly, to the Pharisees (the first controversy, in 2:1–12, involves scribes but does not mention Pharisees). Whereas Josephus leads us to expect the Pharisees' ruling to prevail, it does not prevail against Jesus.

Sabbath Controversies. Two of the controversies concern matters of the Sabbath law (2:23–28; 3:1–6). According to the commandment of God, Jews "shall not do any work" on the Sabbath (Exod 20:8–10), but the Torah itself gives limited guidance as to what constitutes work. It seems from Mark that the Pharisees held both picking heads of grain and healing to fall under the category of work. They pronounce the disciples' activity "unlawful" (Mark 2:24), and seeking a reason to accuse Jesus, they "watched him closely to see if he would heal him on the Sabbath" (3:2). We might expect Jesus and his disciples to submit, as the Sadducees did, to the rulings of the Pharisees on this point, but instead Jesus defends his actions and those of his disciples and thereby offers an alternative interpretation of the law.

In Mark 3:4 Jesus reframes the argument as a binary opposition: "Which is lawful on the Sabbath: to do good or to do evil, to save life or to kill?" There are two alternatives: the former must be lawful and the latter unlawful, and so it is a case of deciding into which category Jesus's miracle will fall. Healing the man with the shriveled hand does not kill and is not evil but does good. Mark confirms Jesus's position on the correct side of this divide by juxtaposing him with the Pharisees and **Herodians** in 3:6 who, by plotting to kill Jesus on the Sabbath, condemn themselves as evildoers.

In the grainfield, Jesus appeals to a legal precedent to defend his disciples' actions (2:25–26; cf. Lev 24:5–9; 1 Sam 21:1–6), but close inspection reveals the odd nature of the precedent he cites. There seems to be little common ground between the two cases: picking heads of grain (which is a potential transgression of Sabbath law) and eating the consecrated bread (which might be construed as a violation of temple regulations). Moreover, although Jesus notes that David and his companions were hungry and in need—a potential mitigating factor—Mark has not suggested that the same is true of Jesus's disciples. They pick heads of grain, but there is no suggestion that they are threshing, winnowing, and milling them for food, let alone eating them as they go along. What Jesus's disciples and David's companions do have in common, however, is that they are accompanying a figure of authority. Just as David, chosen by God, could claim support for his companions in the pursuit of his mission, the presence of Jesus, who was declared God's beloved Son in Mark 1:11, allows his disciples to demonstrate that "the Sabbath was made for man, not man for the Sabbath" (Mark 2:27). The closing verse of this controversy underlines that "the Son of Man is Lord even of the Sabbath" (2:28). If "Son of Man" here is read as a reference to Jesus, then it is Jesus's personal authority (extended to the disciples) that determines behavior. While the populace and the Pharisees submit to the teaching of the Pharisees in such matters, Mark shows Jesus confidently challenging their rulings and exercising his own authority rather than yielding to theirs.

Other Controversies. In the remaining two controversies, Mark makes no direct reference to a point of Jewish law but again contrasts Jesus's behavior with that of the Pharisees. In the first case (2:13–17), the reasoning behind the question, "Why does he eat with tax collectors and sinners?" (2:16), is not stated explicitly. The scribes of the Pharisees may fear for Jesus's reputation; he is associating with people who were readily ostracized by respectable Jewish society. Alternatively, they may fear for Jesus's ritual purity; there is evidence that Jews in the first-century AD attended to a number of practices that ensured the ritual purity of their food. Perhaps neither tax collectors (due to their contact with gentiles) nor "sinners" conformed to the standard expected by the scribes of the Pharisees.

In either case, there is a sense that Jesus, by his association with tax collectors and sinners, is also perceived to be falling short of this standard.

The widespread conformity to Pharisaic teachings and traditions (described by Josephus) might explain the surprise, which is implicit in the question, that Jesus does not avoid tax collectors and sinners. It is also worth noting here that Mark describes Jesus's association with groups on the edges of society, with whom, despite their popularity (according to Josephus), the Pharisees have failed to cultivate "harmonious relations" (*J.W.* 2.166). The scribes of the Pharisees have neglected these who are sick, and it is Jesus who must minister to them.

Similar themes are taken up in the question about fasting (Mark 2:18–22). Here again the anonymous challengers presuppose that Jesus's disciples ought to behave as do the disciples of the Pharisees and the disciples of John the Baptist (2:18). Perhaps this further supports Josephus's witness to general adherence to Pharisaic teaching, or perhaps it acknowledges particular characteristics of Jesus that support similarity with the Pharisees themselves. Jesus's baptism by John in Mark 1 might certainly encourage a comparison with the disciples of John the Baptist.

In any case, the contentious issue is a matter of practice that allows Mark to make a christological point. Jesus's defense of his disciples' actions is grounded entirely in the fact of his own presence; the disciples cannot fast because Jesus, the bridegroom, is with them (2:19). As in the grainfield, the presence of Jesus has special significance for those with him. Jesus looks forward to a time when the bridegroom will be absent (perhaps Mark's deliberate reference to the crucifixion or to a contemporary Christian experience) and then they will fast (2:20). What the disciples do is therefore dictated neither by the Pharisees nor by the disciples of John the Baptist, but is wholly determined by the presence of Jesus.

In 2:21–22 Jesus employs a mini-**parable** or metaphor to explain the overall significance of what is taking place. No one sews an unshrunk (i.e., new) patch onto an old garment because when it is eventually washed with the garment and shrinks, the repair will tear away from the garment that can shrink no further. The new wine, expanding as it ferments, cannot be contained in old and brittle skins. The metaphor implies that behavior must be appropriate: old for old, new for new, feasting with the bridegroom, fasting in his absence. Jesus's presence is a new circumstance that cannot be served by the old practices endorsed by the Pharisees.

If we appreciate the reputation of the Pharisees attested by Josephus, we may observe how their juxtaposition with Jesus in Mark 2:1–3:6 underlines a message about Jesus. The Pharisees are not innovators but respect the elders and ancestral tradition, whereas Jesus has his own authority and his presence necessitates a change in behavior. He heralds something new. Jesus's ministry grows in popularity, despite the dominance of the Pharisees, and withstands challenges from the prevailing wisdom and practice of his day.

For Further Reading

Additional Ancient Texts

Mark 2:1–3:6 is paralleled in Matthew 9:1–16, 12:1–14, and Luke 5:17–6:11. Mark includes further controversies with the Pharisees at 10:2–9, 12:13–17, and especially 7:1–13, which again associates the Pharisees with adherence to ancestral tradition. There is a wealth of further material on the Pharisees in the New Testament, particularly Matthew 23, Acts 5, 22, 23, and 26, and Philippians 3. As well as the passages from Josephus referred to in footnotes above, the passage in *J.W.* 2.162–66 deserves particular attention, as well as *Ag. Ap.* 2.20–21 §282. Other key Second Temple texts include CD A 10:14–11:18; Philo's *Moses* 2.21; and 1 Maccabees 2:29–41.

English Translations and Critical Editions

Josephus. Translated by H. St. J. Thackeray et al. 13 vols. LCL. Cambridge: Harvard University Press, 1926–65.

Mason, Steve, ed. *Flavius Josephus: Translation and Commentary*. 10 vols. The Brill Josephus Project. Leiden: Brill, 2001–.

Secondary Literature

Cook, M. J. *Mark's Treatment of the Jewish Leaders*. NovTSup 51. Leiden: Brill, 1978.

Goodman, M. "A Note on Josephus, the Pharisees and Ancestral Tradition." *JJS* 50 (1999): 17–20.

Kingsbury, J. D. *Conflict in Mark: Jesus, Authorities, Disciples*. Minneapolis: Fortress, 1989.

Marshall, M. *The Portrayals of the Pharisees in the Gospels and Acts*. FRLANT 254. Göttingen: Vandenhoeck & Ruprecht, 2015.

Pickup, M. "Matthew and Mark's Pharisees." Pages 67–112 in *In Quest of the Historical Pharisees*. Edited by J. Neusner and B. Chilton. Waco, TX: Baylor University Press, 2007.

Stemberger, G. *Jewish Contemporaries of Jesus: Pharisees, Sadducees and Essenes*. Minneapolis: Fortress, 1995.

CHAPTER 4

The Testaments of the Twelve Patriarchs and Mark 3:7–35: Apocalyptic and the Kingdom

ELIZABETH E. SHIVELY

From the outset, Mark portrays Jesus's ministry as a conflict between two kingdoms. The Holy Spirit breaks into the world from an open heaven at Jesus's baptism to indwell and thrust him into the wilderness to be tempted by Satan. The Spirit-filled Jesus emerges to make his central proclamation that God's kingdom—or reign—is infiltrating the world (Mark 1:14–15). The reappearance of Jesus, the Holy Spirit, and Satan in 3:22–30 recalls the baptism and temptation accounts, suggesting that this later episode develops the initial wilderness conflict from which Jesus emerged to proclaim God's reign and demonstrate its presence.

This sort of cosmic conflict is the stuff of Jewish apocalypses, like Daniel and portions of 1 Enoch. Similar to Second Temple Jewish literature like the **Qumran** writings, Jubilees, and the Testaments of the Twelve Patriarchs, Mark is not an apocalypse by genre but may be considered "**apocalyptic**" because it uses language and themes that typically appear in apocalypses.[1] By way of analogy, the 2005 film *Serenity* is a science-fiction film that uses themes of the classic Western, so that the universe is portrayed as a frontier into which outlaws ride on their trusted cargo ship. Similarly, Mark is a subgenre of Greco-Roman biography that uses themes of the Jewish apocalypse to portray Jesus's ministry

---

1. J. J. Collins defines an apocalypse as "a genre of revelatory literature with a narrative framework, in which a revelation is mediated by an otherworldly being to a human recipient disclosing a transcendent reality which is both temporal, insofar as it envisages eschatological salvation, and spatial insofar as it involves another, supernatural world" (*The Apocalyptic Imagination: An Introduction to Jewish Apocalyptic Literature*, 3rd ed. [Grand Rapids: Eerdmans, 2016], 5).

as a cosmic conflict. Mark employs typical apocalyptic themes throughout the Gospel—like involvement of supernatural beings, cosmic conflict, and movement toward eschatological salvation—but they cluster in Mark 3:22–30 to establish most clearly the apocalyptic character of Jesus's earthly ministry. In what follows, I seek to illuminate the explanation of Jesus's exorcisms and their function in the conflict between Satan's and God's kingdoms by reading Mark 3:22–30 along with the Testaments of the Twelve Patriarchs (T. 12 Patr.).

The Testaments of the Twelve Patriarchs
"BELIAR SHALL BE BOUND BY HIM"

The Testaments of the Twelve Patriarchs, completed by AD 200, are a collection of farewell speeches from each of Jacob's twelve sons to their children. Because the Testaments of the Twelve Patriarchs have both Jewish and Christian elements, scholars debate whether they were originally Jewish compositions that Christians later edited or Christian compositions based on Jewish sources. In either case, they contain material that predates the New Testament and supply considerable data for understanding its thought world.

Each testament includes an autobiographical section, an ethical section, and an eschatological section. The Testaments of the Twelve Patriarchs explain Israel's disobedience as a supernatural struggle by revealing a world under Beliar's (Satan's) rule in which evil spirits lead people astray from God's commands (which are also portrayed in the terms of Greco-Roman virtues).[2] The patriarchs warn Israel to flee Beliar and please God by obeying his commands; yet they predict that their descendants will inevitably fall into sin, and, in the final version, reject Jesus the **messiah**.[3] Nevertheless, they also predict that God will ultimately remove Beliar and his spirits and free his people from the demonic rule that leads to their ruin, restoring his reign over his people and the world.[4]

For example, the Testament of Zebulon predicts that the Lord will arise and "liberate every captive of the sons of men from Beliar, and every spirit of error will be trampled down. He will turn all nations to being zealous for him" (T. Zeb. 9:8).[5] Elsewhere, the Testaments of the Twelve Patriarchs

---

2. For example, see T. Reu. 4:11; T. Dan 4:7; T. Ash. 1:8–9; T. Benj. 3:3; 6:1.

3. T. Levi 4:2–6; 10:2; 16:3; see also T. Zeb. 9:8–9; T. Ash. 7:2–5.

4. T. Levi 18:12; T. Jud. 25:3; T. Zeb. 9:8; T. Dan 5:10–11.

5. Translation from H. C. Kee, "Testaments of the Twelve Patriarchs," in vol. 1 of *The Old Testament Pseudepigrapha*, ed. James H. Charlesworth (New York: Doubleday, 1983), 775–828 (hereafter *OTP*).

predicts that a redeemer—evidently Jesus Christ—will accomplish this task. For example, the Testament of Judah predicts that an ideal king will restore God's kingdom (T. Jud. 24), in part by throwing Beliar into eternal fire in order to destroy the spirits of error (25:3) so that Israel may rise to life and glorify the Lord forever (25:1–2, 4–5). Likewise, the Testament of Dan anticipates that someone from the tribes of Judah and Levi will "make war against Beliar" and "take from Beliar the captives, the souls of the saints" (T. Dan 5:10–11).[6] As a result, this savior will cause the hearts of the disobedient to turn to God and restore the Edenic paradise so that the righteous may glorify God forever as he lives and reigns among them (T. Dan 5:10–13).

The Testament of Levi describes the removal of Beliar using the term "bind" (T. Levi 18:12). This is the same term that Jesus uses to describe the "binding" (NASB, ESV) or "tying up" (NIV, NRSV) of the strong man in Mark 3:27. Levi predicts that after his priestly descendants fail and reject the messiah, God will raise up a new, ideal priest.

> [9b] In his priesthood sin will cease. Lawless people will rest in their evil deeds, but righteous people will rest in him. [10] He will open the gates of paradise and remove the sword that has threatened since Adam. [11] He will grant to the saints to eat of the tree of life, and the spirit of holiness will be upon them. [12] Beliar will be bound by him, and he will grant authority to his children to trample on evil spirits. [13] The Lord will rejoice in his children, and he will be well pleased by his beloved ones forever. [14] Then Abraham, Isaac, and Jacob will rejoice, and I will be glad, and all the saints will be clothed in righteousness. (T. Levi 18:9–14)[7]

The binding of Beliar (18:12) is concurrent with the final judgment of the wicked and redemption of the righteous (18:9b). As a result of Beliar's binding, liberated people will finally have the power to "trample on evil spirits" that had kept them from obeying God's commands (18:12). Thus, God's people are able to escape the threat of judgment (18:10) and receive the benefits of this paradise—eternal life, a spirit of holiness, righteousness, and God's pleasure. In this context, the act of "binding" is an eschatological

---

6. Kee, "Testaments," 809.

7. My translation. My translation of 18:9b differs from that of Charles, which reads, "And the lawless *shall cease to do evil [and the just shall rest in him]*" (R. H. Charles, *The Testaments of the Twelve Patriarchs*, Ancient Texts and Translations [Eugene, OR: Wipf & Stock, 2005], 47); and that of Kee, "Testaments," 795, which similarly reads, "and lawless men *shall rest from their evil deeds*" (emphasis added). Both the text's grammar and parallelism support my translation.

act of judgment that inaugurates the restoration of the Edenic paradise (18:10, 13–14).

In the Testament of Levi, as in other eschatological sections of the Testaments of the Twelve Patriarchs, the removal of Beliar's reign over human beings functions as a watershed in the restoration of God's reign. The Testaments of the Twelve Patriarchs are not unique in their vision, because 1 Enoch, Jubilees, the Testament of Moses, and the Qumran writings anticipate a similar cosmic regime change.[8] This examination shows that Mark's portrayal of Jesus's ministry as a cosmic conflict is at home in the thought world of **Second Temple Judaism** and reinforces the suggestion that Satan's end is fundamental to Jesus's establishment of the kingdom of God. Nevertheless, Mark also uses apocalyptic language and themes distinctively. Particularly, Mark 3:22–30 explains the function of Jesus's exorcisms in Satan's removal.

Mark 3:7–35

"No One Can Enter a Strong Man's House without First Tying Him Up"

Jesus in the Power of the Spirit. Jesus responds in **parables** to refute the charge of scribes who have circulated a report that he performs exorcisms by the power of Beelzebul, or "Lord of the dwelling" (3:22, 30).[9] Jesus renames this figure as Satan and plays on the image of a dwelling in the parables of the divided kingdom and house. The analogies of a kingdom and a household evoke the image of Satan as the all-powerful prince or head over a community of demons that requires unity and loyalty to rule properly. Although Yahweh is the true Lord of heaven and earth, who reigns over all ("heaven is my throne and the earth is my footstool," Isa 66:1), Satan has become a usurper, a pseudo-lord who reigns over a horde of demons to hold people captive. Mark 3:23–26 convey the absurdity of thinking that Satan (ruler of demons) casts out Satan (group of demons) because divided dominions cannot stand, and it is obvious from continued instances of demon possession that Satan's rule remains intact and operational in the world.

---

8. See especially 1 En. 10:4–6; 55:4; Jub. 23:23–31; 50:5; T. Mos. 10:1; 1QM 1:5, 8–9, 12; 12:9–18; 17:6–7; 18:6–8, 10–11; 19:4–8; 11QMelch.

9. The name "Beelzebul" is challenging, but not impossible, to interpret. See my discussion in *Apocalyptic Imagination in the Gospel of Mark: The Literary and Theological Role of Mark 3:22–30*, BZNW 189 (Berlin: de Gruyter, 2012), 60–62.

The parable of the strong man opposes the scribes' viewpoint: Satan's powerful reign is indeed coming to an end, not through internal division (3:23–26) but through the external attack of one more powerful (3:27). The setting of the parable is the strong man's house (the world), in which Satan holds people as his own possessions until a stronger figure invades his domain. This language echoes Isaiah 49:24–26, in which the Strong One of Jacob rescues Israel from the "strong man," or the mightiest warrior in Jewish tradition. As a result, the redeemed enter the restored city of Zion where the Lord again reigns as king (Isa 52:1–10). Whereas Isaiah presents God as the Strong One who rescues Israel from a human strong man, Mark presents the Spirit-filled Jesus as the stronger one who rescues God's people from a cosmic strong man (see also Mark 1:7).

Like T. Levi 18, Mark 3:27 depicts a redeemer who removes Satan's power from over human beings. Unlike T. Levi, Mark does not describe a history-closing judgment scene but the function of Jesus's exorcisms. In light of Mark's own context, the binding of the strong man most likely refers to the effect of Jesus's exorcisms in fundamentally weakening Satan's realm and guaranteeing its future destruction, rather than to the complete removal of Satan's power in the past or present. The end of Satan's kingdom is inexorably tied to the appearance of God's kingdom, which is imminent rather than fully here (Mark 1:14–15). Indeed, Mark's story neither depicts an impotent Satanic realm nor a patently powerful Jesus during his earthly ministry.[10] Instead, the story follows Jesus to his crucifixion and resurrection, where he deals the decisive blow to Satan's kingdom. The visibly powerful appearances of God's kingdom belong to the future (8:38; 13:24–27; 14:62).

Satan's continuing influence has implications for human beings, because people choose sides in the conflict of kingdoms by their response to the person, power, and authority of Jesus. Accordingly, Jesus names the Holy Spirit as the power by which he exorcises and the consequences when people misname that power, as the scribes have done (3:28–29). The fit of 3:22–30 into the context of 3:7–35 further demonstrates how the battle lines are drawn in the human arena.

New Kingdom Realities. In 3:9 Jesus instructs his disciples to prepare a boat because of the crushing crowd but then does not embark. Instead, he climbs a mountain (3:13) and does not get into the boat until 4:1–2. As a result, 3:7–12 and 4:1–2 act as frames for the material within. The framed material, 3:13–35,

---

10. See, e.g., Mark 4:15 and 8:33, in which Satan retains a measure of power; 1:1–28, 32–34, 39; 3:11–12; 5:1–20; 7:24–30; 9:14–29, which describe continued demon possession; and chs. 11–16, in which Jesus is crucified.

is divided into two parts, separated by a scene-change (3:20). Yet the material also falls into two sets of juxtaposed and overlapping episodes, which invite us to interpret one set (3:13–19, 22–30) in light of the other (3:20–21, 31–35).

The first set of episodes (3:13–19, 22–30) contrasts the Twelve who receive their authority from Jesus with the scribes who receive their authority from Jerusalem. Jesus *goes up* the mountain and authorizes the Twelve to preach and cast out demons, an extension of his own mission to inaugurate God's kingdom (see 1:23–26, 38–39). By contrast, the scribes *come down* from Jerusalem to discredit Jesus's authority to cast out demons, an invalidation of that mission (3:22–23).

The second set of episodes (3:20–21, 31–35) contrasts Jesus's blood family with his newly created "family" (3:20–21, 31–35). Jesus's kin attempt to pull him from his preaching and exorcising, claiming that he is out of his mind. As they call to Jesus from outside the house where he sits with his followers, he symbolically creates a new family.

Mark interlocks these sets of episodes by **intercalating** (that is, inserting) Jesus's conflict with scribes into his conflict with family. While these groups are not alike in every way, they correspond in their efforts to subvert Jesus's assault against Satan's kingdom. Jesus distances himself from both his blood and religious families and instead creates a new family, not determined by blood or by religion but by doing God's will (3:35). The context suggests that doing God's will involves joining Jesus's kingdom mission to battle satanic power. Moreover, the placement of Mark 3:22–30 depicts the movement from one kingdom to another: Jesus liberates people from the domain in which Satan is lord (3:27) and places people in a new domain in which he is Lord (3:31–35).

Later, Jesus envisions his followers living and working faithfully as members of his new household after his death and until his return (13:32–37). The owner or "lord of the house" is the crucified and risen Jesus for whom his people wait (contrast 3:27). Jesus portrays those of his new household continuing to engage in the conflict against satanic power, now empowered by the Holy Spirit—resisting, testifying, suffering, and dying (13:9–13)—until he returns as the Son of Man.

FOR FURTHER READING

Additional Ancient Texts

Texts that share ideas with the Testaments of the Twelve Patriarchs and provide important background material for Mark include: 1 Enoch 10:4–6; 55:4;

Jubilees 23:23–31; 50:5; Testament (Assumption) of Moses 10:1; the War Scroll (1QM) 1:5, 8–9, 12; 12:9–18; 17:6–7; 18:6–8, 10–11; 19:4–8; 11QMelchizedek; Testament of Solomon. See also Daniel 7–12 and Revelation.

English Translations and Critical Editions

Charles, R. H. *The Greek Versions of the Testaments of the Twelve Patriarchs*. Oxford: Clarendon, 1908.

———. *The Testaments of the Twelve Patriarchs*. Ancient Texts and Translations. Eugene, OR: Wipf & Stock, 2005.

Jonge, Marinus de. "The Testaments of the Twelve Patriarchs." Pages 505–600 in *The Apocryphal Old Testament*. Edited by H. F. D. Sparks. Oxford: Clarendon, 1984.

Kee, H. C. "Testaments of the Twelve Patriarchs." Pages 775–828 in vol. 1 of *The Old Testament Pseudepigrapha*. Edited by James H. Charlesworth. Garden City, NY: Doubleday, 1983.

Stone, Michael E. *The Testament of Levi: A First Study of the Armenian MSS of the Testaments of the XII Patriarchs in the Convent of St. James, Jerusalem, with Text, Critical Apparatus, Notes, and Translation*. Jerusalem: St. James, 1969.

Secondary Literature

Collins, J. J. *The Apocalyptic Imagination: An Introduction to Jewish Apocalyptic Literature*. 3rd ed. Grand Rapids: Eerdmans, 2016.

Evans, Craig A. "Inaugurating the Kingdom of God and Defeating the Kingdom of Satan." *BBR* 15 (2005): 49–75.

———. "Jesus's Exorcisms and Proclamation of the Kingdom of God in Light of the Testaments." Pages 210–33 in *The Changing Face of Judaism, Christianity, and Other Greco-Roman Religions in Antiquity*. Edited by I. H. Henderson and G. S. Oegema. Gütersloh: Gütersloher Verlagshaus, 2006.

Jonge, Marinus de. *Jewish Eschatology, Early Christian Christology, and the Testaments of the Twelve Patriarchs: Collected Essays of Marinus de Jonge*. NovTSup 63. Leiden: Brill, 1991.

Kugler, Robert. *The Testaments of the Twelve Patriarchs*. Sheffield: Sheffield Academic Press, 2001.

Shively, Elizabeth E. *Apocalyptic Imagination in the Gospel of Mark: The Literary and Theological Role of Mark 3:22–30*. BZNW 189. Berlin: de Gruyter, 2012.

Twelftree, G. H. *Jesus the Exorcist: A Contribution to the Study of the Historical Jesus*. WUNT 2/54. Tübingen: Mohr Siebeck, 1993.

CHAPTER 5

4 Ezra and Mark 4:1–34: Parables on Seeds, Sowing, and Fruit

KLYNE SNODGRASS

Mark 4 looks odd, even disorganized, and it sounds offensive. In 4:1 Jesus is teaching the crowds from a boat, in 4:10 he is somewhere else with his disciples, but in 4:36 he is back in the boat, taking leave of the crowd. Mark 4:10–12 seems to say Jesus used **parables** to keep people from understanding so they do not turn and find forgiveness, which makes no sense and goes against everything we know about Jesus. Some think these words came from Mark, not Jesus, and that Mark thought parables hide rather than reveal. Some find double predestination in 4:10–12. Further, since the parable's interpretation (4:13–20) looks like an **allegory**, some say the interpretation came from later Christians.[1] Although at first glance the passage is troubling, it is a *powerful and positive text* and is carefully calculated and artistically arranged. It looks odd only if one does not understand Mark's method or know how parables function.

While the Jewish context is absolutely essential to understanding Jesus and the Gospels, Mark 4 presents something of a difficulty. There is little *early* Jewish precedent for anyone telling *narrative* parables like Jesus did, and his subject matter is different. While others spoke of God as king, few Jews prior to Jesus focused on the kingdom of God, and no one spoke of the kingdom as coming, already present, being sought after, being entered into, or being seized the way Jesus did. On the other hand, 4 Ezra with its use of

---

1. In doing so these scholars are following Adolf Jülicher, who in the late nineteenth century argued that parables can have only one point of contact between image and reality, and if there is more than one point, the evangelists are to blame.

parables (or "similitudes") is highly instructive for reading Jesus's parables, even though it was written later, somewhere near the end of the first-century AD. It shows similar use of the images of seed and sowing, a similar focus on the revelation of secrets, a similar emphasis on the necessity of fruit, and it shows both parables being interpreted and that multiple points of contact between image and reality exist with parables and visions.[2]

4 Ezra

"I WILL TELL YOU, NOW, A SIMILITUDE, EZRA"

Fourth Ezra is an **apocalyptic** text containing seven visions and dialogues between Ezra and the angel Uriel. Fourth Ezra, as we know it, is a composite text, displaying both an original Jewish core and Christian additions in chapters 1–2 and 15–16. The full sixteen-chapter version is known as 2 Esdras and belongs to the **Apocrypha**.

Fourth Ezra was written to lament the subjugation of Israel, the existence of evil, Israel's failure to obey God, the fact that the temple was in ruins, God's apparent abandonment of his people, and the difficulty of connecting God's mercy to the destruction of the wicked. Like Habakkuk, Ezra cannot understand Israel's punishment when her conquerors are morally worse. The book is filled with analogical material, some expressed as visions[3] and some parallel to Jesus's parables or similitudes—simple comparisons *without a plot*, like the parable of the mustard seed. There are longer analogies like 4 Ezra 4:13–21 (a juridical parable about the trees and the sea), but examples of *narrative* parables with a plot, like Jesus's longer parables, do not exist. Nevertheless, there are several passages in 4 Ezra that contain wording and ideas similar to the parables involving seed and fruit in Mark 4.

Sowing seed and bearing fruit are key images in 4 Ezra: evil is sown into Adam (4:28–32); people are sown into the world (5:48; 8:41–44); the work of God is sown into hearts (8:6); and the law is sown into Israel (9:30–33). Each of these acts of sowing results in varying amounts of fruitfulness. Some of these passages require a closer look.

Not All Which Were Sown Shall Be Saved. In 4 Ezra 8:41 an angel shares a similitude of a farmer sowing many seeds, not all of which take root:

---

2. Note especially the detailed correspondences between image and reality in 9:37–10:52 and the depiction of Rome and its emperors under the guise of an eagle and its wings in chs. 11–12.

3. Note in 4 Ezra 4:47–50 how the images Ezra sees are described as a "parable" to be explained.

For just as the husbandman sows much seed upon the ground and plants a multitude of plants, and yet not all which were sown shall be saved in due season, nor shall all that were planted take root; so also they that are sown in the world shall not all be saved.[4]

The notion of limited salvation is also communicated earlier through a parable in 8:1–3.

[1] . . . This age the Most High has made for many, but the age to come for few. [2] I will tell you, now, a similitude, Ezra: as, when you ask the earth, it shall say unto you that it produces much more clay from which earthen vessels are made, but little dust from which gold comes; so also is the course of the present age. [3] Many have been created, but few shall be saved!

Both these parables occur in the context of Ezra's lament over the evil of humans, including Israel, and the seeming meaninglessness of life. Both parables are from the angel and explain that salvation will be obtained only by a limited number of those whom God created. In the first analogy about sowing, a farmer casts a large number of seeds to the ground, but some seed fails to take root, which means it does not produce fruit; only some seed sown is actually productive as God intended. The point is that, despite God's love, only a limited number of people were obedient, served God, and will be saved on judgment day. In the second analogy about the clay, the focus is not on productivity but on the higher value of gold, a way to refer to the elect. It is a simple comparison to say just as there is much clay for making pottery and little dust from which gold comes, so many humans were created, but they do not have the value of the elect, the few who would be saved.

I Sow My Law in You. Another parable involving sowing and bearing fruit occurs in 4 Ezra 9:30–34. In this passage Ezra prays to the Lord, imputing speech to him that relates to God's giving of the law to Israel:

[29] And I said: O Lord, you revealed yourself unto our fathers in the wilderness when they went forth out of Egypt, and when they walked through the untrodden and unfruitful wilderness; [30] and you said: O Israel, hear me; O seed of Jacob, attend unto my words!

---

4. Translations of 4 Ezra adapted from R. H. Charles, *The Apocrypha and Pseudepigrapha of the Old Testament*, 2 vols. (Oxford: Clarendon, 1913), 2:542–624.

[31] For, behold, I sow my Law in you, and it shall bring forth fruit in you, and you shall be glorified in it for ever. [32] But our fathers, who received the Law, observed it not, and the statutes they did not keep, and yet [33] the fruit of the Law did not perish, nor could it—because it was yours; but they who received it [34] perished, because they kept not that which had been sown in them.

The image of seed being sown and its bearing fruit to depict education, the dissemination of information, and failure or success was used throughout the ancient world. In this passage from 4 Ezra, just as someone sows seed to produce fruit, God sows the law into people so they would bear fruit and be honored. But people did not keep the law and perished. In this case, though, the fruit could not be destroyed, for it was God's.

Both the form of the parables in 4 Ezra and the images used resonate with the concerns of Mark 4. Both writings have simple comparisons and longer analogies. The depiction of God's revelation being like seed failing to produce fruit is mirrored in Jesus's parable of the sower with its three examples of seed not producing because people were diverted from the message and some seed on good soil receiving the word and producing fruit. Both writings also emphasize hearing the word of God.

Mark 4:1–34

"He Taught Them Many Things by Parables"

Mark 4 is as concerned with evil and failure as 4 Ezra and with the coming end and judgment—at least by implication with the mention of a harvest and the sickle (Mark 4:20 and 29, the latter alluding to Joel 3:13). But Mark's focus is quite different. Both documents deal with the revelation of a secret(s) to select people. In Mark 4:11 it is the secret of the present kingdom, whereas in 4 Ezra 12:36–38 it is secrets about the end time. Both seek to persuade people to receive the revelation from God and to bear fruit.

The Kingdom of God Is Like. . . . Similar to 4 Ezra, in the parable of the sower Jesus likens divine revelation to seed that is sown. However, in Jesus's parable the seed is not the law of Moses but the gospel, the message of the kingdom (Mark 4:33). Also unlike 4 Ezra, in Jesus's interpretation of the parable numerous reasons are given for why the seed fails to produce lasting fruit: Satan takes the word away; the superficiality of humans prevents them from experiencing the word's full impact; human desires inhibit the word from having its effect. The concern is over the failure to produce fruit, a biblical image (especially in Jesus's teaching) for a productive life of obedience.[5]

Similar to Ezra's parable about the clay (4 Ezra 8:1–3), Jesus's parable of the mustard seed is a simple comparison. The contrast in 4 Ezra between much clay and little gold is similar to the contrast of the mustard seed's small beginning and large result. Fourth Ezra's contrast is between many created and few saved, but the mustard seed is about the kingdom of God, that it is hardly observable but has been planted and will assuredly have a huge impact.

With kingdom, we need to understand the vision of God being brought to reality. The kingdom refers to the way things are supposed to be in fulfillment of the OT promises that God would reign among his people, defeat evil, and establish justice. In Mark, the kingdom has arrived (1:15), and the secret (i.e., the revelation) about the kingdom has been given to Jesus's followers (4:11). The whole point of the parables of the growing seed (4:26–29) and the mustard seed (4:31–32) is that, despite appearances, an inevitable process has already begun that will lead to a meaningful harvest of unexpected impact—*the kingdom will eventually be there in all its fullness.*

These two parables seem to have been framed to address doubts about the presence of the kingdom. One can almost hear Jesus's opponents or even his disciples asking, "How can the kingdom be present if there is no evidence of the defeat of evil and Israel's enemies?" These parables assert that with Jesus the kingdom is already in process and will inevitably be completed. The seed is in the ground, and it will produce a bountiful harvest, even if the farmer does not know how. Or, in the case of the mustard seed, despite its tiny size it will produce a large result, probably with the sheltering tree being an image of an extensive and sheltering kingdom. The same emphasis on the present kingdom is implied in the parable of the sower with the word, like seed on good soil, being fruitful and productive (4:20). Jesus's proclamation is an announcement that God's kingdom is here and will not be stopped.

Hearing Parables, Obeying God. What of the rest of the chapter, especially 4:12, which suggests parables prevent understanding, and 4:21–24, which seems disconnected to the rest? Mark has an artistic structure so that one part of his text explains another part. He likes to bracket one section with two others to provide commentary, and the two are parallel to each other and explain each other. Note that 3:31–35, with its emphasis on those *inside* and

---

5. See, e.g., Matt 3:8–10/Luke 3:8–9; 7:16–20/Luke 6:43–44; Matt 12:33; John 15:2–8; Gal 5:22; Eph 5:9. "Fruit" can be used negatively, as in bad fruit from a bad tree.

around Jesus versus those *outside,* is like the description of those *around* Jesus and those *outside* in 4:10–11. These two sections bracket the parable of the sower, and the parable of the sower (4:1–9) and its interpretation (4:13–20) bracket 4:10–12. Then 4:10–12 and 4:21–24 bracket the interpretation of the sower. (See figure 5.1 below.)

Figure 5.1: Bracketing the Flow of 4:1–24

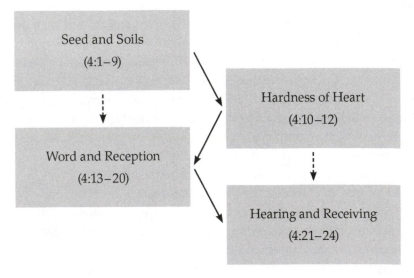

If this seems complicated, remember that most would *hear* the text instead of read it, and the repetition of words would keep people in the flow and enable understanding. Each section is to be heard or read in light of the others, and indeed the focus of the whole section is on *hearing.* The Greek verb for "to hear" occurs thirteen times in 4:3–34. The parable begins and ends with a focus on hearing, and the interpretation contrasts wrong hearing and productive hearing. Verses 21–22 imply that parables hide *in order to reveal,* and 4:23, with its challenge to hear, echoes the conclusion of the parable of the sower in 4:9: "If anyone has ears to hear, let them hear." Then 4:24 warns people to be careful what they hear. The summary in 4:33–34 indicates Jesus taught people even as they were *able to hear* and that he provided further instruction to those who responded positively to his message and followed him. Rather than preventing response to God, the whole section is an urgent appeal to hear correctly and live productively.

The seeming harsh words in 4:12 are a paraphrase of Isaiah 6:9–10, part of Isaiah's own call. These words expressed the people's hardness of heart and refusal to hear in Isaiah's day, and they became the classic way to express *hardness of heart* in later biblical texts. Both Jeremiah (5:21) and Ezekiel (12:2) picked up these words to describe hardness of heart in their own day. The Synoptic evangelists all use Isaiah 6:9–10 sandwiched between the parable of the sower and its interpretation for the same purpose.[6] Far from being intended to prevent hearing, these words are intended to shock people out of hardness of heart and to bring about hearing. English translations do not show it, but Mark 4:3 begins literally, "Hear, see"—the very words from Isaiah 6:9–10. The passage is a warning against hardness of heart that derails obedience.

The point of the parable of the sower and its surrounding context, then, is to state that the only hearing that counts is hearing that produces change in one's life and leads to obedience to the Father. If the kingdom—the vision of God showing his intention for his people—is present and in process of being brought to reality, if this is the content of the preaching of Jesus, then surely the response required is real hearing that leads to obedience. As is well known, the Hebrew verb "to hear" often means "to obey." The hearing this section demands is not passive nor even hearing with joy. It is hearing that leads to productive living in obedience to God (cf. Mark 3:35; 4:20).

These two main points contrast with Ezra's use of seed imagery. Ezra focused on the law and human failure. Mark, by contrast, stresses the certainty of the *kingdom's* success and that humans are *capable* of responding to Jesus's message about the kingdom. Failure to obey corresponds to a person's failure to receive the word, not the failure of the word or of God to ensure a bountiful crop. With the shift from law to kingdom of God, one encounters the central theme of Jesus's teaching and begins to see how his message about the kingdom displaces the centrality of the law.

This section with its focus on productive hearing provides the framework for much of the rest of the Gospel, which shows the importance of this section. The pattern of public preaching followed by private instruction reappears in 7:1–23, 9:33, and 10:1–12. Themes from Mark 4 that reappear in the Gospel include persecution (10:30; 13:9–13), being scandalized by Jesus's word (6:3), hardness of heart (3:5; 6:52; 8:17), having ears and not hearing and eyes and not seeing (8:18), and the deceit of wealth (10:22–23). The hearing theme finds its climax in God's command at the transfiguration concerning Jesus: "Listen to him" (9:7). Accordingly, the parable chapter must be seen as a prelude to the whole Gospel, providing a theological lens through which to understand much that follows.

---

6. These words are also used to describe the failure of the people's response at the end of Jesus's public ministry in John 12:39–40 and at the end of Paul's ministry in Rome in Acts 28:25–27.

FOR FURTHER READING

Additional Ancient Texts

The parables in Mark 4 are paralleled in Matthew 13 and Luke 8. Some of them are also repeated in the Gospel of Thomas (9, 20) and other early Christian literature. Similar ideas are found in Mishnah 'Abot 3.18; 5.15; 1 Enoch 62:7–8; and 1QH 14:14–16. Additionally, for the theme of mystery and knowledge consider Targum Isaiah 6:9–10; 4QInstruction[c] (4Q417) frg. 2 1:10–11; 1QS 4:11; 11:3–7. The failure to understand is evident in NT texts like John 12:39–41; Acts 28:26–27; Rom 11:1–10.

English Translations and Critical Editions

NRSV

Bidawid, R. J. "4 Esdras." In vol. 4.3 of *The Old Testament in Syriac according to the Peshitta*. Edited by M. Albert and A. Penna. Leiden: Brill, 1973.

Klijn, A. Frederik J. *Der lateinische Text der Apokalypse des Esra*. TUGAL 131. Berlin: Akademie-Verlag, 1983.

Metzger, B. M. "The Fourth Book of Ezra." Pages 517–59 in vol. 1 of *The Old Testament Pseudepigrapha*. Edited by James H. Charlesworth. Garden City, NY: Doubleday, 1983.

Stone, Michael E. *The Armenian Version of IV Ezra*. UPATS 1. Missoula, MT: Scholars Press, 1978.

Stone, Michael E., and Matthias Henze. *4 Ezra and 2 Baruch: Translations, Introductions, and Notes*. Minneapolis: Fortress, 2013.

Secondary Literature

Evans, Craig A. *To See and Not Perceive: Isaiah 6.9–10 in Early Jewish and Christian Interpretation*. JSOTSup 64. Sheffield: Sheffield Academic Press, 1989.

Fay, Greg. "Introduction to Incomprehension: The Literary Structure of Mark 4:1–34." *CBQ* 51 (1989): 65–81.

Moule, C. F. D. "Mark 4:1–20 Yet Once More." Pages 95–113 in *Neotestamentica et Semitica: Studies in Honor of Matthew Black*. Edited by E. E. Ellis and Max Wilcox. Edinburgh: T&T Clark, 1969.

Myers, Jacob M. *I & II Esdras: A New Translation with Introduction and Commentary*. AB. Garden City, NY: Doubleday, 1974.

Snodgrass, Klyne. *Stories with Intent: A Comprehensive Guide to the Parables of Jesus*. Grand Rapids: Eerdmans, 2008.

Stone, Michael Edward. *Fourth Ezra*. Hermeneia. Minneapolis: Fortress, 1990.

CHAPTER 6

The Testament of Solomon and Mark 5:1–20: Exorcism and Power over Evil Spirits

MICHAEL F. BIRD

O ne key element of the Gospel of Mark is that Jesus is described as a divine agent with a unique sense of authority and power. The Markan Jesus teaches with unprecedented didactic authority, he forgives people their sins with seemingly divine authority, he has a supernatural ability to control nature, he has the power to heal illnesses, and he has authority over unclean spirits.

The most common display of Jesus's *exousia* (Greek for "power, command, authority") is his ability to expel evil spirits from supplicants of healing (see Mark 1:22, 27; 2:10; 3:15; 6:7). Mark accordingly emphasizes Jesus's power over unclean spirits in several healing stories. Some of these healings are particularly dramatic and showcase Jesus as the powerful Son of God who delivers people from all sorts of malevolent spiritual entities that torment them with physical and mental maladies.

One of the most vivid accounts is the exorcism of the Gerasene demoniac from a legion of demons in Mark 5:1–20. It is the longest healing story in the Gospel, and Mark uses it to exposit many of his key themes related to God, Jesus, mission, and discipleship. The story is similar—in fact, probably *too similar* just to be a coincidence—to a tale about the exorcistic activities of King Solomon in the Testament of Solomon. It is useful to compare Mark 5:1–20 with Testament of Solomon 11.1–7 because they both exhibit ancient understandings of evil spirits and demons as well as demonstrate something of the reception history of Mark's Gospel. So to these texts we now turn.

Testament of Solomon

"The Name for All Demons Which Are under Me Is Legion"

The Testament of Solomon is a classic example of the problem associated with assigning provenance, or place of origin, to a pseudepigraphon. The document as it stands is clearly Christianized (see esp. T. Sol. 11:6; 12:3; 15:10–15; 22:20), indicative of the fact that many **pseudepigrapha** are either Christian compositions about an Israelite figure or else constitute a Christianization of a preexisting Jewish text or tradition (much like the Ascension of Isaiah).[1] Furthermore, in the case of Testament of Solomon 11.1–7, we have a clear example of a text that is dependent upon Mark 5:1–13, yet may also be borrowing from Jewish traditions that associated Solomon with magical lore and exorcisms. **Josephus** narrated Solomon's exploits as an exorcist (*Ant.* 8.45–49); in the **Dead Sea Scrolls** there are psalms attributed to Solomon that are supposedly effective in dispelling demons (11Q11); and there is a passing mention about the "Book of Solomon" which contains the names of forty-nine demons in a text from the Nag Hammadi library (On the Origin of the World 107). Ancient Jews and Christians imagined Solomon as an expert exorcist with a powerful ring that was particularly efficacious in expelling evil spirits (Josephus, *Ant.* 8.47; T. Sol. 1:6–7; b. Giṭ. 68a). In which case, on the date of Testament of Solomon, we are probably looking at a period from the first to third centuries AD.

Solomon Encounters Beelzeboul. In Testament of Solomon we read about how Solomon, while building the Jerusalem temple, received a magical ring from the archangel Michael. Solomon then has encounters with several demons, and he is able to summon the demons, ascertain their names, determine their location on the astral plane, learn about the afflictions they cause, discover the angel that thwarts them, and forcibly press them into the service of constructing the temple. There is a particular focus on the demon named Beelzeboul (i.e., Beelzebub), the Philistine god of Ekron, first mentioned in 2 Kings 1:1–18, but referred to also in Mark 3:22. In Testament of Solomon, Beelzeboul is identical to Satan, the "Prince of Demons" and "highest-ranking angel in heaven," whom God cut off and imprisoned on earth. Beelzeboul is responsible for the destructive power of tyrants, causes the worship of demons alongside men, inspires evil desires, and instigates murder and war. Beelzeboul

---

1. See J. R. Davila, "The Old Testament Pseudepigrapha as Background to the New Testament," *ExpT* 117 (2005): 53–57.

is thwarted by "Almighty God," is sentenced to cut blocks of Theban marble, and when interrogated reveals heavenly secrets to Solomon (T. Sol. 6:1–11).[2]

Interesting for our purposes is Solomon's encounter with a demon who takes on the form of an Arabian lion in Testament of Solomon 11:1–7. When Solomon interrogates the lion demon, he learns that it is "a spirit which can never be bound," that the demon is one who "sneaks in and watches over all who are lying ill with a disease," and who makes it "impossible" for a person to recover from their illness. The lion demon boasts further that it has a host of demons subject to its power: "The name for all demons which are under me is legion" (11:3). Importantly, the demon is thwarted by one called "Emmanouel" (see T. Sol. 6:8; Matt 1:23), who suffered many things done to him by men, has bound the lion demon and his legion, and will yet come to torture them by driving them into the waters at the end of a cliff. Solomon then sentences the demonic legion to carry wood from the forest to the temple and the lion demon is ordered to cut the wood into kindling with its claws.[3]

Points of Contact with Mark. The episode has several strong points of contact with Mark 5:1–13 including: (1) the lion demon cannot be bound (T. Sol. 11:1/Mark 5:3–4); (2) the identification of a "legion" of demons (T. Sol. 11:3, 5/Mark 5:9, 15); and (3) the lion demon and its legion will be tortured and destroyed by being driven off a cliff into water (T. Sol. 11:6/Mark 5:13). It would appear that Testament of Solomon 11:1–7 was intended to describe the prehistory of the demons afflicting Mark's Gerasene demoniac in a legendary account of Solomon's exorcistic powers. In other words, Testament of Solomon 11:1–7 is a combination of imaginative commentary on Mark 5:1–20, speculative demonology about the nature of evil spirits, and ancient hagiography about Solomon.

Mark 5:1–20

"MY NAME IS LEGION . . . FOR WE ARE MANY"

Jesus Encounters a Demoniac. After spending time in Galilee where Jesus was teaching beside the Sea of Galilee (Mark 4:1), Jesus and his disciples cross the sea by boat and arrive in the region of the Gerasenes, part of the

---

2. D. C. Duling, "Testament of Solomon: A New Translation and Introduction," in *The Old Testament Pseudepigrapha*, ed. James H. Charlesworth, 2 vols. (Garden City, NY: Doubleday, 1983), 1:967–68.

3. Duling, "Testament of Solomon," 1:968, 972.

Decapolis—a confederation of Hellenistic cities located on the east and south of the Sea of Galilee, which is gentile territory (5:1–2). Jesus encounters a man who is the epitome of uncleanness: he is a gentile, demon possessed, living among tombs, and in proximity to a herd of pigs. In the words of Herman Waetjen, the man is "an incarnation of uncleanness . . . a complete necrophile, he is the embodiment of living death" and his condition can be described "as the most dehumanized and wretched individual whom Jesus has yet encountered."[4]

The man is possessed by a "legion" of demons, a collective designation for a group of demons that is not random or happenstance but conveys the multitude and malevolence of the evil powers that occupy him, like a Roman legion occupying a foreign land. The demons, much like the demoniac in Mark 1:23–24, move to an immediate posture of defensiveness and fear by kneeling before Jesus and having the man blurt out, "What do you want with me, Jesus, Son of the Most High God? In God's name don't torture me!" (5:7). The naming of Jesus as "Son of the Most High God" is something of a plea of no contest. The demonic legion acknowledges Jesus's identity with an honorific title, not to gain power over Jesus by naming him but to try desperately to convince him that his recognizable superiority renders any possible confrontation pointless.[5] After Jesus solicits the name of the demonic horde, they beg Jesus not to destroy them but instead to send them into the nearby heard of pigs (5:10–12). Here we find a key difference, because in Testament of Solomon 11.3 the lion demon has a legion of demons subject to its will, while in Mark's account the demons name themselves "legion" because of their great number ("My name is Legion . . . for we are many," 5:9). They are a horde with no head.

As Mark's account continues, Jesus then permits the demons to depart into the swineherd, but the pigs then charge off a steep embankment into the sea and perish in the waters (5:13). The pig-herders run off and tell everyone in the city and country what had just happened, so upsetting the local people that they implore Jesus to leave their territory lest they suffer any further economic loss (5:14–17). The healed man wants to accompany Jesus like one of his disciples, but Jesus orders him to go home and tell his people what the Lord has done for him and how he has had mercy upon him (5:18–19). In response, the healed man does precisely this by proclaiming Jesus in the Decapolis (5:20). The story is different from most healing episodes since,

---

4. Herman C. Waetjen, *A Reordering Power: A Socio-Political Reading of Mark's Gospel* (Minneapolis: Fortress, 1989), 114.

5. Waetjen, *Reordering Power*, 114–15.

as Eugene Boring comments, "This is not a story about the response of faith and its transforming power, but about an invasion of alien territory and reclaiming it for the kingdom of God."[6]

Post-Colonial and Apocalyptic Perspectives. In more recent times, the account of the Gerasene demoniac has proved to be fertile soil for liberation and postcolonial interpretations.[7] Generally speaking, in postcolonial interpretation a text is studied with a view to challenging Western perspectives of power and superiority over its former colonies. This is achieved by exposing instances of the West's deployment of self-serving ideological agendas and its sponsorship of imperialist regimes, identifying the hidden protests of the colonized embedded within a text, and hearing the voices of those marginalized by colonial powers and their client rulers as expressed in diverse modes of written media.

Certain textual subtleties may suggest that Mark had similar political and ideological concerns. The horde of demons possessing the gentile man, for example, is called "legion," which is the name of a Roman fighting unit comprised of about six-thousand soldiers. Interestingly, the Roman tenth legion, the *Legio X Fretensis*, was based in Syria-Palestine and had a wild boar as the insignia on its standards and seal.[8] What is more, Josephus alleges that during the Jewish revolt (AD 66–70) Vespasian sent Lucius Annius on a raid against Gerasa where the city and surrounding villages were burned and destroyed (*J.W.* 4.487–89). Events such as these might be part of Mark's memory of the Jewish war and constitute an element of the founding narrative of the churches of the Decapolis and Transjordan.

Mark's story, however, cannot be reduced to an **allegory** of Roman occupation, its demonic nature, and the necessity of expelling it—as has been the tendency in liberation and postcolonial interpretations of this narrative. While there is no doubt that Mark could envisage Roman supremacy as an expression of demonic power, he is also interested in the wider cosmic and eschatological struggle that Jesus is engaged in as the "stronger one" (Mark 1:7) who is able to subdue and ransack the satanic kingdom (3:27).

---

6. M. Eugene Boring, *Mark: A Commentary*, NTL (Louisville: Westminster John Knox, 2014), 150.

7. Richard Dormandy, "The Expulsion of Legion: A Political Reading of Mark 5:1–20," *ExpT* 111 (2000): 335–37; Richard A. Horsley, *Hearing the Whole Story: The Politics of Plot in Mark's Gospel* (Louisville: Westminster John Knox, 2001), 141–48; Ched Myers, *Binding the Strongman: A Political Reading of Mark's Story of Jesus*, 2nd ed. (Marynoll, NY: Orbis, 2008), 190–93. On Mark and postcolonial interpretation more generally, see Simon Samuel, *A Postcolonial Reading of Mark's Story of Jesus*, LNTS 340 (London: T&T Clark, 2007).

8. Gerd Theissen, *The Gospels in Context: Social and Political History in the Synoptic Tradition*, trans. L. M. Maloney (London: T&T Clark, 2004), 110.

The story should not be treated as merely a veiled narrative protest against Roman power, but neither should we insulate social, political, and theological entities since these were intertwined in the **apocalyptic** worldview that Mark shares. Adela Collins offers an apt conclusion:

> The aim of the story is not—at least not primarily—to make a statement about the Romans, but to show how Jesus rescued the man from his plight and restored him to a normal life. Just as, however, the heavenly armies of Daniel and Revelation are correlated with earthly events, so there may be a secondary political implication to the story of the Gerasene demoniac in Mark. It would be a culturally logical step for the audience to link the kingdom of Satan with Rome and the healing activity of Jesus with the restored kingdom of Israel.[9]

Summary. Mark 5:1–20 is one of the most dramatic episodes in the first half of Mark's Gospel by its vivid portrayal of Jesus as the "strongman" who sacks and plunders the demonic realm and in its missional thrust of having Jesus bring the liberating power of the kingdom into gentile territory in the Decapolis. The story perfectly amplifies Mark's account of Jesus's kingdom power evidenced in the prior episode of the stilling of the storm (4:35–41) and prepares the way for Jesus's continued mission among his own people as the **messianic** agent of deliverance by underscoring Jesus's willingness to cross boundaries to bring salvation to those who need it (5:21–6:30).

The Testament of Solomon in general is a window into the world of ancient demonology, and 11:1–7 in particular illustrates how the story of Mark 5:1–20 was received and interpreted by subsequent readers. The Testament of Solomon is vocal where Mark's Gospel is relatively silent—explaining the nature of demons, describing what gives them power, and expounding on how they are to be defeated. The echoes of the Markan story in Testament of Solomon 11:1–7 are a clear example of how Mark 5:1–20 was absorbed into a particular cosmology and demonology where encounters with the demonic were regarded as real if not inevitable. Taken together, a comparison of Testament of Solomon 11:1–7 and Mark 5:1–20 illuminates the power of Jesus to cleanse gentile territory and a gentile man of demonic power, the association of demons with illnesses, demonic possession as sometimes involving a horde of evil spirits, and the name "legion" as connoting the demonic associations of Roman power.

---

9. Adela Yarbro Collins, *Mark*, Hermeneia (Minneapolis: Fortress, 2007), 270.

For Further Reading

Additional Ancient Texts

Other exorcism texts in Second Temple Jewish literature include the Prayer of Nabonidus (4Q242), clearly based on Daniel 4:1–37, where a Jewish man forgives the sins of king Nabonidus and heals him from his affliction. There is a reference to David using his harp to exorcise demons in Pseudo-Philo (LAB 60.1–3). In addition, the *Papyri Graecae Magicae* (available in English in Hans Dieter Betz, *The Greek Magical Papyri in Translation: Including Demotic Spells*, 2nd ed. [Chicago: University of Chicago Press, 1996]) is an invaluable compilation of various texts from the ancient world that describe the process of using spells and rituals to gain power over demons. One also finds implicit mention of other Jewish exorcists in Matt 12:27/Luke 11:19, and in Acts 19:13–20 there is a description of the seven sons of Sceva who tried to exorcise evil spirits in Jesus's name.

English Translations and Critical Editions

Duling, D. C. "Testament of Solomon: A New Translation and Introduction." Pages 935–87 in vol. 1 of *The Old Testament Pseudepigrapha*. Edited by James H. Charlesworth. Garden City, NY: Doubleday, 1983.

McCown, C. C. *The Testament of Solomon*. Leipzig: J. C. Hinrichs'sche Buchhandlung, 1922.

Secondary Literature

Bonner, Campbell. "The Technique of Exorcism." *HTR* 36 (1943): 39–49.

Dormandy, R. "The Expulsion of Legion: A Political Reading of Mark 5:1–20." *ExpT* 111 (2000): 335–37.

Duling, D. C. "Solomon, Exorcism, and the Son of David." *HTR* 68 (1975): 235–52.

Klutz, Todd. *Re-writing the Testament of Solomon: Tradition, Conflict, and Identity in a Late Antiquity Pseudepigraphon*. LSTS 53. London: T&T Clark, 2006.

Newheart, Michael Willett. *"My Name Is Legion": The Story and Soul of the Gerasene Demoniac*. Collegeville, MN: Liturgical Press, 2004.

Twelftree, Graham H. *Jesus the Exorcist: A Contribution to the Study of the Historical Jesus*. Peabody, MA: Hendrickson, 1993.

CHAPTER 7

Mishnah Zabim and Mark 5:21–6:6a: The Rules on Purity

DAVID E. GARLAND

The account of Jesus raising a synagogue leader's twelve-year-old daughter from the dead (Mark 5:21–24, 35–43) wraps around his miraculous cure of an anonymous woman who had suffered from a hemorrhage for twelve years (5:25–34). Both are recognized as "daughters" (5:23, 34, 35), yet their healings represent Jesus's engagement with opposite sides of the socioeconomic scale.

Jairus stands on the higher side of the scale, as a relatively wealthy male religious leader (5:22), with a household able to attract a crowd of mourners to support them in their grief (5:24). Naming him confirms his higher status, which is why he can boldly, if reverently, waylay Jesus with repeated pleas for him to come heal his daughter.

The nameless female is on the opposite side of the scale. The Greek phrases translated "discharge of blood" and "flow of blood" (Mark 5:25, 29 ESV) match the phrasing in Leviticus 15:25 (**LXX**) and 12:7 (LXX) respectively, revealing that the woman suffered from uterine bleeding. The physicians' ineffective treatments have left her destitute (Mark 5:26), and she apparently has no male figure to intercede for her. Her abnormal bloody secretion disqualified her from normal married life, since she must abstain from sexual relations (Lev 20:18). She also would have been cut off from her religious community (Ezek 36:17), banished from the city (Num 5:2; cf. Josephus, *Ant.* 3.261), and barred continuously, not periodically, from the temple and synagogue (m. Kelim 1:8). Because of her condition, the woman knows only shame. She does not dare ask Jesus directly for healing but creeps up from behind to touch his garment, hoping then to steal away unnoticed (Mark 5:27–28).

Despite the stark differences in their socioeconomic and religious status, the synagogue leader Jairus and the hemorrhaging woman have in common their utter desperation, their faith that Jesus has the power to heal, and their fixed resolve to seek help from him. The conjoined accounts convey "that neither being male, ritually pure, religiously well-regarded, nor having means provide any advantage in approaching Jesus. Being female, impure, dishonored, and destitute do not present insurmountable barriers that prevent Jesus from helping."[1]

Both miracle accounts also share an assumed familiarity with the rules of ritual purity in ancient Judaism, knowledge without which the reader is left at an interpretive disadvantage. This essay will therefore examine what the Mishnah teaches on contacting impurity in order to illuminate the significance of Jesus's encounter with two unclean persons.

Mishnah Zabim

"HE CONVEYS UNCLEANNESS BY CONTACT"

Biblical Instructions on Impurity. To glean further theological insight, attention must be paid to the complex intricacies of the biblical laws regarding impurity and later interpretations of them.[2] Ritual impurity was a fundamental concern of Jewish society. "They must purify themselves" (Num 19:12) was an organizing principle of Jewish existence. The regulations were not simply sanitary precautions but prescribed how Israel was to be holy in daily life (Lev 11:45; 19:2; 20:7, 26) to prevent anyone from approaching God in a state of impurity. The purity code reinforces the sense of God's fearsome holiness and majesty that should never be despoiled. Those who were ritually unclean had to distance themselves from what was holy, take precautions to avoid defiling others by contact, and take measures to be restored to a state of cleanness.

Mishnaic Interpretations about Impurity. Jews debated about who and what conveyed impurity, to what degree, and what rites cleansed it (see Mark 7:1–23). Many of these ancient debates are preserved in the Mishnah. The Mishnah is a collection of halakic decisions (the way of walking), arranged and revised around the beginning of the third-century AD. The sayings derive primarily from two groups of rabbis: sages from AD 70–130 and sages

---

1. David E. Garland, *The Theology of Mark* (Grand Rapids: Zondervan, 2015), 125.
2. Herbert Danby (*The Mishnah* [Oxford: Oxford University Press, 1933], 800–804) provides a summary of the rules of uncleanness.

from AD 135 (the end of the war led by Simon bar Kokhba) to AD 200. The latter accounts for two-thirds of the attributed sayings.

The Mishnah is not a new revelation but clarifies how the existing law should be applied in daily life through opinions, precedents, and discussions of questions that have arisen over time. Arranged in six major divisions that are subdivided into seven to twelve tractates, the Mishnah is not simply descriptive but prescriptive. It reflects the majority opinion on what is permitted or forbidden. The key comparator texts about the laws relating to both a woman suffering a flux and contact with a corpse appear in the division known as Ṭeharot (purifications).[3]

Impurity from Touching a Person Suffering a Genital Discharge. Touching was the primary way to transmit uncleanness. The Mishnaic tractate Zabim interprets the laws in Leviticus 15:1–15 and 25–30 concerning ritual uncleanness incurred by abnormal genital emissions. Mishnah Zabim 5:1 asserts that the touch of a *Zab* (literally "flow," referring to a male who has a nonseminal discharge) imparts uncleanness:

> If a man touched a *Zab* or if a *Zab* touched him, if a man shifted a *Zab* or if a *Zab* shifted him, he conveys uncleanness by contact, but not by carrying, to foodstuffs and liquids and vessels that can be made clean by immersing.[4]

This Mishnaic passage contains a dense argument about the levels of impurity transferred by the *Zab* to various objects and persons. It does not address the possibility of a woman with an irregular genital discharge (*Zabah*) touching a strange man, but the basic rules about transferring uncleanness to another apply, paralleling how a woman during her regular menstrual period transfers uncleanness.

Impurity from Touching a Corpse. According to Jewish law, a human corpse spreads impurity to every person or thing that comes directly or indirectly in contact with it (Num 5:1–4; 19:11–22; 31:19–24). Even entering a house containing a corpse conveys uncleanness: "This is the law that applies when a person dies in a tent: Anyone who enters the tent and anyone who is in it will be unclean for seven days" (Num 19:14). The principle underlying

---

3. The Talmud, meaning "instruction" or "learning," consists of the Mishnah plus commentary on it called *Gemara*. The word Talmud usually implies the Babylonian Talmud compiled around AD 500 from traditions dating back to the third century. It follows the Mishnah's structure of six orders. See also ch. 16 of this volume (David Instone-Brewer's "Mishnah Giṭṭin and Mark 10:1–12: Marriage and Divorce").

4. Mishnah translations from Danby, *Mishnah*.

this law is that persons or things overshadowed by a cover (e.g., a tent cover or roof) that also overshadows a corpse contracts the corpse's uncleanness (cf. m. 'Ohal. 15:10). This is stated clearly with respect to a house in the Temple Scroll (11Q19 49:5–21):

> [5] If a man dies in your cities, the whole house in which the deceased dies shall be unclean [6] for seven days; everything there is in the house and everything which goes into the house shall be unclean [7] for seven days. . . . [17] and everyone who come [sic] to the house shall bathe in water and wash his clothes the first day. [18] And on the third day they shall sprinkle over them the waters of purification, and they shall bathe and wash their clothes [19] and the utensils which are in the house. [blank] And on the seventh day [20] they shall sprinkle a second time, and they shall bathe and wash their clothes and their utensils. And they shall be clean by the evening [21] from the dead person, so that they can approach all the pure things. And the men who were not contaminated by [blank].[5]

Discharge and death may seem quite different, but Mishnah Zabim 6:11 equates the impurity contracted from contact with a menstruant, on the one hand, with the impurity contracted from a corpse, on the other: "He that has a connexion with a menstruant is likened to one that suffers corpse uncleanness." The purity system assumes that God, who gives life, must be separated from anything connected to death. Therefore, touching either a menstruant or a corpse involved mandatory ritual cleansing for anybody living under the Jewish purity laws.

Mark 5:21–6:6a

"IF I JUST TOUCH HIS CLOTHES, I WILL BE HEALED"

Jesus's Transgression of Purity Laws. Mark's emphasis on touching in the two miracles is often neglected despite the fact that touching is mentioned six times in 5:21–43. Jairus asks Jesus to "put [his] hands on" his daughter "so that she will be healed and live" (Mark 5:23). Jesus fulfills the request by

---

5. Translation from Florentino García Martínez and Eibert J. C. Tigchelaar, eds., *The Dead Sea Scrolls: Study Edition*, 2 vols. (Leiden: Brill, 1997–98), 2:1267–69.

taking her "by the hand" (5:41). The hemorrhaging woman determines to "touch" Jesus's garment (5:27, 28). Jesus announces that he was "touched," and the disciples marvel that he would ask who "touched" him considering the throng swarming around him (5:30, 31). For a Jew, this emphasis on touching would raise the issue of contracting ritual impurity.

As the biblical and Mishnaic texts cited above demonstrate, the woman's continuous flow of blood makes her a continual font of impurity, since legally her touch imparted ritual uncleanness. For those touched, it took time to be cleansed of the impurity. After being touched by her (5:27), Jesus would be regarded as in a state of uncleanness. He could be restored to cleanness in the evening only after laundering his clothes and bathing in a *miqweh*, a bath used for ritual immersion (see Lev 15:27).

Jesus also has contact with death, the most powerful source of impurity. Jesus not only enters a house where a corpse lies (5:40) but touches the corpse by taking the girl's hand (5:41). In fact, death is implied in Jesus's encounter with the bleeding woman as well, since loss of blood from the womb represents loss of life force, which is analogous to death. According to the law, Jesus would be unclean for seven days and must undergo set rituals to purify himself.

Jesus's Transformation of Purity Laws. Since Jesus does not purify himself after contact with the bleeding woman nor after contact with a dead body as was required, some therefore think that purity issues are irrelevant in this passage. Yet they were critically important in Jesus's context and should not be ignored because of modern presuppositions. Failing to purify oneself after touching a corpse resulted in being cut off from Israel (Num 19:13; m. Ḥag. 2:13). Mark does not portray Jesus as careless or cavalier about purity. Rather, Jesus introduces four revolutionary theological principles relating to ritual purity.

First, the two accounts reveal that Jesus's holy power to heal (imparted even to his cloak) and to raise the dead neutralizes the defilement caused by genital bleeding or by death. The unclean woman becomes clean when she touches him, not the reverse, and the corpse is made alive when Jesus raises up the little girl by the hand.

Mark notes that the woman trembles with fear after being restored miraculously to health (5:33), which leads to a second point: she has touched one whom Mark identifies as infused with God's Spirit (1:10) and whom an unclean spirit identifies as "the Holy One of God" (1:24). Jesus is the embodiment of God's holiness. The woman is not terrified of public chastisement for touching him in her state of ritual impurity; her fear is better understood as awe in the presence of the holy (Gen 15:12; 28:17; Judg 6:22–23; Luke 1:12). Leviticus 15:31 makes clear that when the ritually impure fail to keep the proper distance and defile what is holy, grave penalties, even death, will result. Instead of being struck down, though, the woman was cured. Contact with what is holy "still destroys the impurity, but faith preserves the one bearing impurity from destruction."[6]

Figure 7.1: The Power of Touch

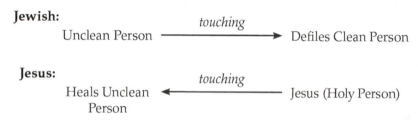

The contagion of ritual impurity cannot be avoided in the daily course of life, but the lesson is that one need not avoid the divine while ritually impure. Jesus cleanses those who have faith in him, and that faith allows them to approach God in whatever state they may find themselves without fear of retribution. If that is the case, then purity regulations become secondary to his holiness.

Third, Jesus's public announcement, "Daughter, your faith has healed you" (5:34), could mislead if not interpreted correctly. It is not the power of the woman's faith but Jesus's holy power that heals her. He does not pray to God for the woman's healing; Mark notes that power went "out from him" (5:30), revealing that he is the source, not a conduit, of the power. Hodges and Poirier comment, "The way in which Jesus's healing power flows into the woman—even without his initially knowing it!—is similar to how her ritual impurity was imagined to flow from her into whomever she touched."[7] Jesus's holy power to heal and purify is present in him.

Fourth, Jesus transfers the role of temple sacrifices in restoring persons to the presence of God. Leviticus 15:28–30 stipulates:

> [28] When [a woman] is cleansed from her discharge, she must count off seven days, and after that she will be ceremonially clean. [29] On the eighth day she must take two doves or two young pigeons and

---

6. Horace Jeffery Hodges and John C. Poirier, "Jesus as the Holy One of God: The Healing of the *Zavah* in Mark 5.24b–34," *JGRChJ* 8 (2011–12): 151–84, at 181.

7. Hodges and Poirier, "Jesus as the Holy One of God," 184.

bring them to the priest at the entrance to the tent of meeting. [30] The priest is to sacrifice one for a sin offering and the other for a burnt offering. In this way he will make atonement for her before the LORD for the uncleanness of her discharge.

Jesus makes no mention of the woman's need to present a sin offering in the temple. She does not have to wait the prescribed seven days. He simply tells her to go in peace (5:34). The verb translated "healed" (5:23, 28, 34) also can mean "saved," which implies a more profound theological meaning of these miracles. Deppe states well the inference that should be drawn: "The new Israel can discern that cleanliness comes from Jesus and not in maintaining the Jewish rituals."[8] He argues that Mark wants to help his audience properly "read the Old Testament in the age of the kingdom."[9] For those with faith in Jesus, the regulations about uncleanness from genital discharges and from corpses have been superseded by Jesus's holy power to cleanse impurity. Her faith in Jesus is sufficient to save her.

The question of Jesus's identity arises explicitly in 6:3 ("Isn't this the carpenter?"). The members of the Nazareth synagogue recognize that Jesus has done "deeds of power" "by his hands" (6:2 NRSV). What Mark conveys in these episodes is that the one who has such power is far more than the son of Mary (6:3); he is the Son of God (1:1). With his touch, Jesus has the power as God to heal and to save.

FOR FURTHER READING

Additional Ancient Texts

On the principle of a woman conveying uncleanness during her menstrual period, see 4Q274 1.1.5–6 in the Dead Sea Scrolls and Mishnah Niddah. On the uncleanness and purification of a house inhabited by a corpse, see the Temple Scroll (11Q19) 49:5–21. Interest in purity is also seen in the cleaning of dishes in CD 10. Purity was extremely important in Jewish life as evidenced by the OT, particularly Leviticus. The discovery of numerous *miqwa'ot* (ritual baths) in Jerusalem and at Qumran dating to the Second Temple period shows the extent to which people went to attain purity.

---

8. Dean B. Deppe, *The Theological Intentions of Mark's Literary Devices* (Eugene, OR: Wipf & Stock, 2015), 437.

9. Deppe, *Intentions*, 46.

English Translations and Critical Editions

Danby, Herbert. *The Mishnah: Translated from the Hebrew with Introduction and Brief Explanatory Notes*. Oxford: Oxford University Press, 1933.

Neusner, Jacob. *The Mishnah: A New Translation*. New Haven: Yale University Press, 1988.

Secondary Literature

Harrington, Hannah K. *The Impurity Systems of Qumran and Rabbis: Biblical Foundations*. Atlanta: Scholars Press, 1993.

Hodges, Horace Jeffery, and John C. Poirier. "Jesus as the Holy One of God: The Healing of the *Zavah* in Mark 5.24b–34." *JGRChJ* 8 (2011–12): 151–84.

Kazen, Thomas. *Jesus and Purity Halakah: Was Jesus Indifferent to Impurity?* ConBNT 38. Winona Lake, IN: Eisenbrauns, 2010.

Klawans, Jonathan. *Impurity and Sin in Ancient Judaism*. New York: Oxford University Press, 2000.

CHAPTER 8

Josephus and Mark 6:6b–29: Herod Antipas's Execution of John the Baptist

MORTEN HØRNING JENSEN

I n Mel Gibson's film, *The Passion of the Christ*, there is a memorable scene, between all the blood and the brute Romans, that catches the viewer by surprise. Leaving the dark Roman court of Pilate, we are taken into a lavishly decorated room full of expensive furniture and pretentious elites wearing fine robes. Indeed, these people are burdened by heavy jewelry of all sorts as they lay around sipping wine from half-empty goblets, though it is still not even noon. There is even a trained leopard in the frame, helping to produce the standard Western impression of an effeminate, Oriental ruler consumed by luxury. We are at the court of Herod Antipas, who has come to Jerusalem to celebrate the Passover, as recounted in the Gospel of Luke (23:6–12).

Though this incident is not part of Mark's Gospel, the stereotype of Oriental kings captured so well in Gibson's film is probably recalled by many when, in the midst of Mark's story of Jesus's Galilean affairs, readers suddenly encounter an almost fairytale-like story of King Herod at his birthday party (6:14). During this event—no doubt after he had consumed too much of the good wine—Herod promises even "half my kingdom" (6:23) to his second wife's charming daughter as reward for having performed, in the presence of his high-end officials and powerful dinner guests, what was probably an erotic dance. Of course, Antipas's hubris is punished as he is tricked into beheading John the Baptist. This, we are told, leaves him "greatly distressed" (6:26).

Admittedly, Mark's story of Herod Antipas initially strikes one as strange, seemingly at odds with the overall outline of Mark's narrative. In this essay

92

we shall examine this **pericope** in the light of our historical knowledge of Herod Antipas and the Herodian rulers in order to answer two main questions: On a historical level, how did Antipas cast "a shadow of death" over John and Jesus? And on a theological level, what was Mark's purpose for including the story of Antipas's execution of John? Particularly, we shall glimpse at the first-century Jewish historian **Josephus**, who happens to have recorded Antipas's murder of John as well, providing us with one of the rare occasions when an incident in the New Testament is corroborated by an independent source.

Before looking at Mark's account, it will be helpful to distinguish between the Herods of the New Testament, since it is easy to get lost among them. These men are often referred to by their dynastical name, Herod, which they took from the founding figure of this royal house, King Herod—or as we normally refer to him, Herod the Great. In short, building on the work of his father, Herod the Great managed to take control of Israel by ousting the old **Hasmonean** royal house, who famously had given Israel its liberty from Greek tyranny in the **Maccabean Revolt** (from 167 BC). According to Josephus, the Jews did not like Herod, calling him a "half-Jew" (*Ant.* 14.403) as a reminder of his family's Idumean origins.

But Herod was favored by the Romans for his ability to keep the Jewish nation in check and politically at peace. This meant that when he died in 4 BC, Augustus finally decided to place his bet on the **Herodians**, even though a delegation of leading Jews had asked to be governed directly by Rome instead. This was not to be, and Herod's realm was divided between three of his sons: Archelaus (Matt 2:22), Philip (Luke 3:1), and our "King Herod" from Mark 6, whose birth name was Antipas.

This division of his father's territory was a disappointment to Antipas. He had hoped to become sole king (cf. Josephus, *J.W.* 2.20) yet was only assigned the second-best part of the kingdom. He was not even officially given the title "king" but only "tetrarch," meaning "ruler of a fourth," as Luke correctly names him (cf. Luke 3:1). Mark's inclusion of the title "king" for Antipas may reflect a popular usage by his subjects. Nevertheless, the two territories Antipas received happened to be those places where Jesus grew up and ministered—Galilee (northern Israel) and Perea (the region east of the Dead Sea where John the Baptist ministered). This, if nothing else, secured Antipas a place in the Gospels, where he is most often mentioned as "Herod" (see figure 8.1). With this brief catalog of the Herods of the New Testament, let us now turn to Josephus's account of Herod Antipas and John the Baptist.

Figure 8.1—The Herodian Dynasty and the New Testament

Name, Official Title, and Tenure	Name and Title in the New Testament
Herod the Great, King (40/37–4 BC)	Matt 2:1–22—King Herod Luke 1:5—Herod, king of Judea Acts 23:35?—Herod
Herod Antipas, son of Herod, tetrarch (4 BC–AD 39)	Matt 14:1–12—Herod, the tetrarch Mark 6:14–29; 8:15—King Herod Luke 3:1, 19–20; 8:3; 9:7–9; 13:31; 23:7–12, 15—Herod, the tetrarch Acts 4:27; 13:1—Herod, the tetrarch
Archelaus, son of Herod, ethnarch (4 BC–AD 6)	Matt 2:22—Archelaus
Philip, son of Herod, tetrarch (4 BC–AD 34)	Luke 3:1—Philip, the tetrarch
Herod Agrippa I, Herod's grandson, king (AD 37–44)	Acts 12:1–23—King Herod
Herod Agrippa II, son of Agrippa I, king (AD 53–ca. 100)	Acts 25:13–26:32—King Agrippa

Josephus

"HEROD FEARED THE GREAT INFLUENCE OF JOHN"

As it turned out, Herod Antipas proved to be a fatal acquaintance for John, and may have been so for Jesus as well (cf. Luke 23:7–16). On a historical level, Josephus's independent narrative of John's execution helps us to appreciate why Antipas cast "a shadow of death."

Josephus's Purpose for Including the Story. Josephus's story of Antipas's execution of John the Baptist is part of a series of events that Josephus presents to prove that Antipas was another unjust and impious Herodian ruler. Through his narrative Josephus is trying to explain why the Jewish nation rebelled against Rome, and to this purpose the impiety of the Herodian rulers is one key piece of evidence. Josephus frames his version of John's execution as an example of what was wrong with the Herodian house, since Antipas is blamed for grossly misinterpreting the situation by blatantly killing a just prophet. Consequently God punished Antipas by destroying his army, just as he later would punish the entire Jewish nation through the first Jewish-Roman War.

Antipas as a Shadow of Death. Believing Herod to be deserving of divine punishment, Josephus ties the story of John to Antipas's conflict with his father-in-law, King Aretas. Aretas had engaged Antipas in battle over Antipas's divorce of Phasaelis (Aretas's daughter) and subsequent remarriage to Herodias (as well as over some boundary disputes), severely destroying Antipas's army (*Ant.* 18.109–15). This defeat is explained by Josephus (and common Jewish opinion) as a result of God's just punishment of Antipas for killing John. According to Josephus, John was a "good man," who urged the Jewish people to live according to virtue, justice, and piety (18.117). He did so by leading people to baptism as a way of purifying the body, their souls having already been cleansed by justice (18.117).

However, Josephus's description of John reveals enough for us to see why Antipas arrived at a different conclusion. John's ministry had produced a significant following, seemingly willing to carry out all his instructions. This caused Antipas to fear that John's movement would lead to rebellion or defection ("Herod feared [John's] strong influence on the people might possibly lead to some kind of rebellion, since it seemed that they would follow every counsel of his," 18.118). He therefore decided it best to act preemptively by having John arrested, imprisoned at Machaerus (Antipas's castle east of the Dead Sea), and put to death (18.119).

© Gyõzõ Võrõs. Used with permission.

According to Josephus, John the Baptist was imprisoned and executed at the fortress Machaerus. It is situated on a hilltop east of the Dead Sea and has in recent years been excavated. This visualization by the excavation team suggests what Machaerus looked like at the time of John.

In essence, Antipas did not understand John as a pious prophet but as a potent political threat with the capacity to stir up a popular uprising.

Mark 6:6b–29

"JOHN THE BAPTIST HAS BEEN RAISED FROM THE DEAD"

Antipas as a Shadow of Death. When Mark introduces us to "King Herod" (6:14), Antipas is already known to cast a shadow of death. In 3:6 we are told that "the Herodians" were plotting with the Pharisees to kill Jesus. We also already know that the story of John will end abruptly, since the initial description of John's ministry of preaching and baptizing in the desert (1:4–11) ends with Mark saying that John had been imprisoned (1:14).

Mark keeps us in suspense as to what actually happened to John in prison until the opportune moment arrives in between Jesus's sending of the twelve on their first independent missionary journey (6:7–13) and their return (6:30–31). The reasons for taking up the story of John at this moment are theologically rich, as we shall see below. For now we will only note an explanation that Josephus helps us to appreciate: as in the case of John, Jesus represents a threat to Antipas's regime due to the success of his ministry. Crowds have gathered in several places (see 1:32, 38–39; 4:1), and as a result of the missionary journey of the Twelve (6:7–13), the fame of Jesus has escalated to new heights (6:30–34). At this point, he is caught in the spotlight of the ruler in Tiberias, to whom "Jesus' name had become well known" (6:14).

The reports that Antipas receives conflict on one central issue—the identity of Jesus—which is what Mark wants us to notice. Who is Jesus? Is he John risen from the dead, Elijah, or one of the prophets? Antipas himself reacts to the rumors: "John, whom I beheaded, has been raised from the dead!" (6:16). This comment prompts Mark to tell us the story behind John's beheading, the blame for which is placed on Antipas's second wife, Herodias, who wanted John killed because of his critique of their marriage. Their marriage was a blatant violation of the law against having sexual relations with one's sister-in-law (Lev 18:16), Herodias having divorced Antipas's half-brother, Philip (not the same as Philip the tetrarch), in order to marry Antipas.

Antipas is described as fearing John since he viewed him as "a righteous and holy man" (Mark 6:20). Antipas even "liked to listen" to John, though he was "greatly puzzled" by him (6:20). Therefore, to get her way with John, Herodias had to trick Antipas by using her daughter's dancing ability to charm him. Herodias's plot ultimately proved successful: John was immediately executed and his head delivered on a platter (6:27–28).

Comparing Mark and Josephus, several literary and historical similarities become obvious. Both accounts circle around the question of Herod Antipas's incapacity to understand John's identity. Both describe John's righteous or good character, his ministry of preaching and baptism, the crowds following him, Antipas's fear of him, and the illegitimacy of his execution. However, Josephus places greater emphasis on the apparent political implications of John's ministry, while Mark places greater emphasis on John's ethical or religious critique of Antipas. Nonetheless, Josephus's narration helps us to appreciate the political potency embedded within Mark's portrayal of the ministries of John and Jesus. As a Roman client ruler, Antipas was "paid" to make sure that the crowds following John (1:5) and Jesus would not band together to form a rebellion—as was the case with Barabbas, who is later presented in the same mold as Jesus (as an "insurrectionist," 15:7).

Mark's Purpose for Including the Story. Let's bring the pieces together. Is the seemingly odd story of Antipas and John out of place in Mark, or is it embedded in the deep logic of the narrative? I will argue the latter. On the one hand, Josephus's independent narrative helps us to see how in Mark's Gospel Antipas looms over Jesus and the disciples as a "shadow of death," just as he did over John. On the other hand, Mark uses Antipas on a theological level to emboss the main question of his narrative: Who correctly understands the identity of Jesus? In the end, Antipas is not able to perceive Jesus correctly. He becomes an example of those casting "a shadow of misunderstanding" over Jesus. This is apparent in several ways.

First, in regard to Antipas as a shadow of death, the murder of John serves to foreshadow the death of Jesus, and of the disciples as well, who will eventually follow in his footsteps (10:39). This trajectory is already prompted by the interrelation between John's imprisonment and Jesus's public ministry (1:14), as well as the Herodians's plot to kill Jesus (3:6). And the same is now highlighted by the groundless murder of John. Will the same not happen to Jesus, then? Further, if John is executed for fulfilling his calling, will the same not happen to the disciples when they take up their own crosses (8:34)? Placed as an **intercalation** between the disciples' sending and homecoming (6:7–13, 30–31), this threat is not to be missed, nor is Jesus's warning against "the yeast . . . of Herod" (8:15).

Second, in regard to the identity of Jesus, Antipas's misunderstanding of him (6:14–16), which clearly prompts the story about John, foreshadows exactly the disciples' reply to Jesus when he asks who people say he is: John, Elijah, or one of the prophets (cf. 8:28). Peter's confession—"you are the Messiah" (8:29)—overtly contrasts with Antipas's misguided identification: He is John, who "has been raised from the dead!" (6:16).

Third, the incapacity of Antipas to come to terms with who John is (cf. the puzzlement described in 6:20) at the very same time heightens the stakes in regard to Peter's misunderstanding of the mission of Jesus (cf. 8:32). The puzzlement that in the end paves the way for Antipas's execution of John mirrors Peter's doubt about the mission of Jesus, which in the end likewise paves the way for his denial (14:66–72).

Finally, there are, in the minute details, some striking antitheses at work. Antipas's lavish banquet stands in stark contrast to the modest banquet of Jesus (6:32–44), just as the humble appearance of the disciples (6:8–9) contrasts with Antipas's mingling with the rich and powerful (6:21).[1] Clearly, whoever Jesus is, he is a very different kind of king from Herod Antipas, having inaugurated a very different kind of kingdom.

In sum, the story of Herod Antipas and John the Baptist is far from trivial or a mere fairytale carelessly thrown into Mark's narrative. On the contrary, it serves to highlight two main themes that Mark wants a disciple to consider: the "shadow of death" that accompanies being sent on mission by Jesus, and the "shadow of misunderstanding" that looms over the odd and hitherto unknown combination of "kingdom and cross," which constitutes the bedrock of Jesus's **messianic** identity. To Mark, Jesus's kingdom was not inaugurated by way of popular uprising, as was the case with the other Jesus (Barabbas; cf. Matt 27:16–17), but by way of the cross and resurrection (Mark 8:27–9:1). Antipas's failure to grasp this much serves to sharpen the reader's attention to a far more important question: Who, if anybody (cf. 14:27), will grasp the "new" (cf. 2:21–22) combination of kingdom and cross?

FOR FURTHER READING

Additional Ancient Texts

Antipas's relationship to John the Baptist is described also by Matthew (14:1–12) and Luke (3:18–20; 9:7–9), as is his interactions with Jesus (cf. Matt 14:1–2; Mark 8:15; Luke 9:7–9; 13:31–33; 23:6–12, 15; Acts 4:27). Josephus's report on Antipas's killing of John is retold by Eusebius (*Hist. eccl.* 1.11).

---

1. See Adela Yarbro Collins, *Mark: A Commentary*, Hermeneia (Minneapolis: Fortress, 2007), 296.

In general, Josephus has included a number of stories that relate to Antipas (see *J.W.* 2.170, 178, 181–83; *Ant.* 18.36–38, 101–25, 136, 148–50, 240–55; *Life* 64–69).

English Translations and Critical Editions

Josephus. Translated by H. St. J. Thackeray et al. 13 vols. LCL. Cambridge: Harvard University Press, 1926–65.

Mason, Steve, ed. *Flavius Josephus: Translation and Commentary.* 10 vols. The Brill Josephus Project. Leiden: Brill, 2001–.

Secondary Literature

Hoehner, Harold W. *Herod Antipas: A Contemporary of Jesus Christ.* Grand Rapids: Zondervan, 1980.

Jensen, Morten Hørning. *Herod Antipas in Galilee: The Literary and Archaeological Sources on the Reign of Herod Antipas and Its Socio-Economic Impact on Galilee.* 2nd ed. WUNT 2/215. Tübingen: Mohr Siebeck, 2010.

———. "HerodAntipas.com: Research on Galilee in the Roman Period." www.herodantipas.com.

Mason, Steve. *Josephus and the New Testament.* Peabody, MA: Hendrickson, 2003.

CHAPTER 9

4QConsolations and Mark 6:30–56: Images of a New Exodus

HOLLY BEERS

In Mark 6:30–56, the Gospel writer narrates Jesus feeding the five thousand and walking on water. A key issue these events introduce concerns Jesus's identity, for who has the authority to perform such acts? And what familiar scriptural images do these events evoke? Specifically, what overtones to Israel's history in the Old Testament might surface in a text where Jesus feeds and comes to his disciples on (or through) water?

The most famous story in the Old Testament where God both feeds his people and rescues them through water is the exodus. After Israel leaves Egypt, they are pursued by Pharaoh's army (Exod 14:5–9), and Israel arrives at a seemingly insurmountable location: a large body of water (traditionally known as the Red Sea). However, God delivers them by dividing the waters so that Israel can pass through them (Exod 14:21–31). Later when they are in the wilderness, God miraculously feeds them several times, most famously with quail and manna (Exod 16:1–36).

These acts of deliverance are remembered throughout the Old Testament in other texts, including a group of chapters in the second half of Isaiah that envisions what is often called a "new exodus" by scholars. Here the first exodus is recalled with language and images that include the return of Yahweh, deliverance through water, and provision of food and water.

Nearer to Jesus's own day, a group of Jews living at **Qumran** filtered the story of God's deliverance from Exodus and Isaiah, incorporating it as a theme into their own texts and community life. One such text is 4QConsolations, a catalog of at least thirteen quotations from the Old Testament with eleven

100

from the second half of Isaiah, on the subject of God's comfort of his faithful people. This essay will compare and contrast the use of a "water text" from 4QConsolations with Mark's story of Jesus walking on water.

4QConsolations

"And from the Book of Isaiah, Consolations"

The text 4QConsolations (4Q176) is one of the **Dead Sea Scrolls**.[1] The author is unknown, and it is possible either that 4QConsolations was composed at Qumran by a member of the sect, or that it was written elsewhere and brought to Qumran. At least two different scribes copied the fragments found at Qumran in cave 4, as evidenced by the two handwriting styles. The handwriting styles allow a tentative date of 100–50 BC, at least as a date for the copying.

The exact genre of this text is debated, not least because of the order of the text as currently reconstructed by scholars. Though the original introduction has been lost, the first preserved portion opens with comments that use a quotation (or near quotation) of Psalm 79:1–3, a passage that laments devastation in Jerusalem and appeals to God to avenge the wrongful shedding of blood—including that of priests! It reads: "And perform your wonder, and do justice among your people and . . . your sanctuary, and contend with kingdoms because of the blood of . . . Jerusalem. See the bodies of your priests . . . and there is no one to bury them."[2]

A New Exodus in Isaiah. Next the author introduces a string of Isaiah quotations with the statement: "And from the book of Isaiah, consolations." Calling them "consolations" is the only interpretive comment given, however, for the quotations themselves follow one after another without any added commentary. The text as it currently stands ends with material that resonates with biblical themes, though most of it is not a quotation. The themes include God's creation of the world, his ordering of human destiny, and his justice in responding to those who love him as well as his destruction of those who hate him. It appears that the only direct quotation (or allusion) is of Zechariah 13:9 (along with language from Isaiah 52).

---

1. For an introduction to the Dead Sea Scrolls, see chapter 1 in this volume by Rikk Watts.
2. Translations of 4QConsolations are mine.

Order of 4QConsolations as Currently Reconstructed by Scholars

	Introduction	Body	Closing
Old Testament passage(s) used	Psalm 79	Eleven Isaiah quotations (from chapters 40–54)	Zechariah 13 and Isaiah 52
Topic	Lament for devastation in Jerusalem (including the killing of priests) and request for God's justice	Consolations and promises to restore God's faithful people after suffering in language that recalls the exodus	Nonbiblical material on oppression and devastation, God's creation of the world, his ordering of human destiny, and his justice (including the allusions/quotations)

The Isaiah quotations begin with Isaiah 40:1–5, a passage famous both for its promise of comfort for the righteous *and* its position at the beginning of a new section of Isaiah (chs. 40–55) that promises restoration after judgment and oppression. The first lines of the quotation read (with reconstructions indicated by square brackets): "[Comfort, comfort, my people], says your God, speak to the heart of Jerusalem, and sho[ut to her that] her [punishment is completed], that her fault is forgiven, that she has received from the hand of Yahweh a double punishment for all her offenses."

The other Isaiah passages quoted include verses from chapters 41, 43, 44, 49, 51, 52, and 54. The linking of these texts suggests that they were viewed as connected by a common theme ("consolations" in Hebrew) and were thus read together by the Qumran community. The restoration promised in Isaiah carries overtones of the exodus from Egypt, yet this new exodus in Isaiah will be an act of deliverance that surpasses the first one.

A New Exodus Deliverance through Water. One of the Isaianic new-exodus promises quoted in 4QConsolations is from Isaiah 43:1–6, and reads in fragments 3–5:

[And now, thus] says Yah[weh who created you, Jacob, and who made you, Israel, "Do not be afraid,] for I have redeemed you. [I have called you by your name, you are mine. When you pass through the water] I am with you, and in the [floods,] they will not drown you.

[. . . I g]ave a human in retu[rn for you, and nations in exchange for your life. Do not be] afraid, [for I am with you.] From the east I will brin[g your descendants, and from the west I will gather you. I will s]ay to the north, ['Give them up'; and to the south,] 'Do not hold back, but [bring back my children from afar, and my daughters from the end of the ea]rth.'"

When compared to Mark 6, this lengthy quotation is significant for at least two reasons. The first is that it uses the language of passing through water and floods (recalling the first exodus) as well as God's promise to be with his people during this time of chaos. The second is the repeated admonition not to be afraid.

Isaiah and Identity. The Qumran community claimed the blessings of this new exodus from Isaiah for themselves. In other words, the way in which 4QConsolations uses Isaiah appears to be consistent with the general use of Isaiah at Qumran: to assist the sect in shaping and legitimating their own identity as the "righteous" within Israel. The group apparently experienced suffering and oppression in various forms (including the killing of their priests), and Isaiah's passages gave them *eschatological* hope. Jewish eschatology in this time was usually not focused on the end of the world per se but instead on the hope of God's imminent judgment on the wicked coupled with the ushering in of a new era of blessing and peace for the righteous within Israel. As the righteous ones, the Qumran sect apparently saw themselves at the forefront of this new age of consolation.

Mark 6:30–56

"It Is I. Don't Be Afraid"

A New Exodus Feeding in the Wilderness. In Mark 6, Jesus miraculously feeds the five thousand (6:30–44) and walks on water (6:45–56). Ears attuned to the Old Testament will hear in these two episodes numerous allusions to Moses and the exodus. For example, the "quiet," "solitary," "remote" place sought out by Jesus (Mark 6:31–32, 35) evokes the deserts through which the Israelites traveled after being liberated from Egypt (Exod 15:22; 16:1–3; 19:1–2). The comparison of the large crowd following Jesus to "sheep without a shepherd" (Mark 6:34) echoes the same expression in Numbers 27:17 where Moses laments Israel's lack of leadership in the wilderness, as well as the shepherding roles attributed to Moses, Joshua, and Yahweh (Num 27:15–23; Isa 40:11; 63:11). Jesus's multiplication of the five loaves and two fish (Mark 6:38, 41) is reminiscent of God's provision of quail and manna for his wandering people (Exod 16:1–36).[3] Jesus's instructing the crowd to sit down "in groups of hundreds and fifties" (Mark 6:39–40) parallels Moses's assembling of Israel into similar quantities (Exod 18:21).[4] Finally, Jesus's dismissing the crowd and then going "up on a mountainside to pray" (Mark 6:46) recalls Moses's ascent of Mount Sinai (e.g., Exod 19:3, 20; 24:12–18; 34:2–4). What we have in this scene, then, is a miraculous feeding that in many ways suggests that through the person and work of Jesus God has inaugurated a new exodus symbolizing the eschatological redemption of his people.

A New Exodus Deliverance through Water. Later in the narrative, after having sent his disciples ahead of him by boat to Bethsaida (Mark 6:45), Jesus sees his disciples straining against heavy winds in the boat while he is still on shore (6:47–48). He walks out to them on the lake, and when he is about to pass by (6:48), they see him and are terrified because they think he is a ghost (6:49). Jesus counsels: "Take courage! It is I. Don't be afraid" (6:50). Then he climbs into the boat, and the winds die down (6:51).

The significance of Jesus walking on water, his comforting response about his identity, and the encouragement not to fear may be unclear without the (new) exodus overtones of the preceding verses. But with them in mind, the central moment of God's rescue of Israel in the exodus is remembered: the crossing of the sea. Of course, Moses leads Israel (and thus delivers them) through the sea (Exod 14:15–31; 15:10, 19–21), but it is Yahweh who has the originating power over the waters.

The Identity of Jesus. What do these new exodus parallels tell us about the identity of Jesus? When Jesus walks to the disciples on water, he is thus embodying what only God can do (Job 9:8; see also Isa 43:16–17; 44:27; 50:2; 51:10; 63:11–12; Ps 77:19–20). In response to their fear, Jesus declares: "It is I. Don't be afraid." The "it is I" could also be translated "I am," and ears familiar with the Old Testament hear the divine name given to Moses in Exodus 3:13–15: "I AM WHO I AM." Significantly, Isaiah 43:1–11 uses both "I am" and

---

3. Isaiah anticipates and heightens this theme of God's provision of food, describing this new exodus as a time when Israel will "feed beside the roads and find pasture on every barren hill" (Isa 49:9), and "neither hunger nor thirst" (49:10; cf. 35:6–7; 41:17–19; 43:19–20; 48:21), for no bread will be lacking (51:14).

4. The Dead Sea Scrolls community also arranged themselves in groups of fifties and hundreds, probably to indicate their self-identification as the gathering of true Israel in the new exodus (CD 13:1; 1QS 2:21–22; 1QM 4:1–5; cf. 4Q521 1 2:13b).

"do not fear" language, and whereas Mark 6 may only be alluding to Isaiah 43, 4QConsolations quotes from this passage:

> [And now, thus] says Yah[weh who created you, Jacob, and who made you, Israel, *"Do not be afraid,*] for I have redeemed you. [I have called you by your name, you are mine. When you pass through the water] *I am* with you, and in the [floods,] they will not drown you" [. . . "I g]ave a human in retu[rn for you, and nations in exchange for your life. *Do not be*] *afraid,* [*for I am with you.*]" (Frag. 3–4, lines 1–2, 4–5, emphases added)

The most powerful identification for Jesus, then, is not Moses but God,[5] and God returning at a specific moment for a specific reason: to bring about the new exodus.

After the wind dies down, Mark narrates that the disciples "were completely amazed, for they had not understood about the loaves; their hearts were hardened" (Mark 6:51–52). This hardening also recalls both the exodus (Pharaoh's hardening; e.g., Exod 4:21; 8:15) and the new exodus in Isaiah, for it is in Isaiah 40 and following where God reverses the hardening of Israel from chapter 6 (cf. Isa 6:9–10).

Mark and 4QConsolations. This new exodus is also the hope in 4QConsolations, though at Qumran this appears to be a hope that is as yet unfulfilled. This reality illustrates a key difference between 4QConsolations and Mark, for Mark narratively makes the point that Jesus is the one who brings that restoration; it is not hope, but hope *fulfilled* (or at least *inaugurated*). And in fact Jesus is greater than Moses, for in Jesus Yahweh himself is present. There are of course also similarities in terms of the ways in which 4QConsolations and Mark employ Isaiah. For example, both texts value Isaiah and use it as an authoritative text that shapes not just the past but also their present circumstances (including chaotic "water" moments) and identity. However, for 4QConsolations the present community of God's faithful is the Qumran **sectarians**, who have separated themselves from the rest of Judaism, while for Mark's Gospel it is the group of disciples who are committed to Jesus and are recruited not from a limited arena but from the whole of society (e.g., Mark 6:6–13; 7:24–37).

---

5. The language in Mark 6:48 of Jesus being "about to pass by them" is also a likely pointer to his divine identity, for it is God who passes by in Exod 33:19–23; 34:6; 1 Kgs 19:11. Since Jesus does not actually pass by them, and it is unclear as to why he would (as they need help and he rescues them), this language most likely carries divine connotations.

Similarities and Differences between 4QConsolations and Mark 6

	Isaiah 43	Identity of God's Faithful People	New-Exodus Hope
4QConsolations	Quoted as an authoritative text	Qumran sectarians separated from the rest of Judaism	Unfulfilled
Mark 6	Alluded to as an authoritative text	Disciples of Jesus recruited from the whole of society	Fulfilled (through Jesus)

FOR FURTHER READING

Additional Ancient Texts

Parallels to the stories of the feeding of the five thousand and walking on water occur in Matthew 14:13–21, Luke 9:10–17, and John 6:1–21. Jesus feeds the four thousand in Mark 8:1–10; Matthew 15:32–39. In addition, Jesus stills the storm in Mark 4:35–41; Matthew 8:18, 23–27; Luke 8:22–25. In Second Temple Jewish literature, the Qumran community organizes themselves into groups of fifties and hundreds in 1QS 2:21–22; CD 13:1; 1QM 4:1–5. Second Baruch 29:1–8 describes the eschatological nourishment (including manna) that God will provide.

English Translations and Critical Editions

Allegro, John M., with Arnold A. Anderson. *Qumrân Cave 4.I (4Q158–4Q186)*. DJDJ 5. Oxford: Clarendon, 1968. Note: Scholars use this in conjunction with John Strugnell, "Notes en marge du volume V des 'Discoveries in the Judaean Desert of Jordan,'" *RevQ* 7 (1970): 163–276. A revised edition of Allegro's work is in preparation by Moshe Bernstein and George Brooke, with the assistance of J. Høgenhaven: *Qumran Cave 4.I: 4Q158–186*, DJD 5a, rev. ed. (Oxford: Clarendon, forthcoming).

García Martínez, Florentino, and Eibert J. C. Tigchelaar, eds. *The Dead Sea Scrolls: Study Edition*. 2 vols. Leiden: Brill; Grand Rapids: Eerdmans, 1997–98.

Lichtenberger, Hermann. "Consolations (4Q176 = 4QTanh)." Pages 329–49 in *The Dead Sea Scrolls: Hebrew, Aramaic, and Greek Texts with English Translations, Volume 6B: Pesharim, Other Commentaries, and Related Documents*. PTSDSSP 6B. Edited by James H. Charlesworth. Tübingen: Mohr Siebeck; Louisville: Westminster John Knox, 2002.

Parry, Donald W., and Emanuel Tov, eds. *The Dead Sea Scrolls Reader 1: Texts Concerned with Religious Law, Exegetical Texts and Parabiblical Texts.* 2nd ed. Leiden: Brill, 2014.

Secondary Literature

Campbell, Jonathan G. *The Exegetical Texts.* Companion to the Dead Sea Scrolls 4. London: T&T Clark, 2004.

Hays, Richard B. *Echoes of Scripture in the Gospels.* Waco, TX: Baylor University Press, 2016.

Høgenhaven, Jesper. "4QTanhumim (4Q176): Between Exegesis and Treatise." Pages 151–67 in *The Mermaid and the Partridge: Essays from the Copenhagen Conference on Revising Texts from Cave Four.* Edited by George J. Brooke and Jesper Høgenhaven. STDJ. Leiden: Brill, 2011.

———. "The Literary Character of 4QTanhumim." *DSD* 14 (2007): 99–123.

Stanley, Christopher D. "The Importance of 4QTanhumim (4Q176)." *RevQ* 60 (1992): 569–82.

Watts, Rikki E. *Isaiah's New Exodus in Mark.* Grand Rapids: Baker Academic, 2000.

CHAPTER 10

The Letter of Aristeas and Mark 7:1–23: Developing Ideas of Defilement

SARAH WHITTLE

The importance of purity and defilement in the ancient world can hardly be overstated. Regulations designed to acquire or maintain purity and avoid defilement controlled everything from birth to death, sex, relationships, access to space, the food one could eat, and moral life. In Mark 7:1–23, Pharisees and scribes from Jerusalem notice that Jesus's disciples are eating with "hands that were *defiled*, that is, unwashed" (7:2). (The Greek term for *defiled* means "unclean," or "common," or "something not devoted to God.") Jesus undermines the Pharisees' attack by showing that following such traditions leads logically to the failure to obey Torah (7:8–9).

Then Jesus delivers his own ruling on purity: "Nothing outside a person can defile them by going into them. Rather, it is what comes out of a person that defiles them" (7:15). He elaborates using bodily functions: "For it doesn't go into their heart but into their stomach, and then out of the body. . . . What comes out of a person is what defiles them" (7:18–20). Jesus defends the disciples and rejects the Pharisees' ruling. Eating with unwashed hands is not relevant, both because it is a tradition of the elders and because defilement emerges not from external things but from within (7:21–23).

Before we decide that Jesus has switched from ritual uncleanness to moral uncleanness, we should consider whether he might still be using literal language. Corpse impurity, leprosy, genital discharge, and menstrual blood all come from within and defile.[1] However, the early Christians clearly

---

1. Roger P. Booth, *Jesus and the Laws of Purity: Tradition, History and Legal History in Mark 7*, JSNTSup 13 (Sheffield: JSOT Press, 1986), 205–13.

interpreted these sayings in an ethical sense, and the vice list at the end of this section confirms the moral framework: the impurity generated from within comes from the *heart* and consists of evil thoughts, sexual immorality, theft, murder, adultery, etc.

But we also have the problem of verse 19: "In saying this, Jesus declared all foods clean." Here Mark appears to abrogate the dietary rules of Torah, the system of ritual purity that classified and separated food that could and could not be eaten by Jews. Leviticus 11:1–47 and Deuteronomy 14:1–20 contain lists of animals classified as clean or unclean based on their characteristics, such as chewing the cud, having a divided hoof, having fins or scales, or swarming. According to the biblical text, even touching the carcass of an unclean animal would lead to temporary defilement.

The issue of whether gentiles were to follow these regulations was much debated in the early church.[2] And that is a problem for an interpretation of Mark as unambiguously ending ritual, dietary purity. Taking it at face value, it certainly seems that Mark considers Jesus as having removed the requirement to avoid ritually unclean food. Apparently this moral turn is part of Mark's broader strategy to show the significance of Jesus's identity as "the Holy One" (1:24) and his alternative purity practices for the kingdom of God. Our comparative text may shed some light on Mark's defilement discourse, particularly the relationship between ritual and moral aspects.

The Letter of Aristeas

"HE HEDGED US AROUND ON ALL SIDES BY RULES OF PURITY"

The Letter of Aristeas, or "Aristeas to Philocrates," as our manuscripts are entitled, is best known for its account of the translation of the Pentateuch from Hebrew to Greek (the **LXX**), purported to have taken place in the mid third-century BC and commissioned by the Egyptian king Ptolemy II Philadelphia (282–246 BC) for the great library of Alexandria. Addressed to Aristeas's brother Philocrates, the Letter of Aristeas contains elements of historiography as well as an extensive apologetic section on the Jewish law. The author is presented as a gentile courtier of Ptolemy, who was sent to Jerusalem to fetch seventy-two Jewish translators from the high priest

---

2. Acts 10:9–16; 15:29; Rom 14:20–21; 1 Cor 8:7–9; 10:27; Col 2:16, 21; 1 Tim 4:1–5.

Eleazar (260–245 BC). In fact, it is likely that the work is Jewish rather than pagan, containing explicitly Jewish concerns and detailed knowledge of Jewish life and customs, and that it was composed between 150–100 BC as Jewish-Hellenistic apologetic. It is a pseudepigraphon—a work attributed by its author to a figure in the past. As such, we shall call the author "Ps.-Aristeas" (Pseudo Aristeas).

Impregnable Ramparts and Walls of Iron. The section we will focus on is Eleazar's apology for the law (Let. Aris. 128–71). It is an extended interpretation of specifically dietary law and is dependent upon Leviticus 11 and Deuteronomy 14. Ps.-Aristeas employs methods of interpretation to show that these laws actually embody Hellenistic morals. The Letter of Aristeas introduces questions about food and drink and animals recognized as unclean (128) on the basis that "our Lawgiver [Moses] . . . fenced us round with impregnable ramparts and walls of iron, that we might not mingle at all with any of the other nations, but remain pure in body and soul" (139).[3] As such, "he hedged us round on all sides by rules of purity, affecting alike what we eat, or drink, or touch, or hear, or see" (142). But in fact, it was not with regard to the clean and unclean animals themselves but "for the sake of righteousness to aid the quest for virtue and the perfecting of character" (144–45).

There is a list of birds that are permissible to eat: they eat grain, are tame, and are distinguished by their cleanliness (146). In contrast, forbidden or unclean birds are carnivorous, cruel, and tyrannize others; preying on the tame, they also injure humans (147). These birds are a *sign* by means of which Jews should understand that they must practice righteousness and justice and refrain from cruelty and violence. These rules are given with the object of "teaching us a moral lesson" (150). Moreover, the division of hoof and the separation of claws teach that the Jews should discriminate their actions with a view to practicing virtue.

The author turns to weasels and mice, first introduced in verse 144. They are quite possibly the *most* unclean creeping things of Leviticus 11:29. The Letter of Aristeas characterizes them as destructive; mice "defile and damage everything" (164). The mention of the weasel relies on ancient biographical tradition about the method of conception.[4] The weasel is particularly defiling, as it "conceives through the ears and brings forth through

---

3. Translation of Letter of Aristeas here and the next two paragraphs are from R. H. Charles, *The Apocrypha and Pseudepigrapha of the Old Testament*, 2 vols. (Oxford: Clarendon, 1913), 2:83–122.

4. See Aristotle, *Gen. an.* 3.6.2; Ovid, *Metam.* 9.322–23; Plutarch, *Is. Os.* 72.

the mouth" (165). And, for this reason "a like practice is declared unclean in men" (166). "For by embodying in speech all that they receive through the ears, they involve others in evils and work no ordinary impurity, being themselves altogether defiled by the pollution of impiety" (166). Here language of evil, impurity, and defilement is piled up. In conclusion, "concerning meats and things unclean, creeping things, and wild beasts, the whole system aims at righteousness and righteous relationships between man and man" (169).

Interpretive Technique. The goal of this interpretation of the law is to point out positive moral values embodied in the dietary rules. There are at least four ideas at work here.

1. Birds and animals serve not only as an *analogy* for the human, but the bird or animal itself is given either negative moral characteristics of tyranny and cruelty or virtues such as being tame and exhibiting cleanliness.
2. Just as birds and animals are designated clean and unclean and are to be separated, so too Jews and gentiles are to be separated.
3. Peculiarly potent defilement is generated from within and comes from the mouth as evil speech.
4. Eleazar's interpretations are Moses's original intentions for the law.

Focusing on the technique of interpretation, the narrator explains that these rules about birds and animals have been "set out figuratively" (150).[5] Though this is often translated "by way of allegory," it has been pointed out that the Letter of Aristeas does not use the term normally used for allegory. Rather, he uses a phrase with "a figurative meaning which has a moral component."[6] We also encounter signs and symbols—with the meaning of signifying, indicating, or pointing to something. Wright says that this is "perhaps the first Jewish work to use this technique of exposing figurative or allegorical meanings of Jewish scripture."[7] As such, it becomes an important precursor to our Markan text. However, we should not forget that the Letter of Aristeas is designed to reinforce *practice*; that is, Ps.-Aristeas's interpretation is concerned with asserting a rational basis for maintaining literal observance of the purity laws.

---

5. Translation here from Benjamin G. Wright III, *The Letter of Aristeas*, CEJL (Berlin: de Gruyter, 2015), 280.
6. Ibid.
7. Ibid.

Mark 7:1–23

"What Comes Out of a Person Is What Defiles Them"

The Jewish temple is the center of holiness and purity. Mark does demonstrate some concern with cultic-ritual purity (the purification of the leper who is to present himself at the temple; 1:44), yet he also explains how to deal with purity in everyday life. His narrative includes unclean animals (5:11–12) and spirits (3:11), persons who are defiled by means of menstrual blood (5:25) and leprosy (1:40), and unclean things (7:4). The story of the Gerasene demoniac includes gentile land, tombs, pigs, and a man possessed by unclean spirits, as several sources of impurity are brought together in one geographic and narrative setting (5:1–19).

Our focus passage (7:1–23) reflects both the concern with the universal threat of the danger of impurity and the Pharisees as Jesus's opponents. All the incidents of Jesus teaching on purity are set in relation to Pharisaic tradition concerning eating (Matt 15:1–20; 23:25–26; Luke 11:37–41). As such, it has been claimed that "the synoptics educate their readers on the Jewish purity practices of their main characters."[8] In contrast, Jesus is portrayed as "the Holy One" (Mark 1:24). Even when confronting sources of defilement, he does not contract impurity, and so he has no need for purification rituals. When he engages unclean people, he restores them to cleanness. This aspect of purity is crucial for Mark's Christology.

Until recently, the consensus was that Pharisees, a sect particularly concerned with purity, emulated the practice of temple priests; that is, their handwashing ritual expanded upon the necessity for priestly hands to be ceremonially washed before holy food was offered as a sacrifice (Num 18:8–13). However, there is evidence that not only Pharisees but also ordinary Jews, for whom there was no requirement to maintain purity in this way, were increasingly observing ritual purity and practicing immersion and hand washing. More likely in this case the issue is the belief that unclean hands could defile food, and the food could then defile the body in a secondary sense. As such, it was more than a concern for unwashed hands. "It is not purity of ordinary food *per se* that is endangered but purity of a whole person is at stake."[9]

---

8. Arseny Ermakov, "Purity in the Synoptic Gospels," in *Purity: Essays in Bible and Theology*, ed. A. B. Latz and A. Ermakov (Eugene, OR: Pickwick, 2014), 89–113, at 94.

9. Ermakov, "Purity," 105–6.

Mark's Jesus not only rejects the Pharisees' logic but sets out his own purity laws: that which goes into a person from the outside does not defile, but that which comes out defiles. With this declaration he is also rejecting the Pharisaic claim that defiled food can defile a person. And if it cannot pollute, it is clean: "In saying this, Jesus declared all foods clean" (7:19). However, just as important, if not more so, is the defiling force of what comes out: the impurity generated from within. "For it is from within, out of a person's heart, that evil thoughts come—sexual immorality, theft, murder, adultery, greed, malice, deceit, lewdness, envy, slander, arrogance and folly. All these evils come from inside and defile a person" (7:21–23). By turning the discussion of handwashing and defiled food—a *ritual* issue—into a statement about defilement coming from within—a *moral* issue in the tradition we observed in the Letter of Aristeas—where does Mark leave us?

It becomes clear from Mark, as well as what is perhaps the earliest example of a Jewish figurative interpretation of ritual-purity texts (i.e., Let. Aris.), that it is difficult to separate the physical, ritual, moral, and figurative aspects of purity and defilement. A general case may be made that ritual and moral defilement have separate origins and prescribed treatments. Sources of ritual impurity are generally natural and unavoidable: contagion is not sinful, it is impermanent and is dealt with by ritual washing and waiting. Moral impurity, on the other hand, involves committing grave sin—or even committing acts that fall into categories of sexual sin, idolatry, and bloodshed—and affects the sinner, the land, and the sanctuary. There is no contact contagion, and it may only be dealt with by punishment or atonement through sin offerings.[10] However, even if we could establish distinct terminology, we have, introduced with the Letter of Aristeas, a moral application of ritual texts that goes deeper than analogy. So these distinctions are further problematized by actual usage in Second Temple Judaism.

Though not perfect, the inside/outside approach is often used to make sense of Mark's sayings. Mark indicates that the heart (7:19, 21) is the inside (7:21, 23), and this is contrasted with the outside (7:15, 18). Earlier in the passage, Jesus has cited Scripture against the Pharisees: "These people honor me with their lips, but their hearts are far from me" (7:6; cf. Isa 29:13 **LXX**). The heart can generate defilement. And for those who place purity on the map of the body, this idea of purity/defilement of heart is important. As Jerome Neyrey puts it, "The concerns of the Pharisees are with body

---

10. Jonathan Klawans, *Impurity and Sin in Ancient Judaism* (New York: Oxford University Press, 2000), 26.

structure, hands, surfaces and lips. These stand in contrast with the heart, the predominant body part for Jesus."[11]

Though we began with the potential of defilement from unclean hands and secondarily contaminated, unclean food, Mark's narrative objective is that followers should not be concerned about defilement resulting from unclean things but rather with defilement that comes out of the heart. So far, so good. But much more serious than the Pharisees' position on defiled hands is the issue of the defiling force of unclean food we have read about in the Letter of Aristeas—the dietary laws of Leviticus. In the Letter of Aristeas, the moral interpretation of the dietary laws served to reinforce their relevance and rational basis: they pointed toward justice and righteousness. Does Mark intend for his interpretative comment, "in saying this, Jesus declared all foods clean," to be understood relatively so as to prioritize the inward, or is he putting an end to observance?

The latter seems to be the case. Apparently, while the Letter of Aristeas encouraged keeping the ritual law so as to maintain moral purity and the separation between Jew and gentile, Mark argues against separation and for his audience to be free to eat all food. There is no indication here that Mark believed that keeping dietary laws was connected to the maintenance of moral purity in the way the Letter of Aristeas did. For Jesus, nothing external could defile: purity was a matter of the heart. And if purity systems maintained boundaries, this was the new boundary. While Jesus berates the scribes and Pharisees for undermining the authority of the Torah, with this move Jesus himself gives the dietary rules of Leviticus a quite different, eschatological goal. Of course, with the Letter of Aristeas, he would have argued that this was faithful to Moses's original intentions for the law. According to Mark the temple as the center of holiness and purity will be replaced by Jesus and his community, a temple "not made with hands" (14:58).

For Further Reading

Additional Ancient Texts

Purity was extremely important in Jewish life as evidenced by the OT, particularly Leviticus. This can be seen in the Second Temple period in the cleaning of dishes, as with CD 10. The discovery of numerous *miqwa'ot*

---

11. Jerome H. Neyrey, *Render to God: New Testament Understandings of the Divine* (Minneapolis: Fortress, 2004), 39.

(ritual baths) in Jerusalem and at **Qumran** dating to the **Second Temple period** shows the extent to which people went to attain purity. See also Philo, *Spec.* 1.256–61; Jubilees 22:16; and Josephus, *J.W.* 2.129. Impurity was especially associated with gentiles and was particularly evident in their proximity to the Temple in Jerusalem. See, for example, Psalms of Solomon 1–2.

English Translations and Critical Editions

Pelletier, André. *Lettre d'Aristée à Philocrate: Introduction, texte critique, traduction et notes.* Sources Chrétiennes 89. Paris: Éditions du Cerf, 1962.

Shutt, R. J. H. "Letter of Aristeas." Pages 7–34 in vol. 2 of *Old Testament Pseudepigrapha.* Edited by James H. Charlesworth. Garden City, NY: Doubleday, 1985.

Secondary Literature

Douglas, Mary. *Purity and Danger: An Analysis of Concepts of Pollution and Taboo.* London: Routledge, 2002.

Ermakov, Arseny. "Purity in the Synoptic Gospels." Pages 89–113 in *Purity: Essays in Bible and Theology.* Edited by Andrew Brower Latz and Arseny Ermakov. Eugene, OR: Pickwick, 2014.

Klawans, Jonathan. *Impurity and Sin in Ancient Judaism.* New York: Oxford University Press, 2000.

CHAPTER 11

Jubilees and Mark 7:24–37: Crossing Ethnic Boundaries

KELLY R. IVERSON

One of the distinguishing features of Mark's Gospel is the way in which Jesus encroaches upon traditional Jewish boundaries. Though not entirely foreign to the other Gospels, Mark places particular emphasis on the activities and sayings of Jesus that underscore his boundary-breaking ministry. Mark's concern to explore Jewish identity markers is evident at numerous places in the narrative,[1] but the issue comes into sharp relief in 7:1–37. Here Jesus interacts with the religious establishment, heals the daughter of a Syrophoenician woman, and restores a deaf and mute man. At first glance the episodes appear unrelated, but the sequence is arranged for theological purposes. As part of his mission not "to call the righteous, but sinners" (2:17), the Markan Jesus transcends social, cultural, ethnic, and religious boundaries to demonstrate his compassion for all in need of a physician (2:17). Before turning to Mark 7:1–37, it will be helpful to consider a Second Temple text that offers perspective on this depiction. Mark's narrative may seem relatively benign from a contemporary perspective, but a wider angle of vision offers context to appreciate the characterization of Jesus.

Jubilees

"SEPARATE FROM THE GENTILES . . . FOR THEIR WORKS ARE UNCLEAN"

The book of Jubilees is a Jewish document that was written sometime during the second-century BC. An apocryphal account purportedly given to Moses during his forty days on the top of Mt. Sinai (1:1–4), the name of

---

1. See, e.g., 1:29–31, 40–44; 2:1–12, 15–17, 23–28; 3:1–6; 5:1–20, 25–34, 35–43.

the book—Jubilees—is derived from the chronological system that is used as the unit of measurement (i.e., forty-nine years; cf. Lev 25) to date many of the events in the text. The content of Jubilees offers a selected retelling of the biblical narrative, extending from creation through the giving of the law (Genesis–Exodus). The author utilizes the basic framework of the biblical account but includes expansions, additions, and explanations that enrich the narrative and reveal the author's theological agenda.

Concern for the Law. The law is a frequent topic of discussion in Second Temple literature; however, Jubilees emphasizes the significance of the law by highlighting the antiquity of Torah. In particular this aspect of the law is accented through the depiction of the Genesis narrative and the so-called heavenly tablets.

One of the interesting features in Jubilees is the way in which the law is retrojected onto the story of Genesis. For example, after Noah departs from the ark, he offers a sacrifice to atone "for all the sins of the land" (6:1–2).[2] Although Genesis 8:20–21 also describes an offering being made by Noah (a burnt offering as opposed to a sin offering), Jubilees reflects a development of thought that is reminiscent of later Levitical practice. Unlike the generalized depiction in Genesis, the author of Jubilees catalogs the specific animals involved in the sacrifice along with the use of oil, wine, and frankincense (6:3). This might seem like an attempt to clarify the scene, but the offering bears a striking similarity to the cultic mandates in Exodus 29:40 and Lev 2:2–15.

This impulse to push back the Sinaitic revelation extends even beyond the Genesis narrative. Unlike the biblical tradition, in which the Torah is codified on stone tablets, in Jubilees the earthly tablets reflect what is engraved in the heavenly realm. These "heavenly tablets" contain a record of all human history (32:21; 45:14), including the events in Jubilees (1:28), along with a prescription for the chronological system of days that are to demarcate the Jewish calendar (e.g., 6:17; 16:28–29; 32:27–29). While the heavenly tablets include the Mosaic law (e.g., 3:9–11; 4:5; 33:10–12), Jubilees also introduces additional laws, which are likewise written on the heavenly tablets and placed alongside Torah. The depiction of heavenly tablets spotlights the fact that the law is a permanent expression of God's ways that are to be obeyed by the community.

Gentile Impurity. Various facets of the law are explicated in Jubilees, but none is more important for appreciating Mark than its depiction of gentiles. Taken as a whole, Jubilees casts a decidedly negative shadow over gentiles

---

2. All Jubilees translations are adapted from R. H. Charles, ed., *The Apocrypha and Pseudepigrapha of the Old Testament in English*, 2 vols. (Oxford: Clarendon, 1913), 2:1–82.

and sets forth stern warnings for interaction with foreigners: "Separate from the Gentiles, and do not eat with them, and do not according to their works, and do not become their associate, for their works are unclean" (22:16).

This attitude toward gentiles is best illustrated in the retelling of Genesis 34. After summarizing the story of Dinah (30:1–6), Jubilees moves on to the legal implications of the episode. According to Jubilees, the children of Israel are to forbid—without exception—any and all intermarriage with gentiles, including converted gentiles (30:11) because it is "written in the heavenly tablets" (30:9). Any man who violates this statute, which has "no limit of days" (30:10), shall be stoned to death, and any daughter or sister given to the gentiles shall be burned "with fire" (30:7–9). Not only does the reproach result in the defilement of a household, it contaminates the nation, causing "plague upon plague, and curse upon curse" (30:15). For such violations of the law there is no remission or forgiveness of sin, except the removal and punishment of those participating in the transgression.

The injunction against intermarriage, as well as intermingling with foreigners in general (22:16), is grounded in the assumed behavior of gentiles. For the author of Jubilees, gentiles revel in the shame of their nakedness (3:31), demonstrate a lack of concern for their own (15:34), show no mercy or compassion (23:23), oppress the people of God (1:13), and worship false deities (1:9). Because of this, they are "sinners" who violate the law and are a reproach to God (23:24; 24:28). Underlying this characterization is the belief that gentiles pose a threat to the well-being of God's people and that the nations have been led astray by evil spirits (15:31–32). The consequence of intermingling with foreigners, and thus violating the law, exposes the individual to defilement and may ultimately lead to the punishment of the nation.

This depiction of gentiles is harsh, and other Second Temple texts offer a more favorable characterization. Nonetheless, in some quarters Jubilees was a text of some influence (e.g., **Qumran**) and offers an example of a perspective that was "in the air" during the composition of Mark's Gospel. At the very least, it provides a backdrop to appreciate Mark's depiction of Jesus.

Mark 7:24–37

"EVEN THE DOGS UNDER THE TABLE EAT THE CHILDREN'S CRUMBS"

If the portrayal of gentiles in the book of Jubilees is negative, the Gospel of Mark moves in an entirely different direction. In fact Mark depicts Jesus as intentionally crossing ethnic, religious, and social boundaries for the sake of extending the blessings of God to gentiles. The expansion of the kingdom is a central focus of 7:24–37, yet the passage must be understood within the context of the preceding narrative (7:1–23).

Declaring all Foods Clean. Throughout Mark, Jesus is often engaged in conflict with the religious establishment (e.g., 2:1–12, 15–17, 18–22, 23–28; 3:1–6). Mark 7 begins in a similar fashion, but the issue prompting the confrontation arises over the question of handwashing. After noticing that the disciples are eating bread with unwashed hands, the Pharisees and scribes inquire about the disciples' failure to observe the traditions of the elders (7:5). Mark, assuming that some in the audience were unfamiliar with the tradition, provides an editorial aside (7:3–4) to explain the practice and to note that the tradition of purification extended even to the washing of cooking utensils.

Jesus responds to the religious leaders, but does not address the question of handwashing. Instead, after branding the authorities "hypocrites" (7:6), Jesus raises the issue of Corban, that is, the tradition of declaring property dedicated to God. Though embraced by the religious leaders, Jesus argues that the tradition is used to deny parental support, which is in conflict with the scriptural command to "honor your father and mother" (7:10). In this sense, what has been instituted through human tradition is in violation of the commandment of God. Though the response does not provide a formal rebuttal to the original question, the matter is intimately related to the subject of handwashing. The implication is that even those practices and traditions that were intended for the benefit of the people have missed the spirit of the law and failed to bring about the desired outcome.

Immediately after rebuking his critics, Jesus calls the crowds to himself and delivers a semicryptic statement: "Nothing outside a person can defile them by going into them. Rather, it is what comes out of a person that defiles them" (7:15). Although no explanation of the saying is provided to the crowd, Jesus enters a home with the disciples to interpret the **parable**. Once inside, Jesus explains that food taken into the body is unable to corrupt a person "for it doesn't go into their heart but into their stomach" (7:19). What comes out of the heart—"sexual immorality, theft, murder, adultery, greed, malice, deceit, lewdness, envy, slander, arrogance and folly"—is responsible for defiling a person (7:21–22). Unlike the religious leaders who assume that unclean objects and/or people may contaminate a person, the Markan Jesus locates the origin of defilement within the human heart. Consequently, a person cannot be defiled via proximity or contact with the unclean since nothing is inherently impure, including food (7:19) and people.

Sharing the Children's Bread. After overturning the food laws, Jesus travels to the region of Tyre where he encounters a Syrophoenician woman whose daughter suffers from an unclean spirit. Although there are similar encounters in the narrative (e.g., 1:29–31; 2:1–12; 5:21–24; 8:22–26), the way the scene develops is unlike any other account in the Gospel tradition. In particular, the encounter with the Syrophoenician woman is striking for two reasons. First, after the woman repeatedly makes her plea (7:26), Jesus appears to respond in a fashion that denies her request. Second, although Jesus heals many people in Mark's Gospel, only here does he respond to a supplicant in parabolic form (7:27), a method of communication intended to shroud and obscure meaning (cf. 4:11–12).

Why does the episode deviate from the typical healing narrative? To appreciate these dynamics, it is imperative to understand that Jesus's response ("first let the children eat all they want . . . for it is not right to take the children's bread and toss it to the dogs," 7:27) is a parabolic description of Israel's (i.e., the children's) unique place in salvation history. In contrast to the gentile nations (i.e., the dogs), the children of Israel have been the primary recipients of God's blessing (i.e., bread). Thus, Jesus's denial is framed within the context of Israel's special relationship with God.

If this is the primary thrust of the response, it still raises the issue of why Jesus appears to reject the woman's request. At no other point in the narrative does Jesus deny a genuine request for healing. Moreover, the response does not align with the broader context in which Jesus heals gentiles (3:7–12) and initiates a journey into gentile territory where he provides healing for an individual with a condition that is similar to the woman's daughter (cf. 5:1–20). Israel may be "first" (7:27), but nothing in the narrative suggests that gentiles are to be excluded from the benefits of the kingdom.

Instead of viewing Jesus's response as a veiled rejection, perhaps a better way of interpreting the statement—at least according to the logic of the narrative—is to understand the statement as a "test," since the very nature of parables and the task of deciphering their features constitute a verbal challenge (4:11–12). This interpretation seems to fit the unfolding narrative in which Jesus declares all foods clean and affirms that the status of a person's spiritual condition is determined by the heart. In view of this teaching and the fact that Jesus has already provided healing to gentiles on more than one occasion, it is preferable to understand the episode as a "test," since neither race nor the food laws can defile a person. Given that there is nothing inherently impure about a person, it seems that the woman's posture (7:25), her address of Jesus as "Lord" (7:28), and her reaction to the apparent denial ("even the dogs under the table eat the children's crumbs," 7:28) are indicative of her purity, perseverance, and dependence upon Jesus. In fact, the woman's rejoinder demonstrates an insight that is unparalleled in the Gospel of Mark. Not only does the woman understand the parabolic challenge—something the disciples are unable to do (7:17–18)—she extends the scenario to include a place for gentiles in God's plan. Jesus's acknowledgment of the woman and the healing of her daughter affirm that she has indeed passed the "test" (7:29).

The episode of the Syrophoenician woman provides a poignant example of Mark's concern for gentile inclusion, but it is hardly the only text related to the theme. In the very next scene Jesus travels to the region of the Decapolis—a place in gentile territory—where he heals a man who is deaf and mute (7:31–37). The additional interaction with gentiles reveals that just as Jesus walks on water, so does he continue to tread upon cultural norms for the sake of extending the kingdom to all who have "ears to hear" (4:9, 23).

As suggested in Mark and Jubilees, the relationship between Jews and gentiles was a crucial issue in the ancient world. Though Jews and gentiles coexisted, the relationship was often characterized by tension. At least for some, foreigners were not just different but were to be engaged with caution, if at all. While Jubilees exemplifies this proverbial fear of the outsider—a common refrain in both ancient and contemporary rhetoric—Mark plays off the perspective and points the audience to a new way of thinking. Instead of promoting a stereotype, the Markan Jesus subverts expectations by repeatedly crossing religious and cultural boundaries, demonstrating that purity is a matter of the heart, not ethnicity, food, or unwashed hands. Although Israel holds a special place in salvation history, the kingdom is not to be identified with a particular people. In contrast to Jubilees, Mark's Jesus extends the blessings of the kingdom to those outside the Jewish community and simultaneously paves the way for the expansion of the church to gentile "dogs."

For Further Reading

Additional Ancient Texts

Other texts characterizing gentiles in a manner similar to Jubilees include the Apocalypse of Abraham and 4 Ezra. Slightly more favorable depictions can be found in 1 Enoch and 2 Baruch.

English Translations and Critical Editions

VanderKam, James C. *The Book of Jubilees: A Critical Text*. 2 vols. CSCO 510. Leuven: Peeters, 1989.

Wintermute, O. S. "Jubilees: A New Translation and Introduction." Pages 35–142 in vol. 2 of *The Old Testament Pseudepigrapha*. Edited by James H. Charlesworth. Garden City, NY: Doubleday, 1985.

Secondary Literature

Donaldson, Terence L. *Judaism and the Gentiles: Jewish Patters of Universalism (to 135 CE)*. Waco, TX: Baylor University Press, 2007.

Iverson, Kelly R. *Gentiles in the Gospel of Mark: "Even the Dogs under the Table Eat the Children's Crumbs."* LNTS 339. London: T&T Clark, 2007.

Juel, Donald H. *Master of Surprise: Mark Interpreted*. Minneapolis: Fortress, 1994.

Segal, Michael. *The Book of Jubilees: Rewritten Bible, Redaction, Ideology and Theology*. JSJSup 117. Leiden: Brill, 2007.

Sim, David C., and James S. McLaren, eds. *Attitudes to Gentiles in Ancient Judaism and Early Christianity*. LNTS 499. London: Bloomsbury, 2013.

VanderKam, James C. *The Book of Jubilees*. GAP. London: T&T Clark, 2001.

CHAPTER 12

SUZANNE WATTS HENDERSON

In Mark, the path to clear understanding of Jesus and his mission is neither predictable nor straightforward. Those closest to him often appear as obtuse and hard hearted as his staunchest opponents. On the other hand, random, unnamed characters—even evil spirits—correctly discern Jesus's identity and mission. In the end, the only human character to name Jesus as "son of God" is a member of the Roman army that has carried out his execution (15:39).

Situated at the heart of the gospel story, Mark 8:1–26 combines episodes that feature Jesus interacting with followers, adversaries, and an unnamed blind man. Taken together, these passages point only allusively, not clearly, to what Jesus is up to in Mark. Jesus's second miraculous feeding (8:1–10; cf. 6:30–44) seems to constitute the very "sign from heaven" some Pharisees request in the next scene (8:11–13). But Jesus flatly denies it, saying that "no sign will be given to [this generation]" (8:12). When he regroups with his followers on a boat, Jesus not only warns against the "leaven" of the Pharisees and of Herod, but he also rants about his disciples' misunderstanding in terms that liken them to those "outside": no perception, hardened hearts, failures in hearing and vision (8:14–21; cf. 3:5; 4:11–12).

A clear narrative break occurs as the entourage arrives in Bethsaida. Scholars take Mark 8:22–26 as the Gospel's central literary hinge, where the story swings from Jesus's ministry in and around Galilee toward his destiny in Jerusalem. Unique to Mark's Gospel, this passage features a two-staged healing of an unnamed blind man. At first try, Jesus restores only partial, blurry sight; it takes a second attempt for the man to see "everything clearly" (8:25). As the story ends, Jesus sends the man home, but emphatically not "into the village" (8:26). This curious passage both builds on the chapter's interest in clear sight (see 8:18) and anticipates the shift toward Mark's central section (8:27–10:52), where Jesus makes clear that the cross lies at the heart of his mission. Our discussion will thus focus on this obscure healing story as a "way in" to Mark's epistemology.

Damascus Document

"LISTEN TO ME AND I SHALL OPEN YOUR EYES"

Jewish prophetic tradition is full of texts that use metaphors of blindness and sight to contrast unfaithful Israel with those who discern and reflect God's righteous ways (see, e.g., Isa 6:10; Jer 5:21). Moreover, restoration of sight to the blind is a marker of God's power unleashed on earth (e.g., Isa 29:18; 35:5; 42:7). These and other passages likely lie behind the Damascus Document (CD), a text found in fragmentary form among the **Dead Sea Scrolls** that will serve as the companion text for our Markan story.

The Damascus Document (also known as the "Zadokite Fragments") is the only **sectarian** text discovered near **Qumran** that was also found elsewhere—in this case, in the library of a Cairo synagogue, in 1896 (thus the label "CD," for "Cairo Damascus" document). It combines exhortation with legal provisions for those "who entered the new covenant in the land of Damascus" (6:19).[1] While scholars disagree about the audience's precise geographic and chronological setting, the text clearly signals that the community has repudiated the ways of Second Temple religious leaders in Jerusalem and follows a figure known as the Teacher of Righteousness.

Blind Persons Who Grope for a Path. Besides its metaphorical use of blindness and sight, the Damascus Document offers a fitting counterpoint to our Gospel passage for at least three reasons. Like Mark, the text invokes the **apocalyptic** frame that sees that history is pressing toward full revelation, as God's reign will soon take root on earth. Like Mark, the writer sees the audience as those who make their way, over time, toward faithfulness. And like Mark, the document features a prominent human figure

---

1. Translations of the Damascus Document are from Florentino García Martínez and Eibert J. C. Tigchelaar, eds., *The Dead Sea Scrolls: Study Edition*, 2 vols. (Grand Rapids: Eerdmans, 1997–98), 1:551–74.

who issues a countercultural call to that way of faithfulness. Let us consider several excerpts that offer interpretive handles for our study of Mark's baffling passage.

In the opening column, the writer sets the temporal stage by noting that 390 years after the Babylonian exile, God has "caused to sprout from Israel and from Aaron a shoot of the planting, in order to possess his land and to become fat with the good things of the soil" (CD 1:5–8). But such a sated destiny apparently still awaits, as this faithful remnant squares up to its iniquity in the meantime. Thus we learn that "they were like blind persons and like those who grope for a path over twenty years" (1:9–10). It is while in this condition of blindness that God has "raised up for them a Teacher of Righteousness, in order to direct them in the path of his heart" (1:11).

See and Understand the Deeds of God. Bearing this mantle of instruction, the Teacher exhorts the community this way: "Listen to me and I shall open your eyes so that you can see and understand the deeds of God . . . so that you can walk perfectly on all of his paths" (CD 2:14–16). The Teacher then appears throughout the document as the "interpreter of the law" (6:7) who promotes the "exact interpretation of the law in which the forefathers were instructed" (4:8; cf. 6:14, 18). This language sets the community at odds, in the Teacher's view, with the religious leaders in power in Jerusalem, who "sought easy interpretations, chose illusions, [and] scrutinized loopholes" (1:18–19). Scholars generally think the writer targets the Pharisees, whose oral traditions constituted what many saw as a "looser" interpretation of the law. The Damascus community, then, is a conservative one, on guard against what the writer calls "Belial's three nets": fornication, wealth, and the defilement of the temple (4:15–18).

The Damascus Document thus addresses a community emerging from blindness to sight (see also CD 16:2). The two conditions coexist in the writer's view; they have "returned to the law of Moses" at the point of entering the community, even as they gain clearer vision through the Teacher's ongoing instruction. By pointing away from the corrupt and lascivious ways rampant in Jerusalem, the Teacher of Righteousness offers a cure that accompanies a strict interpretation of Jewish law within the community. Epistemology in the Damascus Document is anchored not just in Torah but in a particular—and exacting—interpretation of this foundational **covenant**. Those who have eyes to see will, the writer implies, ultimately "possess [God's] land and . . . become fat with the good things of his soil" (1:7–8).

Mark 8:1–26

"DO YOU HAVE EYES BUT FAIL TO SEE, AND EARS BUT FAIL TO HEAR?"

Like the community addressed in the Damascus Document, Mark's audience was probably at odds with, and physically removed from, mainstream Jewish thought and practice. At this pivotal juncture in the Gospel, then, we find a story about restored sight that occurs in stages rather than all at once. More than just evidence of Jesus's healing powers, the encounter works metaphorically to shed light on the way of discipleship for those who would follow Jesus in his own day and in generations to come. Our discussion will explore four dimensions of Mark 8:22–26 that grow clearer in dynamic interface with our Qumran text.

"Outside the Village." From start to finish, this healing occurs at the margins of the social order. The passage begins with Jesus in Bethsaida, where unnamed patrons petition Jesus "to touch" a blind man. But rather than restoring the man's sight in town, Jesus's first touch brings the man's removal, by the hand, to a place "outside the village" (8:23). What is more, the story ends with a rather odd prohibition: Jesus tells him explicitly, "Don't even go into the village" (8:26). Why the dislocation? What does geography have to do with epistemology?

Mark's **apocalyptic** worldview is in play here, but with a twist. On the one hand, Mark's Jesus often distinguishes sharply between insiders and outsiders. Only those "around him," for instance, have been given "the secret of the kingdom of God," while "those on the outside" have been prevented from "perceiving" it (4:10–12). Yet such hard-and-fast lines grow blurry elsewhere in the Gospel, and especially in this chapter, where Jesus accuses his own disciples of not seeing, even though they have been in his very presence (8:17–18). As with our Qumran text, the "outsider" status of the blind man—and the Markan audience—seems to play a role in their ability to see clearly; disoriented social location may lead, paradoxically, to true "insider" vision.

"His Hands." On the question of restored sight, Jesus plays just as indispensable a role as does the Teacher of Righteousness, but his tactile approach stands out in sharp relief from the Teacher's "exact interpretation." Mark mentions physical touch three times in this brief passage: Jesus leads the man "by the hand" (8:23) before twice putting "his hands on" him (8:23, 25). Throughout the Gospel, Jesus conducts kingdom power through human contact—most recently by distributing loaves, through the disciples, to the hungering crowd (8:6).

126

This corporeal contagion of wholeness suggests that, for Mark, the perception of God's reign on the earth involves not just the mind or spirit but the body as well. Epistemology goes beyond correct cognition to involve active, physical participation in manifesting God's power to institute human well-being. After all, when Jesus recalls for his disciples the abundant leftovers after each feeding, he twice asks probingly, "How many basketfuls of pieces did *you pick up*?" (8:19, 20). Their failure to "see or understand" (8:17) stems, it seems, from their failure to consider their own tactile part in Jesus's display of kingdom power.

"Like Trees Walking Around." After the first touch, the man regains sight, but only partially. Like the Damascus community that "gropes for a path" even after discerning their iniquity, the man's interim condition allows him to see people rather than darkness, albeit people who "look like trees walking around" (8:24). Scholars typically take this seeing-but-not-seeing interlude as emblematic of the disciples themselves, and by extension, of Mark's community. Not only has the Gospel already featured their murky understanding (6:52; 8:17–18), but the passage that follows will combine Peter's affirmation of Jesus as the "Messiah" (8:29) with his pointed rejection of Jesus's suffering destiny, which Jesus in turn ascribes to Satan's influence (8:32–33).

The interim reality for Mark's own community must have confirmed this experience of partial sight. After all, they had cast their allegiance with an executed criminal, and we infer from this Gospel that they were persecuted as a result. Desperate as they must have been for the full disclosure of God's reign on earth, they surely stumbled on the path of faithfulness, partly making their way in the dark. That this story casts the man's blurry vision as a middle step along the way to clear sight must have injected a word of grace and hope into otherwise austere circumstances.

"Looked out . . . Expansively." Clarity arrives, for the blind man, after Jesus touches him for a second time. At first glance Mark's account of what happens seems repetitive: "And he looked through and he was restored and he looked out expansively on everything" (8:25; author's transl.). What does Mark convey through these two different compounds of the Greek verb "to look" or "see"? And what kind of expansive vision does the therapy secure?

As Joel Marcus has shown, ancient writers often linked clear—and perceptive—vision with an "extramission theory of vision."[2] In this view,

---

2. Joel Marcus, "A Note on Markan Optics," *NTS* 45 (1999): 250–56, at 251.

vision occurs from the inside out, and perspicuity depends on the absence of internal impediments to clarity (see also Matt 7:5; Luke 6:42). This observation adds an important dimension to the story that is lacking in the NIV, which simply says, "his eyes were opened." Rather than a passive recipient of clear sight, the man appears as an active participant in his own epistemic progression.

If Jesus's physical touch is the delivery method for curative power, then that power is activated only when the man "looked through" to the vast world outside of himself. In apparent contrast with the concerns of the Damascus Document, Mark's interest in clear vision extends beyond maintaining sectarian distinction. For this man, restored sight brings "everything" into view—that is, creation as the expansive horizon where God's restorative power is operative.

Of course, in Mark's story that horizon will feature the cross front and center—not just for Jesus but also for those who follow on his way (Mark 8:34–38). While in the Damascus Document, the Teacher's death (20:1, 14) initiates a time of final judgment based on the standard of "perfect holiness" (e.g., 20:2), Jesus's death in Mark establishes the sacrificial pattern of God's power as the criterion for true discipleship and the means of salvation. Clear vision thus carries a cost. "Seeing through" means casting loyalty with God's power rather than Rome's or Jerusalem's. And here lies the Gospel's most distinctive claim: "Whoever wants to save their life will lose it, but whoever loses their life for me and for the gospel will save it" (8:35).

For Further Reading

Additional Ancient Texts

Within Mark, this healing story works with the healing of blind Bartimaeus (10:46–52) to serve as a pair of narrative bookends for the Gospel's central section. Though none of the other NT Gospels include the two-staged healing, each reports instances in which Jesus restores human sight (e.g., Matt 9:27–31; Luke 18:35–43; John 9:1–12); consistently, they detect in these encounters evidence of Jesus's **messianic** power (e.g., Matt 11:5; Luke 7:22). The Markan story has certain parallels with Tobit 11:7–15, where sight returns after a similar sequence of therapeutic tactics—in this case, breathing rather than spitting and rubbing a salve rather than merely touching. Finally, **Philo** shows a keen interest in clear vision, which comes from the inside out, for both God and humans (e.g., *Migr.* 39; *Post.* 57).

English Translations and Critical Editions

Eisenman, Robert. "The Damascus Document." Pages 355–78 in *The Dead Sea Scrolls and the First Christians: Essays and Translations*. Edison, NJ: Castle Books, 2004.

Garcia Martínez, Florentino, and Eibert J. C. Tigchelaar, eds. *The Dead Sea Scrolls: Study Edition*. Volume one. Grand Rapids: Eerdmans, 1997.

Secondary Literature

Glenney, Brian, and John T. Noble. "Perception and Prosopagnosia in Mark 8.22–26." *JSNT* 37 (2014): 71–85.

Keller, Marie Noël. "Opening Blind Eyes: A Revisioning of Mark 8:22–10:52." *BTB* 31 (2001): 151–57.

Larsen, Kevin W. "A Focused Christological Reading of Mark 8:22–9:13." *Trinity Journal* 26 (2005): 33–46.

Marcus, Joel. "A Note on Markan Optics." *NTS* 45 (1999): 250–56.

Matera, Frank J. "The Incomprehension of the Disciples and Peter's Confession (Mark 6:14–8:30)." *Biblica* 70 (1989): 153–72.

Wise, Michael O. "The Origins and History of the Teacher's Movement." Pages 92–122 in *The Oxford Handbook of the Dead Sea Scrolls*. Edited by Timothy H. Lim and John J. Collins. Oxford: Oxford University Press, 2010.

CHAPTER 13

Sirach and Mark 8:27–9:13: Elijah and the Eschaton

SIGURD GRINDHEIM

Mark's story now takes an important turn. Up until Peter's confession, Jesus's actions have had the human characters dumbfounded, wondering about who he might be (Mark 1:27; 2:7; 4:41; 7:37). People's suggestions regarding his identity include John the Baptist, Elijah, and one of the prophets (8:28; cf. 6:14–15). Now it is time for Jesus to have a conversation with the disciples and teach them about his identity. Challenged to take a stand, Peter comes forward and affirms that Jesus is the **Messiah** (8:29). Anyone who has previously studied Matthew's Gospel may jump to the conclusion that Peter's confession is a great one (cf. Matt 16:17), but we should not miss the fact that Mark's account is much more subdued. Peter receives no praise at all, and the disciples are warned not to tell anyone (8:30). The reader of Mark's Gospel knows that Peter's confession is correct (1:1), but the meaning of the title Messiah needs to be understood adequately.

The first qualification of the title is provided by Jesus himself. He explains that he must suffer, be rejected, and be killed before he will rise again (8:31). Mark's Messiah is a suffering Messiah. His true identity is fully revealed on the cross, when the Roman centurion proclaims that he surely was the Son of God (15:39). As a consequence of this understanding of the Messiah, discipleship must be understood as consisting of suffering as well (8:34–38).

The next qualification comes in the form of an account of Jesus's transfiguration (9:2–8). This passage and the preceding narrative must be read in close connection, as they are linked together with the phrase "after six days" (9:2). Accompanied by Peter, James, and John, Jesus went up to a high mountain where his clothes became shining white, and Elijah and Moses emerged and talked to him. Out of a cloud came a voice, echoing the voice from Jesus's baptism: "This is my Son, whom I love. Listen to him!" (9:7). The Messiah is also God's beloved Son and spokesman.

The presence of Elijah (and Moses) on the mountain with Jesus calls for an explanation. It will help to know something about the views that many Jews held about Elijah and his role in the **eschaton**.

Sirach

"YOU ARE APPOINTED TO ABATE THE WRATH . . . AND RESTORE THE TRIBES OF JACOB"

The most extensive evidence regarding Elijah is found in the book of Sirach, also known as Ecclesiasticus (from a Latin word that probably means "the church book"). A collection of wisdom sayings, this work has much in common with the book of Proverbs. The author was Jesus son of Eleazar, son of Sirach (Sir 50:27), who wrote in Hebrew between 196 and 175 BC. His grandson translated the work into Greek sometime after 132 BC (prologue). Many scholars believe that Sirach represents a theological outlook that is close to that of the Sadducees. Although widely read by ancient Jews, the book was never canonized in Judaism but is included in the so-called **deuterocanonical** books in the Catholic and Eastern Orthodox traditions. As "Sirach" is the Greek form of the Hebrew "Sira," the book is also frequently referred to as "Ben Sira" ("ben" is a Hebrew word meaning "son").

Sirach 44:1–50:24 contains praises of the great men of Israel's past (the author does not find room for any women). One of these men is Elijah, who received extensive treatment (48:1–11):

> [1] Then Elijah arose. He was a prophet like fire, and his word burned like a torch. [2] He brought a famine upon them, and he reduced them to a small number by his zeal. [3] By the word of the Lord, he kept heaven at bay. In the same way, he brought down fire three times. [4] How glorified you were, Elijah, in your astonishing works, and who may boast of being like you? [5] You raised a dead man from the grave and from the realm of the dead by the word of the Most High. [6] You brought kings down to destruction and men of renown from their sickbed. [7] You heard a rebuke at Sinai and judgments that brought vengeance at Horeb. [8] You anointed kings to bring

131

retribution and prophets to succeed you. [9] You were taken up in a flaming whirlwind with a chariot drawn by horses on fire. [10] It is written that you are appointed to abate the wrath before it comes in fury, to turn a father's heart to his son and restore the tribes of Jacob. [11] Blessed are those who see you and those who pass away in love, for also we will certainly live.[1]

Elijah's Marvelous Deeds. The above portrait of Elijah is drawn from the many accounts of his marvelous deeds in 1 and 2 Kings. "He was a prophet like fire" because he called fire to come down from heaven and consume the men that were sent to him from King Ahaziah (2 Kgs 1:10, 12). He caused a famine (1 Kgs 18:2) when he told King Ahab that there would be no rain for the next few years (1 Kgs 17:1). During his famous dispute with the prophets of Baal, he brought fire down from heaven to consume the sacrifice that had been prepared on the altar (1 Kgs 18:38). When he was staying in Zarephath and a widow provided his food, the widow's son died, but Elijah's prayers made his life return to him (1 Kgs 17:22). He "brought kings down to destruction" when he announced the death of Ahab: "In the place where dogs licked up Naboth's blood, dogs will lick up your blood—yes, yours!" (1 Kgs 21:19). King Ahaziah had been injured and was bedridden when Elijah told him that he would never leave his bed (2 Kgs 1:4; cf. 1:16). At Horeb, Elijah received the word of God and was sent to anoint kings of Aram and Israel as well as a prophet to succeed himself (1 Kgs 19:9–18). In the end, he did not die but was taken up to heaven in "a chariot of fire and horses of fire" (2 Kgs 2:11).

Elijah's Role in Israel's Restoration. As announced by the prophet Malachi, Elijah would return before the day of the Lord and "he will turn the hearts of the parents to their children, and the hearts of the children to their parents" (Mal 4:6a). In so doing, he will avert the wrath of God, who warns: "Or else I will come and strike the land with total destruction" (Mal 4:6b). At the same time, he will "restore the tribes of Jacob." The idea echoes Isaiah 49:6, where this task is given to the servant of the Lord and concerns both the return of the exiles and the ethical and religious restoration of the people. The last verse in the text above (Sir 48:11) is uncertain. From the surviving Hebrew manuscripts, we cannot be sure who the subject of the verb "live" is. The translation above follows the Greek translation of Sirach. However, there is a great deal of uncertainty about whether Sirach would have believed in the afterlife.

---

1. My translation.

Mark 8:27–9:13

"Elijah Does Come First, and Restores All Things"

Elijah as an End-Time Character. Sirach's account of Elijah shows that he was expected to appear in the end times, an expectation that was rooted in the prophecies of Malachi. It appears that Mark shares this understanding of Elijah. Mark also quotes from the prophet Malachi when he introduces John the Baptist (Mark 1:2; cf. Mal 3:1). The implication is that John the Baptist is Malachi's eschatological messenger, later identified as Elijah (Mal 4:5). In other words, Mark was familiar with the traditions regarding Elijah as a character that belonged to the end times. The disciples knew about these traditions too (Mark 9:12). When Elijah shows up at Jesus's transfiguration, therefore, his presence may be an indication that this event had eschatological significance. Moses was also associated with the end times, as God had promised to raise up a prophet like him (Deut 18:18). In Malachi 4:4–6, Moses and Elijah are both mentioned. The presence of Elijah and Moses in Mark's account therefore alerts us to the fact that God's eschatological intervention is about to take place. In a surprising twist, God announces that he is delegating the eschatological revelation to his beloved Son (Mark 9:7).

A Demoted Elijah. The most striking contrast between Mark and Sirach is that Mark does not show Elijah any particular respect at all. He is mentioned, and he appears together with Moses when Jesus is transfigured, but neither he nor Moses receives any particular attention or praise. They are just there. Instead, all the focus turns to Jesus. Mark's account of the transfiguration concludes on the significant note that "they no longer saw anyone with them except Jesus" (9:8).

In light of the high view of Elijah that is attested in Sirach, the silence in Mark is deafening. Both he and Moses are reduced to silent extras in the scene of Jesus's transfiguration. According to Sirach, no one compares to Elijah (Sir 48:4), and Moses was also viewed as an extremely exalted character in Jewish tradition. God told Moses, "I have made you like God to Pharaoh" (Exod 7:1), and **Philo** has an extensive discussion about what it means that Moses could be called "God" (*Mut.* 128; cf. 4Q374 2.2.6). (The glory of Moses is also a theme in Sir 44:23–45:5.) No one knew where Moses was buried (Deut 34:6), and a Jewish tradition holds that he was lifted up to heaven, like Elijah (Assumption of Moses). But in Mark, neither Elijah nor Moses is anything compared to Jesus. The implication is, at the very least, that Jesus is the ultimate spokesperson for God, God's final messenger who brings God's revelation to its climax.

But we may be justified in seeing an even deeper significance in Mark's portrait of Jesus. If Jesus is so much greater than the greatest human beings, then who might he be? Mark's account provides a hint: "His clothes became dazzling white, whiter than anyone in the world could bleach them" (9:3). Scholars have offered many comparisons to the splendor of Jesus's appearance, but they often ignore the most significant. In the Old Testament there is only one character that stands out because of his extraordinary white attire. The prophet Daniel had a vision of the Ancient of Days (i.e., God), whose "clothing was as white as snow; the hair of his head was white like wool" (Dan 7:9). (In the New Testament, angels are also seen in white clothes, but not in the Old Testament.) When Mark adds that Jesus's clothes were "whiter than anyone in the world could bleach them," it may be another indication of Jesus's nonearthly (in other words, heavenly) nature.

Elijah and the Messiah. What Mark does not say about Elijah is quite significant, but what Sirach does not say about Elijah is worth noticing too. A common interpretation holds that Elijah was known as the forerunner of the Messiah. In the Gospel of Matthew, John the Baptist is identified as Elijah (Matt 11:14; cf. Luke 7:27; Mark 1:2), and John the Baptist was the forerunner of Jesus, so the conclusion that Elijah was the forerunner of the Messiah seems natural.

However, when we turn back to Sirach, we find no reference to the Messiah. There appears to be an end-time role for Elijah; he is "appointed to abate the wrath before it comes in fury, to turn a father's heart to his son and restore the tribes of Jacob" (Sir 48:10). The wrath that comes in fury must be the wrath of God, the wrath of his final, eschatological judgment. Before this final judgment, Elijah will have his role. He will abate the wrath of God as he causes people to repent. He will help bring reconciliation among family members who are in conflict with each other. In this way he will bring restoration to the people of Israel, a restoration that takes place when they turn back to God. John the Baptist "restore[d] all things" (Mark 9:12) when he brought people to repentance by announcing the coming wrath (Luke 3:1–20), so we can understand why he was identified as Elijah. However, it does not follow from the Old Testament alone that Elijah was the forerunner of the Messiah.

The expectations regarding Elijah stem from the prophet Malachi. Through him God announces: "I will send my messenger, who will prepare the way before me. Then suddenly the Lord you are seeking will come to his temple; the messenger of the **covenant**, whom you desire, will come"

(Mal 3:1). Later the prophet conveys a related message from God: "See, I will send the prophet Elijah to you before that great and dreadful day of the LORD comes. He will turn the hearts of the parents to their children, and the hearts of the children to their parents; or else I will come and strike the land with total destruction" (Mal 4:5–6). "My messenger" and "Elijah" appear to be the same character, the one who will come before "the great and dreadful day of the LORD." In the context of the prophet Malachi, this day is not the day of the Messiah (Malachi has no obvious references to the Messiah) but to the eschatological judgment of God.

In Jewish sources that are earlier than the New Testament, we find no connection between Elijah and the Messiah. But it would appear that Mark himself hints of such an association when the disciples ask Jesus, "Why do the teachers of the law say that Elijah must come first?" (Mark 9:11). However, it was not the identification of Jesus as the Messiah that got the disciples talking about Elijah; it was his reference to the resurrection. Those Jews who believed in the resurrection thought that all the dead would be raised in God's judgment (cf. Dan 12:2), but we do not have any indication that Jews at Jesus's time believed in the individual resurrection of the Messiah. In Judaism the coming of Elijah therefore did not have anything in particular to do with the Messiah, but it had everything to do with what God was going to do at the end of time.

The presence of Elijah at the mountain provides important clues to the identity of Jesus and the nature of his ministry. It shows that Jesus came to fulfill the prophecies regarding God's own eschatological intervention on earth when he would come to bring judgment and salvation.

FOR FURTHER READING

Additional Ancient Texts

Elijah's eschatological role is mentioned very briefly in the following ancient Jewish texts: 4Q558 1.2.4; CD-A 6:11 (not mentioned by name, but "the one who teaches justice" may be Elijah); 1 Enoch 90:31 (not mentioned by name, but the ram may be Elijah); m. Soṭah 9:15; Soperim 19:9; b. 'Erubin 431-b; Pesiqta Rabbati 35:4; Targum Pseudo-Jonathan Exodus 40:10; Targum Pseudo-Jonathan Deuteronomy 30:4; Targum Lamentations 4:22.

English Translations and Critical Editions

NETS
NRSV

Beentjes, Pancratius C. *The Book of Ben Sira in Hebrew: A Text Edition of All Extant Hebrew Manuscripts and a Synopsis of All Parallel Hebrew Ben Sira Texts*. VTSup 68. Leiden: Brill, 1997.

Ziegler, Joseph, ed. *Sapientia Iesu filii Sirach*. 3rd ed. Septuaginta 12.2. Göttingen: Vandenhoeck & Ruprecht, 2016.

Secondary Literature

Allison, Dale C., Jr. "Elijah Must Come First." *JBL* 103 (1984): 256–58.

Bryan, Steven M. *Jesus and Israel's Traditions of Judgement and Restoration*. SNTSMS 117. Cambridge: Cambridge University Press, 1992.

Faierstein, M. M. "Why Do the Scribes Say That Elijah Must Come First?" *JBL* 100 (1981): 75–86.

Fitzmyer, Joseph A. "More about Elijah Coming First." *JBL* 104 (1985): 295–96.

Grindheim, Sigurd. *Christology in the Synoptic Gospels: God or God's Servant?* London: T&T Clark, 2012.

———. *God's Equal: What Can We Know about Jesus's Self-Understanding?* LNTS 446. London: T&T Clark, 2011.

Miller, David M. "The Messenger, the Lord, and the Coming Judgement in the Reception History of Malachi 3." *NTS* 53 (2007): 1–16.

Skehan, Patrick W., and Alexander A. Di Lella. *The Wisdom of Ben Sira: A New Translation with Notes and Commentary*. AB 39. New York: Doubleday, 1987.

CHAPTER 14

Tobit and Mark 9:14–29:
Imperfect Faith

―⚬⚬⚬―

JEANETTE HAGEN PIFER

The writer of Mark underscores faith as a central and abiding theme of the Gospel. This is evident from the very outset of the narrative with Christ's proclamation of the kingdom: "'The time has come,' he said. 'The kingdom of God has come near. Repent and *believe* the good news!'" (1:15). This proclamation of the kingdom sets the stage for Christ's demonstration of God's kingdom-rule, shown through healings, exorcisms, and eventually through Jesus's death and resurrection. In each miracle Mark makes clear that it is only after faith is evident that Jesus responds in a marvelous display of power (2:5; 5:34). On the other hand, Christ expresses astonishment at the lack of faith exhibited by many (4:40; 6:6). The overall picture we glean is that faith, though absent in much of Israel, is the essential posture for discipleship to Christ.

One account of healing within Mark's Gospel deserves particular attention, based on its placement within the narrative and the unique commentary faith receives. In chapter nine, Mark relays the story of a father petitioning Jesus to heal his son who is possessed by a mute spirit (9:14–29). In this essay we will examine the passage to find out what new-covenant faith looks like and what makes it unique.

In preparation for our discussion of faith in Mark, we will look at another remarkable story of faith from the Second Temple period—the story of Tobit. The book of Tobit is an apocryphal narrative that was written between 250 and 175 BC.[1] It tells the story of the piety and suffering of the Naphtalite

---

1. The text was probably first written in Aramaic, but modern translations rely upon the Greek text of Codex Sinaiticus.

Tobit, who was taken captive with his family after the Assyrian conquest of the northern kingdom of Israel in 722 BC. Tobit's story pairs well with Mark 9:14–29, with its demonstrations of prayer and faith in the face of adversity, as well as its unique encounter with the demonic.

Tobit

"I Know and Believe That Everything That God Has Said Will Be Fulfilled and Will Be"

The book of Tobit traces the lives of three main characters: Tobit, his son Tobias, and a relative, Sarah. It opens with Tobit testifying of his own faithfulness to walk in the ways of truth and righteousness (1:3). A life of faithfulness, however, did not spare him from suffering. One evening, after realizing that an Israelite had been murdered and left on the streets, Tobit took it upon himself to see him properly buried. That same night, a sparrow dropped excrement in Tobit's eyes, damaging his vision (2:10). As a result of this impairment, he became financially dependent on his wife, who thus questioned the worth of his piety. Despairing of his situation, Tobit resorted to praying that he would die (3:6).

A parallel story is found in the life of Tobit's relative, Sarah. The young woman had suffered at the hand of a demon named Asmodeus, who was in love with her and had jealously killed each of her seven successive grooms on the nights of their weddings. Sarah, too, despaired of living and prayed for death (3:10, 13–15).

In answer to their desperate prayers, God sent the angel Raphael (3:16–17), who disguised himself as a relative in order to accompany Tobias on a journey. One night, while the two rested by the Tigris River, a large fish leapt from the water, attempting to swallow Tobias's foot—a strange event that proved to be providential. The angel instructed Tobias to catch the fish, cut it open, and remove its gall, heart, and liver—these would become the instruments of deliverance for Sarah and healing for Tobit.

As the journey continued, Raphael led Tobias to the home of Sarah's father, Raguel, to present the beautiful young woman as the rightful bride for the young man. Raphael assured Tobias that he would survive their wedding night if they prayed for God's mercy and safety (6:18) and then burned the fish's liver and heart. Tobias obeyed Raphael's instructions, kneeling in prayer with Sarah, and the odor of the fish repelled the demon (8:3).

Eventually the travelers returned to Tobit, having saved the gall of the fish in order to heal his blindness. After applying this "medicine," Tobit's eyes were opened and he praised God.

Faith Expressed through Prayer and Obedience. There is much to be learned about faith from this story. Tobit, Sarah, and Tobias each express their trust in God through petitionary prayer, and in each case God compassionately responds. Instead of directly answering their despairing prayers for death, however, God miraculously heals Tobit of his blindness and delivers Sarah from demonic oppression. Tobias also expresses faith through prayer for deliverance on his wedding night and in his obedience to Raphael's instructions.

Faith in God's Plan and Power. Faith for something greater than individual needs is also found in this story. It has been widely noted that the fate of Tobit and his family is representative of the fate of the nation of Israel: Tobit's suffering is symbolic of covenant curses and exile, and his healing is symbolic of the nation's blessing and restoration.[2] Thus in the final scene of the story, Tobit, after having witnessed God's restorative power firsthand, declares his faith in God's word: "I know and *believe* that everything that God has said will be fulfilled and will be, and not one word of the prophets' utterances will fail" (14:4).[3] Tobit believed God's promises about the children of Israel being returned to dwell forever in the land of Israel and their oppressors being punished. The temple would be rebuilt, all the nations of the world would be converted, and ultimately all would worship God in truth (14:5–7). In this climactic speech we learn that in Tobit faith in God's power and plan is faith in both individual and national healing.

We see through this story that faith involves a personal dimension of trust in the power and compassion of God. Faith is expressed by prayer and obedience. In prayer, the petitioner shows dependence on the mercy and power of God. We also see that there is a greater dimension than simply the fulfillment of personal needs and desires; faith is confidence in God's plan for the restoration of his people, which results in the ultimate display of and human response to his glory. We will see similar emphases in Mark's account of faith.

---

2. Richard Bauckham, "Tobit as a Parable for the Exiles of Northern Israel," in *Studies in the Book of Tobit: A Multidisciplinary Approach,* ed. M. Bredin, LSTS 55 (London: T&T Clark, 2006), 140–64.

3. Translations of Tobit are the author's own.

Mark 9:14–29

"I DO BELIEVE; HELP ME OVERCOME MY UNBELIEF!"

After the rapid succession of miracles in the first eight chapters of Mark, a climactic moment occurs in 8:29 when Peter declares that Jesus is the Christ. This identification of the one who fulfills God's plan for redemption is critical for understanding the new-covenant concept of faith. From this point, Jesus begins to prepare his disciples for his crucifixion, teaching them that he must "suffer many things" (8:31). Furthermore, he instructs them that true disciples must also "deny themselves and take up their cross and follow" him (8:34).

The story of Jesus's healing the boy with a mute spirit (9:14–29) expands upon the themes of suffering, death, resurrection, and discipleship first announced in chapter eight. The episode begins with Jesus descending from his transfiguration where he finds a crowd arguing with his disciples. The conflict had arisen because the disciples were unable to exorcise the demon. Jesus's response to the situation, "you *unbelieving* generation . . . how long shall I stay with you?" (9:19), sets the stage for a lesson about faith.

Faith in the One Who Is Able. The faith of the father is first explicitly exhibited when he entreats Jesus: "But if you can do anything, take pity on us and help us" (9:22). The theme of "being able" is repeated five times in this passage alone, and throughout the Gospel Mark emphasizes Jesus's power over the natural and spiritual realms. The first recorded miracle of Jesus's public ministry that Mark describes is of an exorcism in Capernaum on the Sabbath (1:21–28). This and the following series of miraculous healings and exorcisms display his unique power as the Son of God (1:24; 5:7).[4] Christ alone is the one with the power and the authority to make demons flee and illness vanish.

The father's cry for help (9:22) prompts Jesus's call to faith: "Everything is possible for one who believes" (9:23). Some have questioned whether the faith that makes all things possible is that of Jesus or the petitioner, but the text is clear that faith is necessary on the part of the one in need. This faith grabs ahold of the power of the one who has authority over all. Tobit's dying declaration that "everything that God has said will be fulfilled" reflects this same confidence in God's omnipotence (Tob 14:4).

---

4. Throughout Mark's Gospel, Jesus's encounters with the demonic serve to manifest his kingdom power and reign (cf. Zech 13:2).

Imperfect Faith. The father's response, "I do believe; help me overcome my unbelief!" (9:24), gives deep insight into the nature of faith. It exposes the reality that human faith is imperfect, and thus it highlights the necessary posture of reliance and humility. The father's faith is demonstrated by his persistence to see his son healed and his trust that Christ is the true source of that healing. Being unable, however, to convey perfect faith, the father presents himself as dependent on the only one with the power to deliver his son.

In acknowledging both the presence and absence of faith, Joel Marcus notes, echoing Luther, that the father is *simul justus et peccator,* "at once righteous and a sinner." Marcus writes: "The father of the epileptic boy is therefore, in this double-mindedness, a perfect symbol for the Christian disciple. Whereas logically faith and unbelief are opposites, in Christian experience they are simultaneous realities; the one who believes is always concurrently involved in a battle against disbelief."[5] True faith in Jesus honestly acknowledges its own deficiencies in a continual disposition of humility and dependence. In a similar way, we saw an imperfect faith demonstrated by Tobit and Sarah, who in their despair turned to God, even if their request fell short of God's plan to deliver them.

Christological Faith. While humility and dependence are often portrayed as weakness, in Mark's Gospel this kind of faith yields a victory that is integrally linked to Jesus's death and resurrection. This connection is prepared for in the way Mark precedes this episode with Christ's revelation of his passion and resurrection (8:31) and is reinforced by Christ's second announcement of his dying and rising in the verses that follow (9:30–31). In this way, Jesus's death and resurrection appropriately form an *inclusio* for this lesson on faith.

This christological *inclusio* extends beyond simple literary artistry—it is also evident in the way Mark depicts the result of the exorcism: "The boy looked so much like a corpse that many said, 'He's dead'" (9:26). This is immediately followed by a scene that resembles a resurrection: "But Jesus took him by the hand and lifted him to his feet, and he stood up" (9:27). This scene conveys a symbolic connection between faith and Christ's death and resurrection. The very juxtaposition of weakness and power seen in the cross and resurrection describes even the faith of the believer; faith in Christ is an identification with Christ both in his death and new life. In this way, faith is a unique expression of one's own powerlessness and a dependence

---

5. Joel Marcus, *Mark 8–16: A New Translation with Introduction and Commentary,* AYBC 27A (New Haven: Yale University Press, 2009), 663.

on divine power through Jesus Christ. This conception of faith marks the most significant development from Tobit's presentation of faith. While Tobit is confident that God will ultimately restore his people and display his glory, Mark reveals the agent of eschatological restoration to be Jesus Christ.

Faith and Prayer. After the boy is dramatically healed, Jesus withdraws with the disciples, who ask him in private why they were unable to cast out this demon. Jesus's response expands upon the demonstration of the imperfect but dependent faith of the father. Jesus answers: "This kind can come out only by prayer" (9:29). We have no indication that Jesus himself prayed for the boy to be healed, though this is explained by the fact that he is the object and not the subject of prayer. However, the boy's father does pray (9:24), and his "believing-yet-disbelieving posture" is meant to model the way Christians stand before God in prayer.[6] Prayer is the expression of faith. Similarly, Tobit, Sarah, and Tobias each expressed their faith through prayer, actively petitioning God to respond to their needs.

Summary. In our examination of Tobit and Mark, we have seen a consistent presentation of faith as dependence upon the goodness and power of God. Both texts underscore the personal and universal dimensions of faith—the one who trusts can experience this power of God personally, but ultimately faith is about trusting in God's plan to deliver his people from oppression. Tobit trusted that the Israelites would be delivered from the oppressive Assyrians. Mark's text highlights God's ultimate plan to deliver from sin, demons, and death all those who trust in him through Jesus, the Christ. Mark uniquely stresses that Jesus responds to an imperfect, but humble and dependent faith that is expressed through prayer.

Ultimately, Jesus's death and resurrection form the foundation for Christian faith. Even in this pre-crucifixion event, Mark symbolically portrays Christ's death and resurrection as the object and expression of faith. Faith identifies with Christ both in his death and resurrection because this is the new reality for the believer—overcoming spiritual death and receiving new life in Christ.

FOR FURTHER READING

Additional Ancient Texts

For further study on the Jewish understanding of faith, many texts deal with the faith of Abraham specifically. See Philo, *On the Life of Abraham*; 1

---

6. Marcus, *Mark 8–16*, 665.

Maccabees 2:52; Sirach 44:19–20. Other passages on faith in Mark include 1:15; 2:5; 4:40; 5:21–43; 10:46–52; 11:20–24; 11:27–33; 16:9–18.

English Translations and Critical Editions

NETS

NRSV

Hanhart, Robert. *Tobit*. Septuaginta 8.5. Göttingen: Vandenhoeck & Ruprecht, 1983.

Weeks, Stuart, Simon Gathercole, and Loren Stuckenbruck, eds. *The Book of Tobit: Texts from the Principal Ancient and Medieval Traditions with Synopsis, Concordances, and Annotated Texts in Aramaic, Hebrew, Greek, Latin, and Syriac*. FSBP 3. Berlin: de Gruyter, 2004.

Secondary Literature

Di Lella, Alexander A. "Two Major Prayers in the Book of Tobit." Pages 95–116 in *Deuterocanonical and Cognate Literature: Yearbook 2004*. Edited by Friedrich V. Reiterer. Berlin: de Gruyter, 2004.

Fitzmyer, Joseph A. *Tobit*. CEJL. Berlin: de Gruyter, 2003.

Marshall, Christopher D. *Faith as a Theme in Mark's Narrative*. SNTSMS 64. Cambridge: Cambridge University Press, 1989.

McDowell, Markus. *Prayers of Jewish Women*. WUNT 2/211. Tübingen: Mohr Siebeck, 1989.

Moore, Carey A. *Tobit: A New Translation with Introduction and Commentary*. AB 40A. New York: Doubleday, 1996.

Morgan, Teresa. *Roman Faith and Christian Faith: Pistis and Fides in the Early Roman Empire and Early Churches*. New York: Oxford University Press, 2015.

Schweizer, Eduard. "Portrayal of the Life of Faith in the Gospel of Mark." *Interpretation* 32.4 (1978): 387–99.

CHAPTER 15

Rule of the Community and Mark 9:30–50: Discipleship Reordered

JEFFREY W. AERNIE

One of the unique elements of Mark's Gospel is its depiction of the relationship between Jesus and his disciples. At three points in the Gospel Jesus predicts his death and resurrection (Mark 8:31; 9:31; 10:32–34), and his disciples respond in distinctly negative ways—with insolence (8:32–33), fearful silence (9:32), and misplaced arrogance (10:35–41). Each episode of misunderstanding by the disciples, however, is followed by a dramatic description of the nature of Jesus's ministry (8:34–38; 9:35–37; 10:42–45). Jesus's distinct statements at these points about the nature of his ministry create a pattern for a reordered form of discipleship.

Mark 9:30–50 contains the second of Jesus's predictions of his death and resurrection. Perhaps in light of Jesus's earlier rebuke of Peter's negative response to Jesus's first prediction (8:32–33), the disciples respond at this stage only with fearful silence (9:32). As the narrative progresses, their fearful silence quickly becomes shamed silence as they fail to respond to Jesus's inquiry about the content of their conversation on their way from Galilee to Capernaum. Knowing that the disciples had been debating about which of them was the greatest, "Jesus called the Twelve and said, 'Anyone who wants to be first must be the very last, and the servant of all'" (9:35). This concise declaration encompasses a central element of Jesus's reordered vision of discipleship. His followers are defined not by cultural markers of greatness but rather by a willingness to embody self-sacrificial humility. Mark 9:36–41 provides further illustrations of this reordering as Jesus welcomes both one who is culturally insignificant (a child) and one who remains outside his inner circle of followers (an unnamed exorcist). The final section of the passage (9:42–50) offers a series of interrelated warnings that highlight the demands that this self-sacrificial humility entails, namely, to reject sin and seek peace.

The unique nature of Mark's description of discipleship in this passage can be illuminated by comparing it with the shape of other Jewish communities within the **Second Temple period**. There are many different segments of cultural and religious society within Second Temple Judaism (e.g., **Essenes**, **Pharisees**, **Sadducees**). One significant group is that associated with certain textual manuscripts discovered in caves near **Qumran** along the Dead Sea. This community's focus on its structure offers interesting points of similarity and dissimilarity with Jesus's assertion about the nature of discipleship in Mark 9:30–50. One of the key texts for understanding the nature and structure of this segment of Second Temple Judaism is the Rule of the Community (1QS).

Rule of the Community

"No One Will Be Demoted from His Position; No One Will Be Promoted above His Place."

The Rule of the Community is a document that offers insight into several of the structural and practical elements of the community (or communities) that lived near the site at Qumran where the **Dead Sea Scrolls** were discovered. Due to its attestation in several distinct manuscript fragments (1QS; 4Q255–64; 5Q11; 5Q13), the Rule of the Community appears to have been developed in different stages over the course of the community's existence. The longest remaining copy of the text is attested in the manuscript 1QS, which dates to around 100–75 BC and likely represents the final stage in the development of the textual tradition. Although 1QS is a composite document that may postdate the community's inception, a significant portion of the manuscript describes the formal regulations that may have originally been used to establish and sustain involvement in the community. Several segments of the text provide specific insight into the formal order of the community and a description of how members were incorporated into the community's life and practice. These descriptions of the community's order and structure provide a textual foil for the portrait developed in Mark 9:30–50.

Ordered Inclusion. Entry into the **sectarian** community at Qumran was determined through an ordered set of commitments and regulations that shaped the identity and position of hopeful initiates (1QS 1:16–2:19). The regulations that governed one's inclusion into the community were stringent. The process of initiation required a minimum of two years of probation in which both the leaders of the community and the community itself examined the candidates to determine their suitability for inclusion in the group (6:13–23). If an initiate was accepted after completion of this probationary period, then that person would be inserted into the community at an appropriate place within the group's established hierarchy: "They will enroll him at the appropriate rank amongst his brothers with respect to the Law, justice, purity, and for sharing his wealth" (6:22).[1] This emphasis on the structured inclusion of the initiate was intended to assist in creating a community capable of seeking God with all its heart and soul (1:1–2) and fulfilling everything that God commanded (1:17). The wider content of 1QS suggests that these aims were achieved through engagement with specific beliefs and disciplines meant to foster a distinct corporate identity.[2] The rigorous initiation requirements allowed the community to determine the sincerity and potential contributions of its members.

Another description of the process for initiation in the community highlights the focus on the status of new initiates: "They are to be enrolled in order, one before another, according to their understanding and deeds, so that they may all obey one another, the lower obeying the greater" (5:23). The life of the community was conditioned by a specific focus on the rank of each member. Each person was required to participate within the community only with respect to their position in the established hierarchy. The status of the members conditioned their engagement in communal meetings, their participation in communal meals, and their access to communal property. Those unwilling to participate faithfully in this aspect of the community were viewed as standing outside the people of God (2:25–3:12). Inclusion within the community was dependent on the specific guidelines, beliefs, and practices created by the community itself. One could voluntarily join the community only through persistent dedication to its ordered reality.

Ordered Status. Commitment to the community at Qumran was not restricted to the initiation process. Each member was required to renew his commitment to the community annually:

---

1. All translations of 1QS are mine.
2. Carol A. Newsom, *The Self as Symbolic Space: Constructing Identity and Community at Qumran*, STDJ 52 (Leiden: Brill, 2004), 186–90.

[19] They will do as follows year after year, all the days of Belial's reign. The priests will join [20] first in the order according to their spiritual status, one after the other. The Levites will join after them, [21] and third all the people will join in the order, one after the other, in their thousands, hundreds, [22] fifties, and tens, so that each Israelite may know his own position in the community of God, [23] an eternal council. No one will be demoted from his position; no one will be promoted above his place. [24] For they will all be in a community of truth, genuine humility, gracious love, and righteous intention [25] toward one another in a holy council, and they will all be members of an eternal fellowship. (2:19–25)

This description of renewed commitment highlights the ordered reality of the community's structure. The renewal process was an exercise undertaken by the community but through a specifically ordered sequence. The stated movement from the priests to the Levites to the people emphasizes the focus on rank within community. Entry into the community was voluntary, but each member had a particular status within the group from which it would be inappropriate to deviate.

A subsequent section of 1QS reiterates this focus on the concept of ordered rank in its description of the procedure used at meetings held by the community:

[8] The priests will sit in the first seats, the elders in the second, and then the rest [9] of all the people will sit according to their position. In this order they will be asked for any judgement, deliberation, or matter which has to do with the many, each man offering his knowledge [10] to the council of the community. No one should interrupt his neighbor's words before his brother has finished speaking. Neither should one speak before another of [11] higher rank. (6:8–11)

Here again the hierarchal nature of the community derives from the social and communal rank of the individual members—first the priests, then the elders, and then the rest of the community. As with other segments of Second Temple Judaism and other institutions within the Greco-Roman world, participation in the community at Qumran was dependent on the ordered status of its members. Variance from this structured reality would likely have been understood as an affront to the theological identity and structure of the community. Those who did not participate faithfully would have been regarded as unclean and rejected from the life of the community.

MARK 9:30–50

"ANYONE WHO WANTS TO BE FIRST MUST BE THE VERY LAST, AND THE SERVANT OF ALL"

Reordered Status. Jesus's second prediction of his death and resurrection in Mark 9:30–32 compels his disciples to consider the reordered nature of the community that Jesus's ministry creates. In response to the disciples' argument about their status, Jesus presents a dramatic inversion of the type of people that will be included in the community of God's kingdom. Drawing the disciples' attention to a child, Jesus asserts that "whoever welcomes one of these little children in my name welcomes me" (9:37). Within the cultural context of the first-century AD, children were frequently seen as socially inferior and insignificant. The force of Jesus's illustration, therefore, does not rest on the potential humility or innocence of the unnamed child but rather on the child's lack of social status. Whereas the disciples have been focused on obtaining a status of greatness ("on the way they had argued about who was the greatest," 9:34), Jesus urges them to reverse the focus of their evaluation. Followers of Jesus are measured not according to their conformity to a specific hierarchal structure but according to their connection with Jesus himself. In contrast to the emphasis on rank that develops in the Rule of the Community, the community of Jesus's followers is defined by its imitation of the social inversion manifest in Jesus's crucifixion in which he becomes the paradigmatic "servant of all" (9:35). Participants in this community are neither encouraged to progress to an elevated position in the social hierarchy nor to remain in their current state. Instead, Jesus's disciples are urged to embody a lower position in the community so that they can engage even with those who have no status in their cultural and religious context.

Reordered Inclusion. Unlike the rigid corporate boundaries developed in the Rule of the Community, the defining boundaries around the community of Jesus's followers are extremely porous. Inclusion into this community is defined not through a stringent set of requirements used to determine a candidate's suitability to participate in the life of the group. Although the disciples castigate the unnamed exorcist because he was not a member of Jesus's closest followers—"he was not one of *us*" (9:38)—Jesus rebukes them. Jesus establishes membership in the community along different lines.

The process of inclusion into this community is defined not by a series of annual examinations but by commitment to Jesus himself.

That is not to say, however, that there is no requirement for faithfulness in the community that Jesus develops. The interrelated series of warnings in Mark 9:42–50 highlight that the stringent focus on faithfulness seen in 1QS also shapes the community of Jesus's followers. The sincere commitment and persistent dedication that marked the community at Qumran are reflected in Jesus's warnings to the disciples. The hyperbolic demands to depart with a hand, foot, or eye if it would prevent them from entering the kingdom evoke the strict calls to purity developed in the Rule of the Community. The shape of these two communities and the status of their respective participants are widely divergent, but the emphasis on faithfulness to the wider community is a feature that resonates through both the Gospel of Mark and the Rule of the Community.

Jesus's dramatic statement in Mark 9:35 and the subsequent illustrative material reflect a reordering of values. To be a disciple of Jesus requires a reorientation of one's entire existence. The community of followers that Jesus seeks to create in Mark 9:30–50 derives its identity and ethos neither from the surrounding cultural context nor from extant religious structures. In contrast, the identity of this community is marked by the sacrificial service of Jesus's own life, death, and resurrection. The order of the kingdom community is defined not by rank—first to last or greatest to least—but by its inversion.

FOR FURTHER READING

Additional Ancient Texts

For external depictions of the wider Essene movement to which the community at Qumran is likely connected, see the descriptions in **Josephus** (*Ant.* 13.171–73; 18.19–22; *J.W.* 2.119–61) and **Philo** (*Prob.* 75–91). Other sectarian documents, such as the Damascus Document and the War Scroll, provide further insight into the theology and practice of the Qumran community. Mark 9:30–50 is paralleled in Matthew 17:22–23; 18:1–9 and Luke 9:43–50; 17:1–2. For other passages in Mark on the reordered nature of discipleship, see Mark 3:20–35; 8:31–38; 10:32–45; 12:28–34.

English Translations and Critical Editions

Burrows, Millar, with the assistance of John C. Trevor and William H. Brownlee, eds. *The Dead Sea Scrolls of St. Mark's Monastery. Volume II:*

Plates and Transcription of the Manual of Discipline. New Haven: American Schools of Oriental Research, 1951.

Charlesworth, James, ed. *The Dead Sea Scrolls: Rule of the Community and Related Documents (Hebrew, Aramaic, and Greek Texts with English Translations).* PTSDSSP. Tübingen: Mohr Siebeck, 1995.

García Martínez, Florentino, and Eibert J. C. Tigchelaar, eds. *The Dead Sea Scrolls: Study Edition.* 2 vols. Leiden: Brill, 1997–98.

Parry, Donald W., and Emanuel Tov. *The Dead Sea Scrolls Reader.* 6 vols. Leiden: Brill, 2004.

Secondary Literature

Hempel, Charlotte. "Community Structures in the Dead Sea Scrolls: Admission, Organization, Disciplinary Procedures." Pages 67–92 of vol. 2 in *The Dead Sea Scrolls after Fifty Years: A Comprehensive Assessment.* 2 vols. Edited by Peter W. Flint and James C. VanderKam. Leiden: Brill, 1998.

Henderson, Suzanne Watts. *Christology and Discipleship in the Gospel of Mark.* SNTSMS 135. Cambridge: Cambridge University Press, 2006.

Hurtado, Larry W. "Following Jesus in the Gospel of Mark—and Beyond." Pages 9–29 in *Patterns of Discipleship in the New Testament.* Edited by Richard N. Longenecker. Grand Rapids: Eerdmans, 1996.

Knibb, Michael A. *The Qumran Community.* Cambridge: Cambridge University Press, 1987.

Newsom, Carol A. *The Self as Symbolic Space: Constructing Identity and Community at Qumran.* STDJ 52. Leiden: Brill, 2004.

Tigchelaar, Eibert. "The Dead Sea Scrolls." Pages 204–27 in *Early Judaism: A Comprehensive Overview.* Edited by John J. Collins and Daniel C. Harlow. Grand Rapids: Eerdmans, 2012.

CHAPTER 16

Mishnah Giṭṭin and Mark 10:1–12: Marriage and Divorce

DAVID INSTONE-BREWER

Jesus's interactions with the Pharisees become increasingly acrimonious throughout Mark's Gospel. The Pharisees had previously asked him three questions, all concerning food: whom he ate with (2:16); why his disciples were plucking grain on the Sabbath (2:23–24); and why they did not wash their hands before eating (7:5). The Pharisees' next three questions are characterized by Mark as a "test": they demanded a sign to test his status (8:11); finally, they tested him with trick questions (12:13–15). The intervening question about divorce ("Is it lawful for a man to divorce his wife?") is also a called a "test" (10:2), presumably because the Pharisees knew that they were trapping him into stating an unpopular viewpoint. We will see that in his reply Jesus rejected the most popular type of divorce, on which most people relied to ensure their marriage contract had an escape clause, without which even his disciples were wary of getting married (according to Matt 19:10).

Jesus's dispute with the Pharisees about divorce is recorded in a form that is familiar in ancient records of rabbinic disputes. The typically brief account contains only highly abbreviated main points. Readers are expected to mentally expand these, provide the links between them, and recognize the source of any allusions. In this essay, we will compare Mark 10:1–12 with select tractates from the Mishnah in order to throw light on these allusions.

Mishnah

"A MAN SHOULD NOT DIVORCE HIS WIFE EXCEPT . . ."

Rabbinic debates were transmitted first orally, then written in the Mishnah, Tosefta, and two Talmuds. The oral version was perhaps the most fixed form, because a community of scholars recited the traditions and corrected one another. The later, written discussions include comments on any differences in these recited traditions (see, e.g., m. Ḥul. 8:1; m. 'Ohal. 8:1). All four written sources follow the same structure, and the latter two are commentaries on the Mishnah, so the earliest traditions tend to occur in more than one source.

Mishnah	Tosephta	Jerusalem Talmud	Babylonian Talmud
Earliest traditions	Mishnah	(Mishnah assumed)	(Mishnah included)
Written ca. AD 200	+ extra traditions	+ discussions of it	+ discussions of it
	ca. AD 300	at Jerusalem	at Babylon
		ca. AD 350	till ca. AD 450

A debate about divorce occurs among the largest oral source—a series of over six-hundred disputes between the schools founded by Hillel and Shammai.[1] This debate is recorded in the Mishnah tractate Giṭṭin:

> The School of Shammai say, A man should not divorce his wife except he found in her a thing of indecency, as it is said: *For he finds in her an indecent thing* [Deut 24:1]. And the School of Hillel say, Even if she spoiled his dish, since it says: *For he finds in her an indecent thing* [Deut 24:1]. (m. Giṭ. 9:10)[2]

Recognized Grounds for Divorce. The background to this debate was a new ground for divorce that was invented by the Hillelites, which was

---

1. The rabbis Hillel and Shammai lived in the first-century BC, and their disciples were among those called "Pharisees" by the Gospel writers.
2. All translations of the Mishnah are the author's literal translation of the text available at www.RabbinicTraditions.com/index.php?m.Git.9.10. Italics indicates citation of the OT.

commonly called a divorce for "any cause." This is roughly equivalent to a modern "no-fault" divorce because there was no need to prove any specific grounds for divorce. The recognized grounds for divorce were adultery (based on Deut 24:1) as well as the breaking of one's other marriage vows to provide food, clothing, and marital love (based on Exod 21:10–11). These obligations were written into typical marriage contracts of the time, as illustrated in the following papyrus:

> According to the law of Moses and the Judeans and I will feed you and clothe you and I will bring you (into my house) by means of your *ketuvah* and I owe you the sum of 400 denarii . . . together with the due amount of your food and your clothes and your bed. (P.Yadin 10 [AD 126])[3]

The *ketuvah* represented the money paid by a husband who failed to keep these stipulations and was consequently divorced by his wife. After the first century, only men could initiate divorces, though a court could have him beaten with rods until he "wanted" to divorce her (m. 'Arak. 5:6). Men could similarly divorce a wife who failed to keep her equivalent marriage vows, and in this case the husband did not pay her the *ketuvah*. However, the Hillelites found a way for men to divorce wives who had not broken any vows.

Divorce for "Any Cause." The phrase in Deuteronomy 24:1 that provided the ground of divorce for adultery is a little strange in Hebrew. In verbatim English it reads: "If . . . he finds in her indecency of a thing." The Shammaites interpreted this verse in the same way that most English translations do, as if it said "a thing of indecency," which they understood as a reference to adultery. The Hillelites agreed that it referred to adultery, but argued that the word "thing" was superfluous, and if one takes the order of the words seriously one could conclude that "thing" referred to a separate, unspecified ground for divorce. The word "thing" (Hebrew *davar*) has a wide range of meanings, including "word," and in legal contexts it could mean "a cause." Therefore, the Hillelites said that this phrase in Deuteronomy 24:1 implied two reasons for divorce: "adultery" and "any cause."

The new "any cause" divorce introduced by the Hillelites quickly gained popularity. First-century Jewish writers **Philo** and **Josephus** both referred to it—and Josephus employed it twice. Even women liked this new type of

---

3. Yigael Yadin, Jonas C. Greenfield, and Ada Yardeni, "Babatha's Ketubba," *Israel Exploration Journal* 44 (1994): 75–101.

divorce, because under such conditions there was no need to expose their domestic lives in a court case, allowing them to preserve their dignity, as well as because in such divorces women were awarded their *ketuvah*. This is presumably why Joseph was praised for wanting to divorce Mary "quietly" (Matt 1:19).

Josephus (*Ant.* 4.253)	Philo (*Spec.* 3.30)	Pharisees (Matt 19:3)
He who desires to be divorced from the wife who is living with him, for whatsoever cause . . .[4]	Another commandment is that if a woman after parting from her husband for any cause whatever . . .[5]	Is it lawful to divorce one's wife for any cause? (ESV)

Mark 10:1–12

"Is It Lawful for a Man to Divorce His Wife?"

Grounds for Divorce. Mark's Gospel assumes the reader knows all about the rabbinic debates on divorce discussed above and that they understand the meaning of the opening question from the Pharisees: "Is it lawful for a man to divorce his wife?" (10:2). As it stands, this question is as misleading as, "Is it lawful for a sixteen-year-old to drink?"—because all humans need to drink. It would be pedantic to add the words "alcoholic beverages" to this modern expression, because everyone knows that this is the subject of the question. Equally, in the early first century it would have been pedantic to specify that the question "Is it lawful for a man to divorce his wife?" concerned divorce "for any cause," because this was the big divorce debate of the day. Therefore, everyone knew that this much was implied.

However, by the time Matthew's Gospel was written, this addition was necessary to include because the "any cause" divorce had won the day, and the debate was quickly forgotten. Matthew added another phrase to aid his readers: "I tell you that anyone who divorces his wife, *except for sexual immorality* [i.e., indecency], and marries another woman commits adultery" (Matt 19:9). This exception clause is a fairly verbatim Greek translation of

---

4. H. St. J. Thackeray and Ralph Marcus, trans., *Josephus: Jewish Antiquities, Books 4–6*, LCL (Cambridge: Harvard University Press, 1930).

5. F. H. Colson, trans., *Philo: On the Decalogue. On the Special Laws, Books 1–3*, LCL (Cambridge, Harvard University Press, 1937).

what we might call the Shammaite slogan: "*Except* he found in her *a thing of indecency*" (m. Giṭ. 9:10—this is especially close to the Greek of Matt 5:32). The Shammaites argued that there was no extra ground for divorce in Deuteronomy 24:1—that is, this verse referred to divorce for nothing "except for indecency," which is to say adultery. In Matthew it is clear that Jesus sided with the Shammaites on this issue. Mark's conclusion reflects the same: "And he said to them, 'Whoever divorces his wife and marries another commits adultery against her, and if she divorces her husband and marries another, she commits adultery'" (10:11–12 ESV).

The consequence of Jesus's stance was dramatic because this new Hillelite law was already used by almost everyone. When Jesus rejected it, he was saying in effect that Hillelite divorces were invalid. Therefore, as Jesus points out, if they subsequently "married" someone else, they were actually committing "adultery," because their previous marriage was still valid. This could be succinctly stated as: "Divorcees who remarry are committing adultery"—a summary that occurs with slight variations in all the Synoptic Gospels (Matt 5:32; 19:9; Mark 10:11–12; Luke 16:18). In Mark this conclusion is revealed only to the disciples, in private (Mark 10:10–12).

No Shammaites survived the destruction of Jerusalem in AD 70, so even rabbinic lawyers soon forgot this debate. This is illustrated by a discussion between a pair of third-century rabbis where they clearly misunderstand the Shammaite slogan "nothing except indecency," supposing the Shammaites had only allowed divorce for adultery (y. Soṭah 1.1, 1a). However, we know that Shammaites also recognized the neglect of food, clothing, and love as grounds for divorce (based on Exod 21:10–11), because they discussed in earlier traditions the minimum quantities that might lead to divorce (m. Ketub. 5:5–8). The church fathers misunderstood the phrase in a similar way, though this was not surprising because they did not realize that Jesus was citing the Shammaite slogan "nothing except indecency" (cf. Matt 19:9). This meant they did not know that the original context of this debate concerned how many grounds for divorce could be found in Deuteronomy 24:1, a contextual insight many interpreters continue to miss today.

Instructions on Marriage. It is clear from Mark's summary that most of Jesus's answer to the Pharisees was unrelated to the original question. He was asked about divorce, but Jesus responded by talking about marriage. He was concerned about two topics where he disagreed with almost all Jews, and not just Hillelites: hard-heartedness and polygamy.

Most Jews felt that divorce was a right and even pious act if adultery had occurred. Jesus contrasted this with the way that God forgave the repeated infidelities of his bride Israel, as described in Jeremiah 3–4, till her eventual divorce (Jer 3:8). Jesus's allusion to God's dealing with Israel was made in Mark 10:5 by his use of the single word "hard-hearted" ("your hearts were hard," NIV). This word is found nowhere in previous Greek literature, but was invented by the **Septuagint** translators and used only three times (Deut 10:16 **LXX**; Jer 4:4 LXX; Sir 16:10). Only the use in Jeremiah concerns divorce, so ancient Jewish readers could not have missed the link. This was like using the English word "scapegoat" (which was similarly invented by Bible translators)—it is difficult to use this word without referring in some way to Leviticus 16. Jesus said, in effect, Jeremiah showed that divorce was allowed for "hard-hearted" breaking of marriage vows, like unrepentant Israel's repeated sinning—though not for occasional minor offenses accompanied by contrition.

Jesus also argued against polygamy, which was generally accepted and practiced by Jews in Palestine. This is substantiated by the most complete family archive that has survived from antiquity, belonging to Babatha, who buried her basket of documents in a cave near **Qumran**. These documents reveal that she was widowed and subsequently married a man who already had one wife.[6] Polygamy was opposed by only two groups of Jews: those at Qumran and those living outside Palestine where Roman law made polygamy illegal. Each group argued from Scripture in different ways, and Jesus referred to both.

At Qumran, in the Damascus Document, they reasoned for monogamy by combining two Old Testament texts:

> 4:21 The foundation of creation is "male and female he created them" [Gen 1:27]. 5:1 And those who entered (Noah's) ark went in two by two into the ark [Gen 7:9]. (CD 4:21–5:1)[7]

Their argument was that the phrase "male and female" has the same meaning in both scriptural texts (Gen 1:27; 7:9), so the flood story tells us that marriages should always consist of only a pair of people. Mark helped his readers recognize this trope by using a similar opening: "from the beginning of creation" (10:6 ESV).

---

6. For Babatha's marriage contract, see Yigael Yadin, Jonas C. Greenfield, and Ada Yardeni, "Babatha's Ketubba," *IEJ* 44 (1994): 75–101. For the Greek Babatha documents, see http://papyri. info/ddbdp/p.babatha.

7. Translation from J. M. Baumgarten and D. Schwartz, "Damascus Document (CD)," in *The Dead Sea Scrolls: Hebrew, Aramaic, and Greek Texts with English Translations, Volume 2: Damascus Document, War Scroll, and Related Documents*, ed. James H. Charlesworth, PTSDSSP 2 (Tübingen: Mohr Siebeck; Louisville: Westminster John Knox, 1995), 19, 21.

Jews in the diaspora used a less complex method. When they translated Genesis 2:24, they added the word "two," as found in Mark 10:8: "And the two will become one flesh." This was added in the Septuagint, then in the Syriac and Latin, and later even in the Aramaic Targums, but never in Hebrew texts.

When this highly abbreviated debate is expanded, using the same methodology used for expanding similar debates recorded by ancient rabbis, we find a wide-ranging discussion taking place in Mark 10:1–12. Some rabbis ask Jesus where he stood in the debate about the new Hillelite "any cause" divorce, but Jesus is interested in affirming marriage. He alludes, in Mark 10:5, to the marriage of God to Israel that did not end in divorce until the nation had broken her vows repeatedly and unrepentantly—that is, "hard-heartedly" (Jer 4:4 LXX). He then argues for monogamy in Mark 10:6–8 by citing texts used by other Jews for the same purpose (Gen 1:27; 2:24).

Jesus also points out that God is a witness at all marriages, so "let no one separate" them (Mark 10:9). The use of this imperative does not mean that it is impossible for divorce to occur, but it indicates that no human *should* cause a marriage breakup. This coheres with Jesus's rejection of the Hillelite no-fault divorce, which makes broken marriage vows the only grounds for divorce. In Jesus's teaching, a wronged partner may decide to divorce, but only after he or she suffers hard-hearted breaking of vows, which *should* never happen.

This passage stands out in Mark as the only place where Jesus addresses a matter of morality, whereas Matthew and Luke included other ethical concerns, mostly from Q.[8] It is also the only specific ethical teaching of Jesus directly referred to in the Epistles (cf. 1 Cor 7:10). It is therefore likely that this teaching had profound practical consequences for the readers of Mark. Yet, as we have seen, familiarity with ancient rabbinic debates is essential for fully understanding Jesus's instructions on marriage and divorce.

For Further Reading

Additional Ancient Texts

Parallel sources for m. Gittin 9:10 are found at Sipre Deuteronomy 269; y. Sotah 1.1, 1a. Other early-Jewish marriage contracts can be found in Naphtali Lewis, Yigael Yadin, Jonas C. Greenfield, eds., *The Documents from the Bar Kokhba Period in the Cave of Letters: Greek Papyri*, Judean Desert

---

8. Q is short for the German "Quelle," i.e., a hypothetical "source" used.

Studies 2 (Jerusalem: Israel Exploration Society, 1989). The divorce certificate by a Jewess is translated in David Instone-Brewer, "Jewish Women Divorcing Their Husbands in Early Judaism: The Background to Papyrus Ṣe'elim 13," *HTR* 92 (1999): 349–57. A Qumran discussion of polygamy similar to Jesus's occurs in CD 4:20–5:6.

English Translations and Critical Editions

Blackman, Philip. *Mashnayoth*. New York: Judaica, 1979.

Danby, Herbert. *The Mishnah: Translated from the Hebrew with Introduction and Brief Explanatory Notes*. Oxford: Oxford University Press, 1933.

Neusner, Jacob. *The Mishnah: A New Translation*. New Haven: Yale University Press, 1988.

RabbinicTraditions.com includes the Mishnah and Babylonian Talmud from the Soncino editions, and the Tosefta and Jerusalem Talmud from Neusner. The website shows parallel relationships and is searchable in English and Hebrew/Aramaic.

Secondary Literature

Archer, Leone J. *Her Price Is beyond Rubies: The Jewish Woman in Greco-Roman Palestine*. JSOTSup 60. Sheffield: Sheffield Academic Press, 1990.

Heth, William A., and Gordon J. Wenham. *Jesus and Divorce*. London: Hodder & Stoughton, 1984.

Instone-Brewer, David. *Divorce and Remarriage in the Bible: The Social and Literary Context*. Grand Rapids: Eerdmans, 2002.

CHAPTER 17

Eschatological Admonition and Mark 10:13–31: Riches, Poverty, and the Faithful

MARK D. MATHEWS

J esus's challenge to the overzealous rich man in Mark's Gospel and his subsequent explanation of the difficulty of salvation for the rich in general leave those in its wake both sorrowful, amazed, and exceedingly astonished (10:22, 24, 26). How are the disciples, or we for that matter, to reconcile the disparity between wealth as a sign of blessing in the Old Testament and early Judaism on the one hand, and this apparent rejection of riches in the New Testament on the other? This essay is aimed at helping to bridge that divide. The answer to the question is found in seedling form in the prophetic tradition of the Hebrew Bible, but takes firm root in the literature of **Second Temple Judaism**, notably in the Enochic document known as Eschatological Admonition (1 Enoch 108).

Eschatological Admonition
"THOSE WHO LOVE GOD HAVE LOVED NEITHER GOLD NOR SILVER"

Wealth and the Covenant. The Deuteronomic tradition, prescribed originally and most clearly in the book of Deuteronomy, makes clear that **covenant** faithfulness to God will be manifested in the life of his people through inheritance of the land, peace, and freedom from political domination. More importantly, the faithful were also promised material blessing. This blessing was expressed in the form of agrarian abundance, bountiful progeny

(Deut 28:3–11), as well as silver and gold (8:13). Thus the many examples of the faithful within Israel were accompanied by descriptions of their wealth (e.g., Gen 13:5–6; 26:12–14; 2 Chr 9:13–22).

In the prophetic tradition we begin to see a critique of rich Jewish leaders who oppress the poor among God's people. Yet this critique is not against riches themselves, nor does it call for a rejection of the same. It serves merely as a description of the abuses of authority among the Jewish leaders due to their avarice. In these denunciations the wealth of the leadership is labeled as unjust in order to establish that their riches are not a result of the blessing of God (Hos 12:7–8; Amos 4:1; Mic 2:1–2; 6:12; Zech 11:5).

When we come to the Second Temple period, however, we find a dramatic shift in covenantal discourse in which the faithful are described as those who reject riches, and the rich are categorically labeled as arrogant, oppressive sinners. Eschatological Admonition provides a window into this shift of worldview in relation to the faithful of God.

Enochic Tradition. Eschatological Admonition is a final appendix to the Enoch corpus (1 En. 108) and is only extant in the Ethiopic tradition with no known attestation in Aramaic or Greek manuscripts. In addition it is not found at **Qumran** among the **Dead Sea Scrolls**. It is likely among the latest additions to the Enochic tradition and perhaps even contemporary with the Synoptic Gospels, which are dated in the latter part of the first-century AD.

This document introduces new ideas into the Enochic tradition and likely represents the convictions and concerns of a community that viewed itself as a later expression of the communities reflected in the earlier traditions of 1 Enoch. The different concerns of this writer and his community, however, have been incorporated into the Enochic tradition probably due to its sustained discussion regarding the suffering of the righteous and issues concerning wealth and poverty. Unlike earlier Enochic traditions—the Epistle of Enoch (1 En. 91–105) in particular—that present the righteous as a distinct group who are oppressed by the rich, in Eschatological Admonition suffering and a lifestyle of poverty are a determined status, being indicative of one's relationship to God and the covenant.

Wealth and Love for God. In Eschatological Admonition, for example, those considered to be faithful to God are described in economic terms as "those who have loved neither gold nor silver nor any of the good things which are in the world" (108:8).[1] This language denotes a voluntary position

---

1. All translations of 1 Enoch are from Daniel C. Olson, *Enoch: A New Translation* (North Richland Hills, TX: BIBAL, 2004).

of marginalization in which loving God and loving silver and gold are mutually exclusive (cf. Luke 16:13). This document also mentions blessings that are recorded in "the books" (1 En. 108:10) that are contrasted with books that record the deeds of sinners (108:7). This suggests an expectation of future reward that does not take place in the present age but only comes as a result of perseverance in testing. Proving oneself faithful, it is presupposed, manifests itself in a categorical rejection of wealth or any other pleasures in the present age. The faithful, who are aware of the temporal nature of this age, look forward to a future reward in heaven.

While the opponents of the faithful are categorized as "sinners" and "those who do evil," their description does not overtly include economic references so frequently portrayed in the Epistle of Enoch (1 En. 97:8–10). Moreover, the writer also emphasizes obedience to Torah as a distinguishing mark of the faithful community (108:2). The absence of any second-person address to opponents—such as "you rich" or "you sinners"—or any critique of their oppression of the faithful suggests that this later Enochic community was not experiencing any programmatic persecution. It did, however, attach itself to the Enochic tradition in order to establish its identity as those who reject wealth in their faithfulness to God. The antithesis constructed between loving God or wealth, heaven or the world, and the promise of reward in the future indicates that the mark of the faithful here is both obedience to Torah and a categorical rejection of riches. This marks a development from earlier Enochic traditions in which the mark of the faithful is their experience of persecution by the rich.

MARK 10:13–31

"HOW HARD IT IS FOR THE RICH TO ENTER THE KINGDOM OF GOD!"

There are several points of consideration that arise between Eschatological Admonition and Mark 10:13–31, not least of which is the obvious call for the rich person to divest himself of his wealth in order to attain eternal life. This position of detachment from riches, so clearly articulated by Eschatological Admonition in the statement "those who love God have loved neither gold nor silver nor any of the good things that are in the world" (1 En. 108:8), is plainly expressed through Jesus's encounter with the rich man.

Discipleship and Divestment. The rich man leads with his accounting of his obedience to the commandments as a testimony of his love for God

(Mark 10:17–20). But Jesus exposes the man's true love by demanding that obedience to Torah must be accompanied with a detachment from his wealth: "Go, sell everything you have and give to the poor, and you will have treasure in heaven. Then come, follow me" (10:21; cf. 1 En. 108:2, 8). Would the man be willing to divest himself of his possessions in order to attain eternal life, have treasure in heaven, and be with God? The answer is clearly no, for the narrator tells us that "the man's face fell" and "he went away sad, because he had great wealth" (Mark 10:22). The man's attitude reflects one where the keeping of the law and having wealth can coincide, unlike that found in Eschatological Admonition. This gives the impression that Jesus's request finds alignment with a similar tradition.

At the same time, Jesus is not antagonistic with the rich man. On the contrary, the text says Jesus "loved him" (10:21). However, the one thing standing between the man and faithfully following Jesus was his unwillingness to divest. This can be seen in Jesus's further comment that it is easier for a camel to fit through the eye of a needle than it is for a rich man to enter the kingdom of God (v. 25). In other words, the accumulation of individual wealth and discipleship are incompatible: "How hard it is for the rich to enter the kingdom of God!" (v. 23). Jesus also promises that those who renounce their possessions and follow him will suffer persecution in this life (v. 30), an idea that is also present in Eschatological Admonition (1 En. 108:8). Yet the Markan tradition does not link that persecution to those who are rich and powerful. Rather, the persecution of the faithful will rise from their commitment to Jesus and his kingdom.

Possessions in This Life. There are, however, factors that demonstrate a point of view more tempered in the Markan tradition than what we find in Eschatological Admonition. Jesus promises in Mark 10:30 that those who renounce their possessions ("homes" and "fields") will receive a hundredfold return not only "in the age to come" ("eternal life") but also "in this present age" (this life). The "already" of this already/not yet scheme likely refers to the access fellow disciples would have to one another's assets. We know that Martha owned a home (Luke 10:38), as did Peter (Matt 8:14) and John (John 19:27). Moreover, Joanna and Susanna, among others, were said to provide for Jesus and his disciples out of their own wealth (Luke 8:3). Thus, Jesus's promise implies that as the faithful carry out their kingdom duties, they will have access to places where they can seek shelter and sustenance from fellow believers (cf. Heb 13:2; 3 John 5–8). This displays more of a communal sharing of possessions than it does an outright rejection of wealth *per se* (cf. Acts 2:44–47; 4:32–37).

Reconciling Traditions. So how does one reconcile the fact that Jesus's disciples maintained some possessions yet he tells the rich man that he must divest himself of all his assets and give them to the poor in order to attain eternal life? Some have suggested there are differing levels of discipleship that Jesus calls his followers to obey.[2] While many of the disciples maintained homes and others provided for Jesus's ministry out of their wealth, Jesus calls some to renounce everything. But this suggestion for differing levels of discipleship is untenable since those closest to Jesus are those who display and spread the word of the kingdom after Jesus's death. Moreover, there is no mention of "other" disciples who had to renounce "all" in a greater way than the Twelve. In fact, Peter makes the very claim that "we have left everything to follow you!" (Mark 10:28). The question, then, is whether "everything" has more to do with leaving everything literally or with taking a determined position to "love God," not "gold nor silver nor any of the good things that are in the world" (1 En. 108:8). In other words, this challenge may be more directed toward social status and one's willingness to endure shame for the sake of the kingdom, a position that is clearly articulated in Eschatological Admonition (1 En. 108:10–11).

The contrast between the rich man and the children in Mark 10:13–16 provides us with some additional insight. Jesus received the children willingly, while his disciples rebuked those bringing them to him. Surely Jesus was too important and too busy to be bothered by insignificant children. But the rich man is given a pass. There is no objection by the disciples of his approach. In fact, they are "amazed" that he is not a potential candidate for God's kingdom (10:24, 26). Jesus, then, is turning the expectations of the socioeconomic world upside down. Children were at the bottom of the social hierarchy in the ancient world.[3] Moreover, they had no attachments to possessions, nor did they have any to offer. They only have need. This seems to suggest a contrast between the honor of the rich man and the shame of the children. A similar pattern of thought is found in Eschatological Admonition, in which the righteous have "experienced abuse and insult" from opponents and were "put to shame" (108:10). Moreover, they were "not rewarded with such honor as their faithfulness deserved" (108:11). If honor-and-shame categories are being expressed in Mark, it may be possible to suggest that Jesus's request is in line with streams of tradition similar

---

2. See, e.g., Robert H. Gundry, *Matthew: A Commentary on His Literary and Theological Art* (Grand Rapids: Eerdmans, 1982), 388.

3. Christian Laes, *Children in the Roman Empire: Outsiders Within* (Cambridge: Cambridge University Press, 2011), 174.

to Eschatological Admonition. Thus, it is not the powerful and rich who will enter the kingdom but those who have no status and nothing to offer (cf. "many who are first will be last, and the last first," Mark 10:31). This is why the rich man's unwillingness to become like the poor excludes him from the kingdom.[4]

Perhaps the most interesting thing to note in this Markan passage is that we find two opposing traditions concerning wealth and covenantal faithfulness standing side by side. On the one hand, Jesus challenges the rich man's love for God by demanding he divest himself of his wealth in what seems to be a complete rejection of accumulating individual wealth. His failure to do so is said to demonstrate his unfitness for entrance into the kingdom. On the other hand, the disciples' shock over the inability of the rich man—or the rich in general—to enter the kingdom suggests they are viewing wealth from a Deuteronomic perspective. Mark's contrast between the two traditions suggests that Jesus is undermining Deuteronomic ideas that view material wealth as a sign of covenant faithfulness, while also raising sociological implications that, coupled together, demonstrate who is fit to enter God's kingdom.

For Further Reading

Additional Ancient Texts

The Second Temple period supplies a wide variety of texts that deal with the issue of wealth, though some have opposing expectations. While the earlier Enoch traditions, such as the Book of Watchers (1 En. 1–36), lays the groundwork for the distinction between rich and poor as wicked and righteous, respectively, the Epistle of Enoch (1 En. 91–105) provides the most explicit depiction of the rich as arrogant, oppressive sinners. The Wisdom of Ben Sira (Sirach) provides the clearest expression that affluence is the expected lot of the faithful in the present age. Some scholars suggest that these two traditions should be read in conversation with one another. The Wisdom of Solomon also attests to an underlying expectation of wealth in relation to wisdom while contrasting the righteous and wicked in terms of material wealth.

---

4. Giving to the poor out of one's wealth is something that is stressed in Sirach (4:1–6; 29:10–13). In the Enoch tradition, the rich are portrayed as never considering helping the "lowly" righteous (1 En. 96:5), and the latter would likely not accept it even if it were offered (1 En. 104:6).

English Translations and Critical Editions

Knibb, M. A. *The Ethiopic Book of Enoch*. 2 vols. Oxford: Clarendon, 1978.

Nickelsburg, George W. E., and James C. Vanderkam. *1 Enoch: A New Translation*. Minneapolis: Fortress, 2004.

Olson, Daniel C. *Enoch: A New Translation*. North Richland Hills, TX: BIBAL, 2004.

Secondary Literature

Hengel, Martin. *Property and Riches in the Early Church: Aspects of a Social History of Early Christianity*. London: SCM, 1974.

Mealand, David L. *Poverty and Expectation in the Gospels*. London: SPCK, 1980.

Murphy, Catherine M. *Wealth in the Dead Sea Scrolls and in the Qumran Community*. STDJ 40. Leiden: Brill, 2002.

Schmidt, Thomas E. *Hostility to Wealth in the Synoptic Gospels*. JSNTSup 15. Sheffield: JSOT Press, 1987.

Stuckenbruck, Loren. *1 Enoch 91–108*. CEJL. Berlin: de Gruyter, 2007.

CHAPTER 18

Rule of the Congregation and Mark 10:32–52: Glory and Greatness in Eschatological Israel

JOHN K. GOODRICH

The middle portion of Mark's Gospel (8:22–10:52) famously narrates Jesus's journey "on the way" toward Jerusalem (cf. 8:27; 9:33, 34; 10:17, 32, 46, 52), which is accompanied by his analogous teaching on "the way of discipleship." This middle section can be roughly divided into three smaller units that cycle through several core **christological** themes and are conspicuously bookended by parallel healings of two blind men (see figure 18.1).

Figure 18.1: The Structure of Mark 8:22–10:52[1]

Gradual, Secret Healing of a Blind Man (8:22–26)			
Affirmation about Jesus	8:27–30	9:2–29	10:17–18, 26–28
Passion Prediction	8:31	9:30–31	10:32–34
Disciples Fail to Understand	8:32	9:32	10:35–40
Renewed Call and Instruction	8:33–9:1	9:33–50	10:41–45
Full, Public Healing of a Blind Man (10:46–52)			

The latter part of the third cycle (10:32–45) is the high point of this middle section, containing the most explicit predictive passion material in the entire Gospel (10:32–34) as well as one of the better-known private interactions from

---

1. Adapted from M. Eugene Boring, *Mark: A Commentary*, NTL (Louisville: Westminster John Knox, 2006), 231.

the entire Synoptic tradition (10:35–45). In this passage, James and John approach Jesus to make a special request of him. Their petition—"Let one of us sit at your right and the other at your left in your glory" (10:37)—seems as awkward as it does ambitious. Indeed, since the entire lot of disciples was admonished shortly beforehand for arguing about their individual greatness (9:33–35), this question causes one to wonder why the brothers would have dared to broach the topic again, requesting not only that Jesus do for them "whatever [they] ask" (10:35) but that he assign them special seats "in [his] glory" (10:37).

One gets a better sense of the motivation behind the brothers' appeal when it is realized that aspirations for **eschatological** glory and greatness were common in early Judaism, not least in the **Dead Sea Scrolls**. The reader has already been introduced to the Rule of the Community in earlier essays of this book. The nature of the interaction between Jesus, James, and John can be helpfully illuminated through a comparison with a related **Qumran** text—the Rule of the Congregation.

Rule of the Congregation

"THEY SHALL SIT BEFORE HIM, EACH ACCORDING TO HIS GLORY"

The Rule of the Congregation, also known as the Messianic Rule, is an important Qumran work originating some time before 75 BC. Its importance is obvious from the fact that nine fragmented copies have survived from Cave 4 alone (4QSa–i = 4Q249a–i), and that the most complete extant manuscript (1QSa = 1Q28a) was sewn into the same scroll as the famous Rule of the Community (1QS), where together with a second text known as the Rule of the Blessings (1QSb) it functions as an appendix to the much lengthier 1QS document. Accordingly, the Rule of the Congregation, though containing only two columns amounting to fifty-two lines of Hebrew, has an importance quite disproportionate to its length.

Eschatological Leadership and Qualifications. The content of the Rule is especially pertinent to the organization of the Qumran community. But what makes this document so extraordinary is its eschatological orientation: Rule of the Congregation was written to provide policies and instructions on education and community formation for "the Congregation of Israel *in the end of days*" (1:1).[2] In other words, the document concerns the organization

---

2. All translations of 1QSa are from James H. Charlesworth, ed., *The Dead Sea Scrolls:*

of God's people during the period following the arrival of Israel's promised eschatological leadership, both its priest and its prince (i.e., **Messiah**), yet prior to the final approaching battle between Israel and its enemies. Thus, what is prescribed herein is a socioreligious hierarchy—including levels of participation in community life and service based on the various developmental stages of the individual—which was to be installed during the last days.

The instructions on personal religious development progress from the youngest to the oldest members of the community. Participation of the congregation's youngest members, for example, is to be restricted to their religious education: "From [his you]th they [shall instru]ct him in the Book of Hagu (i.e., the community instruction manual) and according to his age they shall enlighten him in the statute[s of] the covenant. And [according to his understanding they shall] teach him their precepts" (1:6b–8a). By age twenty, the age of adulthood when one has learned "[good] and evil," participants were permitted to register with their tribal clan, become citizens of the congregation, and marry (1:8c–11a). Once members reached twenty-five years of age, they could begin to "perform the service of the Congregation," meaning they could participate (at the most menial level) in the community militia (1:12b–13a; cf. 1:21, 26). Then, by age thirty, one's service opportunities truly broadened:

> And at thirty years (of age) he shall draw near to decide a legal case and ju[dgme]nt, and to take a firm stand among the heads of the thousands of Israel, the rulers of hundreds, the rulers of fi[f]ties, [and the rulers of] tens, (and to be one of the) judges and officers for their tribes, in all their families, [according t]o the Sons of [Aar]on, the priests. (1:13b–16a)

We see here that there were leaders of diverse ranks to be appointed in eschatological Israel, including various kinds of political heads, military rulers, as well as tribal judges and officers.[3] The Rule nowhere states how competitive or desirable these positions of responsibility were, only that the appointments were to be made by the priestly leadership. Nonetheless, given the stress on honor and social status (cf. 1:18; 2:14–21), we can assume that higher levels of authority would have been coveted by most adult men.

Hebrew, Aramaic and Greek Texts with English Translations, Volume 1: Rule of the Community and Related Documents, PTSDSSP 1 (Tübingen: Mohr Siebeck; Louisville: Westminster John Knox, 1994). Emphasis added.

3. For "thousands," "hundreds," and "fifties" as military units, see Num 31:5, 14, 48, 52–54; Deut 33:17.

In addition to age, various other criteria were used to determine a person's assignment. "And according to his (i.e., the member's) understanding along with the perfection of his way, he shall strengthen his back to take (his) posi[tion for service] of his work among his brothers. . . . And as the years of a man increase, according to his ability [they shall assign] him his duties in the [service] of the Congregation" (1:17–19). By "ability," the Rule means physical, mental, and religious competency (cf. 1:19–22). This implies that not all members of the Congregation were equally qualified for leadership positions. In fact, only specially skilled and pious persons could participate in the more exclusive Council of the Community (i.e., the Council of the *Yaḥad*, 1:27–2.3), while those with religious impurities and significant bodily ailments, including those "crippled in the legs or the hands, lame or blind or deaf or dumb" (2:5–6), could not participate directly in the main meetings of the Congregation (2:3–10). This is not to suggest that the leadership ethos promoted for eschatological Israel was blatantly discriminatory. Those with various afflictions could participate in the Council through intermediaries (2:9b–10), and the Rule directs that "each man shall honor his fellow" regardless of whether his rank is "important or unimportant" (literally, "great or small"; 1:18). Nonetheless, "glory" and "greatness" were bestowed in accordance with one's piety, knowledge, and skills.

The Messiah's Leadership Ethic. The organizational hierarchy and leadership ethos are perhaps most apparent in the statutes regarding the feasts of the Council of the Congregation (2:11–22), the larger, more inclusive assembly for which entrance and participation in the dining area were to follow a specific protocol. The Rule explains how the Priest shall enter first as "the head of all the Congregation of Israel and all [his] br[others]" (2:12–13), followed by the subordinate priests, who "shall sit be[fore him each man] according to his glory" (2:13–14). Next, the Messiah shall enter, followed by the remaining laity, who shall enter and be seated "each according to his glory" (2:15–17). Even consumption of the meal must follow a strict rank-based order: "Fo[r he (i.e., the priest) shall] bless the first portion of the bread and the new wi[ne, and shall stretch out] his hand to the bread first of all. And aft[er (this has occurred)] the Messiah of Israel [shall stret]ch out his hands to the bread. [And after that] all the Congregation of the Community [shall ble]ss (and partake), each ma[n according to] his glory" (2:19–21). Thus, the Messiah and his priestly counterpart reinforce the communal hierarchy as they take their places of priority and preeminence during the conciliar meal.

The above emphasis on glory and greatness in Rule of the Congregation demonstrates how despite the Qumran community's rhetoric of brotherhood and social *equality*, they nonetheless maintained a stress on rank and status that manifested itself in a distinctive political *inequality*.[4] Such hierarchies should not surprise us, since they were commonplace within all ancient Mediterranean societies, including early-Jewish communities. Mark's Gospel shares some of these emphases, while also subverting them in some rather striking ways.

Mark 10:32–52

"WHOEVER WANTS TO BECOME GREAT AMONG YOU MUST BE YOUR SERVANT"

Eschatological Leadership and Qualifications. Numerous points of contact exist between the Rule of the Congregation and Mark 10:32–52. Like the Rule text, the Gospel of Mark concerns itself with the leadership of restored Israel. God's eschatological kingdom is precisely what James and John have in view when referring to Jesus's "glory" (10:37; cf. "kingdom" in Matt 20:21). Indeed, in its only other two occurrences in Mark, "glory" is associated with both the power and parousia of the Son of Man (8:38; 13:26). Moreover, in antiquity sitting beside a monarch connoted great authority (cf. Ps 110:1). Thus, when James and John ask to sit "at your right" and "at your left in your glory" (10:37), the brothers are requesting to participate in none other than Jesus's own eschatological reign.

To be fair, it is not entirely surprising that James and John would have made such a bold request. As our analysis above has shown, beliefs in eschatological thrones and hierarchies were current in early Judaism, often rooted in Daniel's prophecy that "the sovereignty, power and greatness of all the kingdoms under heaven will be handed over to the holy people of the Most High" (Dan 7:27; cf. 7:9, 26).[5] Moreover, it should be remembered how immediately before our passage Jesus tells the disciples about the reversal of fortunes they will receive "in the age to come" (Mark 10:28–31), and how throughout the Gospel Jesus repeatedly confronts Israel's scribal and priestly leaders, implying that they will eventually be removed and replaced (cf. 12:9). As they approached Jesus, then, James and John were probably assuming they would have a hand in governing restored Israel (cf. Matt 19:28; Luke 22:30).

---

4. Yonder Moynihan Gillihan, *Civic Ideology, Organization, and Law in the Rule Scrolls: A Comparative Study of the Covenanters' Sect and Contemporary Voluntary Associations in Political Context*, STDJ 97 (Leiden: Brill, 2012), 484.

5. For the many allusions to Daniel 7 in Mark 10:35–45, see Brant Pitre, "The Ransom for Many, the New Exodus, and the End of Exile," *Letter & Spirit* (2005): 41–68, at 44.

Jesus, however, explains that "[t]hese places belong to those for whom they have been prepared" (10:40). In other words, Jesus, though not necessarily declining their request, indicates that such positions are not his but the Father's to grant. Nonetheless, before revealing the source of these appointments, Jesus shares that such kingdom positions have specific qualifications. In the first place, elevated rank is conditioned upon suffering in the present life: "Can you drink the cup I drink or be baptized with the baptism I am baptized with?" (10:38). The cup and baptism here symbolize suffering (cf. 14:23–24, 36). Thus, Jesus shares that being *glorified* with him demands that they also *suffer* with him (cf. Rom 8:17–18), a fate the brothers themselves were prepared—in fact, predestined—to undergo (Mark 10:39). Even so, it is probably not so much the ambition of James and John that Jesus finds problematic but their ignorance about the cost involved.

The brothers also seem to be inappropriately motivated by a competitive desire to outrank the other disciples. Such was the impetus of the Twelve's previous debate about greatness (9:33–34), and their follow-up argument in 10:41 probably centers on the same issue, revealing an unhealthy self-interest incompatible with the nature of the kingdom.

Jesus therefore begins to offer instructions on the kind of leadership to be exercised by his followers. The "rulers of the Gentiles," Jesus explains, "lord it over" their subjects, and "their high officials" are known to "exercise authority" in the same manner (10:42). "Not so with you," Jesus warns the Twelve. "Instead, whoever wants to become great among you must be your servant, and whoever wants to be first must be slave of all" (10:43–44). Jesus here introduces a leadership ethic that contrasts with that which is exercised by the leaders of the nations. Although the Romans theorized about "servant leadership,"[6] foreign rulers were habitually tyrannical and abusive—as demonstrated in Jesus's third passion prediction (10:33).[7]

Once again, because Jesus affirms the one who "wants to become great" and "wants to be first," ambition is not his concern. Instead, his concern is for his followers to lead in the interest of *others* rather than themselves. God's leaders must exhibit humility and servitude, such that they become the servants and slaves of the people they lead—in intention, if not in form.

---

6. Cf. David Seeley, "Rulership and Service in Mark 10:41–45," *NovT* 35 (1993): 234–50; Adam Winn, "Tyrant or Servant? Roman Political Ideology and Mark 10.42–45," *JSNT* 36 (2014): 325–52.

7. See also Tessa Rajak, "The Angry Tyrant," in *Jewish Perspectives on Hellenistic Rulers*, ed. T. Rajak et al. (Berkeley: University of California Press, 2007), 110–27.

The Messiah's Leadership Ethic. This mode of servant leadership is modeled on and motivated by Jesus's own self-giving. In the same way that Jesus, the authoritative "Son of Man," came not "to be served, but to serve, and to give his life as a ransom for many" (10:45), so kingdom leaders must not exercise their authority selfishly but sacrificially. Although they might not be mocked, spat on, flogged, and killed like Jesus (10:34), kingdom leaders must be willing to be expended for the benefit of those they lead.

An apt example follows at the end of our passage. Hearing the persistent cries of a blind beggar on the roadside (10:47–48), Jesus mercifully grants his request to see (10:51–52). By humbly ministering to Bartimaeus—who due to his affliction could not have belonged to the inner circle of the eschatological Congregation of Israel (1QSa 2:5–9)—Jesus wins a devoted follower on his journey to Jerusalem while demonstrating how to be a "slave of all" (10:44).

In sum, while the Rule of the Congregation and Mark 10:32–52 share a vision for the political hierarchy of eschatological Israel, they fundamentally disagree on the qualifications for leadership and how authority is to be exercised. The Rule rewards knowledge, skills, and piety, stressing the priority and preeminence of those with greater status, beginning with the priest and Messiah. Mark's Gospel, on the other hand, promotes servant-style leadership rooted in the Messiah's own self-giving. Although elevated rank and status will be issued in God's kingdom, Jesus subverts imperial and Jewish practice by teaching that eschatological glory and greatness are obtained, counterintuitively, through humble service in the present.

FOR FURTHER READING

Additional Ancient Texts

For the Synoptic development of Jesus's teaching on greatness, see Matthew 20:20–28; Luke 22:24–30. On the leadership of the Qumran community, see also the Community Rule and the Damascus Document. For non-Qumranic Jewish leadership (esp. the high priesthood) during the **Hasmonean period**, see 1 Maccabees 14; Sirach 50:1–28.

English Translation and Critical Edition

Barthélemy, D. "1Q28a. Règle de la Congrégation (1QSa)." Pages 108–18 in *Qumran Cave 1.* DJD 1. Edited by D. Barthélemy and J. T. Milik. Oxford: Clarendon, 1955.

García Martínez, Florentino, and Eibert J. C. Tigchelaar, eds. *The Dead Sea Scrolls: Study Edition.* 2 vols. Leiden: Brill, 1997–98.

Secondary Literature

Gillihan, Yonder Moynihan. *Civic Ideology, Organization, and Law in the Rule Scrolls: A Comparative Study of the Covenanters' Sect and Contemporary Voluntary Associations in Political Context.* STDJ 97. Leiden: Brill, 2012.

Hempel, Charlotte. *The Qumran Rule Texts in Context: Collected Studies.* TSAJ 154. Tübingen: Mohr Siebeck, 2013.

Hill, Craig C. *Servant of All: Status, Ambition, and the Way of Jesus.* Grand Rapids: Eerdmans, 2016.

Kaminouchi, Alberto de Mingo. *But It Is Not So among You: Echoes of Power in Mark 10:32–45.* JSNTSup 249. London: T&T Clark, 2003.

Moore, Mark E. *Kenotic Politics: The Reconfiguration of Power in Jesus's Political Praxis.* LNTS 482. London: T&T Clark, 2013.

Santos, Narry F. *Slave of All: The Paradox of Authority and Servanthood in the Gospel of Mark.* JSNTSup 237. London: Sheffield Academic Press, 2003.

Schiffman, Lawrence. *The Eschatological Community of the Dead Sea Scrolls.* SBLMS 38. Atlanta: Scholars Press, 1989.

CHAPTER 19

1 Maccabees and Mark 11:1–11:
A Subversive Entry into Jerusalem

TIMOTHY GOMBIS

Jesus's entry into Jerusalem is one of the more well-known scenes in the Gospels. Each of the four Gospel writers gives an account of it (Matt 21:1–11; Luke 19:28–40; John 12:12–19) and Christians celebrate it yearly on Palm Sunday. Many Bible translations assign the title "Triumphal Entry" to passages that describe Jesus's entry into the city, including Mark 11. Yet the manner in which Mark narrates the incident is anything but triumphal. In fact, Jesus's entry is a *subversion* of triumphalism. Mark indicates that the disciples and others who are celebrating are not doing what Jesus wants them to do in this passage, and when Jesus arrives into the temple courts he merely looks around and leaves. This underwhelming climax to the scene resonates with a major narrative feature of Mark: the Gospel portrays Jesus as resisting the efforts of various characters (the **Pharisees**, his disciples, the crowds, Peter, and Satan) to turn him into the sort of **Messiah** who will fulfill their hopes for a military hero who can build a movement, rally troops, and achieve freedom from Rome and blessing for God's people in the land.

Mark portrays Jesus as a Messiah who disappoints the hopes fostered among Jewish groups by the Maccabean heroes. First Maccabees is a Jewish text that tells the story of the priest Mattathias and his sons who led a rebellion against the **Seleucids**, the Syrian occupying power ruling Judea early in the second-century BC. The **Hasmonean** heroes—Mattathias's sons—succeed in freeing Judea from occupation and establishing an independent state in 142 BC.[1] When they recapture Jerusalem, Simon enters the city to an

---

1. The family and descendants of Mattathias are known as the Hasmoneans, probably because of an ancestor named "Hashmon," though 1 Maccabees does not use this name.

enthusiastic reception that is strikingly similar to Jesus's entrance in Mark 11. The military leaders and their exploits lauded in 1 Maccabees shaped Jewish hopes for a conquering hero, the sort of Messiah many hoped Jesus would be. His entry into Jerusalem, then, is yet another instance in Mark in which Jesus resists popular opinion and public pressure to conform to cultural hopes and dreams.

1 Maccabees

"THE JEWS ENTERED IT WITH PRAISE AND PALM BRANCHES, AND WITH HARPS AND CYMBALS"

The Revolution Begins. After being ruled for a time by the Ptolemies from Egypt, Judea was governed by the Seleucids from Syria from about 198 BC. With the emergence of a new king—**Antiochus IV Epiphanes**, in 175 BC—the suffering of the Jews intensified. He sought ever-greater control over Judea through the imposition of an alien culture and the elimination of Jewish religious practices. The pressure to conform to **Hellenistic** culture being imposed by Antiochus split the Jewish people, with some wanting to accommodate to the foreign rulers and many others wanting to maintain their distinctiveness (1:11–15).

With Judea in the grip of cultural crisis, a representative of the king came to a town called Modein, to the northwest of Jerusalem, to make an offer to the local priest (2:15–18). If Mattathias were to support the king and make a pagan sacrifice, thus encouraging wider loyalty, then Antiochus would greatly honor him and enrich his family. Mattathias refused to demonstrate loyalty to the king (2:19–22), after which the following dramatic scene unfolded.

> [23] When he had finished speaking these words, a Jew came forward in the sight of all to offer sacrifice on the altar in Modein, according to the king's command. [24] When Mattathias saw it, he burned with *zeal* and his heart was stirred. He gave vent to righteous anger; he ran and killed him on the altar. [25] At the same time he killed the king's officer who was forcing them to sacrifice, and he tore down

---

Josephus provides this detail in *Ant.* 12.265 (John R. Bartlett, *1 Maccabees*, GAP [Sheffield: Sheffield Academic Press, 1998], 18).

the altar. [26] Thus he burned with zeal for the law, just as Phinehas did against Zimri son of Salu. (1 Macc 2:23–26, emphasis added)

Mattathias then called upon all who were zealous for the purity of Israel to gather and be led out into the wilderness, thus beginning the **Maccabean revolt** against the Seleucid rule of Judea. This began in 167 BC, and over the next twenty-five years they drove out their foreign oppressors and established an independent state in 142 BC.

Judas the Hammer. First Maccabees chronicles the exploits of Judas, the third son of Mattathias, in 1 Maccabees 3:1–9:22. Judas took over leadership of the rebellion after the death of his father. He was a strong leader and powerful warrior, earning the nickname "Maccabeus," which means "the hammer" (3:1). After the slaughter of all the men in a town that refused him and his followers passage, Judas razed the city and then made his way to Mount Zion and entered "in joy and gladness and offered burnt offerings" (5:54).

Simon Enters the City. After the death of Judas, his brothers Jonathan and Simon led the revolt. Under Simon's leadership, Judea attained political independence:

In the one hundred seventieth year the yoke of the Gentiles was removed from Israel, and the people began to write in their documents and contracts, "In the first year of Simon the great high priest and commander and leader of the Jews." (13:41–42)

Simon subsequently completed the final military operations necessary to actualize the independence of Judea and Jerusalem. After he secured the temple and removed the foreign soldiers, he purified the temple from its pollution by foreigners. He then led a celebratory entrance into it:

On the twenty-third day of the second month, in the one hundred seventy-first year, the Jews entered it with praise and palm branches, and with harps and cymbals and stringed instruments, and with hymns and songs, because a great enemy had been crushed and removed from Israel. Simon decreed that every year they should celebrate this day with rejoicing. (13:51–52)

The heroes and legendary narratives of 1 Maccabees shaped Jewish imagination in the first century, during which Judea was again an occupied land, this time by Rome. In a culture hungry for liberation, hopes were high for a heroic figure who had the charisma to gather together a fighting force and the military skill to drive the Romans from the land. Mark's narrative of Jesus as a cross-directed Messiah preaching a cross-shaped kingdom and calling for cross-carrying disciples subverts these hopes at every turn.

Mark 11:1–11

"JESUS ENTERED. . . . HE LOOKED AROUND AT EVERYTHING, BUT . . . WENT OUT"

A Subversive Messiah. Throughout the Gospel of Mark, Jesus follows a healing or exorcism with strong exhortations to keep quiet about his identity. For example, after he raised up Jairus's daughter (Mark 5:21–43), he "gave strict orders not to let anyone know about this, and told them to give her something to eat" (5:43). Judea longed for liberation from Roman occupation, and Jesus did not want his ministry to generate revolutionary fervor so that big crowds got out of control with the demand for a messianic movement shaped by Maccabean violence. Jesus preached the gospel of the kingdom that called all to take up their crosses—to die to revolutionary desires, to give up hopes for military triumphs over the Romans.

The Confused Disciples. Jesus's **parable** of the sower and soils in Mark 4:1–20 (esp. 4:11–12) is paradigmatic for the Gospel narrative. The cross-shaped gospel goes out and finds cultivated hearts, and those who are of the kingdom will perceive it and respond to it, while those outside the kingdom will hear it "in parables," being confused by it. Ironically, as Mark progresses, it is the disciples who grow increasingly confused about Jesus and his messianic mission. Peter confesses that Jesus is indeed the Christ (8:29), but when Jesus speaks of his betrayal and death, Peter rebukes him (8:32). Jesus in turn rebukes Peter, calls him "Satan," and reveals that his heart and mind are set on the wrong sort of kingdom (8:33). This episode sheds light on the satanic temptation earlier in 1:12–13. Mark provides no details there, but readers who grow increasingly familiar with Mark, having repeatedly gone through the narrative, will come to associate Peter's rebuke of Jesus with Satan's aims in tempting Jesus.

In Mark, Satan is not concerned with preventing Jesus from being Messiah, the Son of God. Rather, Satan aims for Jesus to be a *spectacular* Messiah, one who can rally a fighting force to drive out the Romans. Satan desires Jesus to be consumed by self-advancement and self-preservation and to avoid going to the cross at all costs. Jesus calls Peter "Satan" because he has previously heard this temptation. Satan is opposed to Jesus going to the cross because that is how God overthrows the reign of Satan.

Mark has been accused of portraying the disciples too negatively. But characterizing them as confused by Jesus is the device whereby Mark demonstrates that there are several opposing agendas at work to shape Jesus into a Messiah who will meet Jewish hopes and expectations oriented by the Maccabean narrative. The disciples, after having initially responded by following Jesus (Mark 1–3), begin to grow increasingly confused by him, starting after the parable of the soils (4:1–20). Their vision of what Jesus is all about is determined by worldly forms of honor and triumph. Each time Jesus predicts his suffering and death, the disciples disagree with him, misunderstand him, or ignore what he has said and discuss who will be most prominent in the kingdom (8:31–33; 9:30–33; 10:32–45). The Pharisees also attempt to turn Jesus into a worldly Messiah, calling for him to give them a sign (8:11–12). Their request is a demand for Jesus to meet their expectations, to do something spectacular and impressive rather than feeding desperate crowds and healing the sick.

A Misunderstood and Subversive Entrance. These narrative features come to a head in Jesus's entrance to Jerusalem. Mark narrates Jesus entering the city as a faithful Davidic ruler while the disciples and crowds attempt once again to turn Jesus into a conquering military hero, foisting on him their hopes for liberation from Rome. Jesus does nothing to play to the audience, which is how he has treated crowds throughout Mark. They have been largely an obstacle to his ministry rather than a positive indication of success (cf. 1:36–38; 3:20; 5:21–43). Jesus enters the city in the manner of the prophecy in Zechariah 9:9, which speaks of a humble, royal ruler:

> Rejoice greatly, Daughter Zion!
>   Shout, Daughter Jerusalem!
> See, your king comes to you,
>   righteous and victorious,
> lowly and riding on a donkey,
>   on a colt, the foal of a donkey.

The crowds spread their cloaks on the road, and some waved palm branches, in the same way that the crowds welcomed the conquering Simon upon his entrance into the city (1 Macc 13:51). They acclaimed Jesus in terms of Psalm 118, which celebrates God's deliverance through military victory.

First Maccabees does not indicate what songs were sung when Simon entered the temple, but one of them very well may have been Psalm 118, part of which the crowds shout in Mark 11:9 ("Blessed is he who comes in the name of the LORD!"; Ps 118:26), among other acclamations longing for "the coming kingdom of our father David" (Mark 11:10).

The disciples likely played a role in whipping up the crowds to acclaim Jesus as a conquering king entering the city triumphantly. After all, they had misunderstood him throughout his ministry and may be doing the same here. Mark suggests that those celebrating Jesus's entrance are not acting according to Jesus's agenda.[2] The crowd consists of "those who went ahead and those who followed" (11:9). Many of these had been traveling to Jerusalem with Jesus, and just before this episode Mark notes that "the disciples were astonished, while those who followed were afraid" (10:32). In Mark these reactions indicate a lack of understanding of Jesus (cf. 5:20; 6:50–52). Further, in 10:32b–37, when Jesus states that he is going to Jerusalem to die, James and John make their stunningly selfish request for places of honor in the kingdom.

Locations of physical proximity to Jesus are important in Mark. Jesus has called his disciples to be "with him" (3:14), which means doing what Jesus says, along with acting and thinking according to his agenda. When Mark indicates therefore that the ones who "went ahead" and "those who followed" were acclaiming Jesus as a triumphant king, he does not situate them "with Jesus," indicating that they are acting according to their own agendas.[3] They are forcing Jesus into the image of their culture's messianic hopes and aspirations.

Many have noted that Jesus's actions in this narrative are anticlimactic. He merely enters, looks around, and leaves (11:11). But Jesus has his own agenda, just as he has had throughout Mark. He is the chief agent of the kingdom of God, the one through whom God is carrying out his purposes, and those purposes do not include military triumph. In the immediate

---

2. Mark does not comment on Jesus's lack of reaction, but commentators routinely note the anticlimactic character of the episode. In addition, (1) Mark's first audiences would have expected Jesus to respond to the crowd's shouts, given the Maccabean history. (2) The crowd celebrates "the coming kingdom," whereas in Mark the kingdom has already arrived in Jesus (1:15), indicating they are expecting a glorious triumphant reign. (3) Jesus is indeed "he who comes," but he comes after the one who prepares "the way for the Lord" (Mark 1:3). Jesus, then, represents the God of Israel returning to his temple, and (4) he returns in judgment (Mal 3:1–2), which Jesus enacts in the following episode (Timothy C. Gray, *The Temple in the Gospel of Mark: A Study in Its Narrative Role* [Grand Rapids: Baker Academic, 2010], 20–22).

3. Francis J. Moloney, *The Gospel of Mark: A Commentary* (Grand Rapids: Baker Academic, 2012), 219.

context, Jesus is not coming to purify or reclaim the temple as Simon and his brothers did in 1 Maccabees. Jesus has come in the same way that the God of Israel arrives to inspect the fruit of his people before rendering a judgment (Isa 5:1–7). After departing the city, he will return the next day to render God's verdict of judgment on the temple, first symbolically (11:12–14) and then actually (11:15–19).

Mark portrays Jesus as the Son of Man who came to serve and not to be served (10:45). He is a cross-directed Messiah whose behavior and preaching fly in the face of hopes for violent overthrow of the occupying Romans. The subversive character of Jesus's entry into the city in Mark 11:1–11 is clear when read against Simon's entrance in 1 Maccabees 13:51, and when Mark is read alongside 1 Maccabees.

FOR FURTHER READING

Additional Ancient Texts

Psalms of Solomon 17 reflects a Jewish **eschatological** hope for God's kingdom to come and envisions a Davidic ruler who will drive out wicked rulers and restore justice. Second Maccabees 4:21–22 records another entry into Jerusalem, this one by Apollonius, who arrives to shouts from the crowds. **Josephus** also records several entrances into Jerusalem by rulers who are welcomed by the people with acclamations (*J.W.* 1.72–74; *Ant.* 16.12–15; 17.193–95).

English Translations and Critical Editions

NETS

NRSV

Kappler, Werner, ed. *Maccabaeorum liber I–IV.* Septuaginta: Vetus Testamentum Graecum, Band 9. Göttingen: Vandenhoeck & Ruprecht, 1990.

Secondary Literature

Borchardt, Francis. *The Torah in 1 Maccabees: A Literary Critical Approach to the Text.* DCLS 19. Berlin: de Gruyter, 2014.

Gray, Timothy C. *The Temple in the Gospel of Mark: A Study in Its Narrative Role.* Grand Rapids: Baker Academic, 2010.

Harrington, Daniel J. *The Maccabean Revolution: Anatomy of a Biblical Revolution.* Wilmington, DE: Michael Glazier, 1988.

Kinman, Brent. *Jesus' Entry into Jerusalem: In the Context of Lukan Theology and the Politics of His Day.* AGJU 28. Leiden: Brill, 1995.

Myers, Ched. *Binding the Strong Man: A Political Reading of Mark's Story of Jesus*. Maryknoll, NY: Orbis Books, 1988.

Trampedach, Kai. "The War of the Hasmoneans." Pages 61–78 in *Dying for the Faith, Killing for the Faith: Old-Testament Faith-Warriors (1 and 2 Maccabees) in Historical Perspective*. Edited by Gabriela Signori. BSIH 206. Leiden: Brill, 2012.

Tomes, Roger. "Heroism in 1 and 2 Maccabees." *Biblical Interpretation* 15 (2007): 171–99.

CHAPTER 20

Psalms of Solomon and Mark 11:12–25: The Great Priestly Showdown at the Temple

NICHOLAS PERRIN

For contemporary readers, Mark 11:12–25 raises a handful of questions. First, Jesus curses a fig tree simply because it fails to bear fruit (11:12–14, 20–21)—out of season no less! Is there an explanation for this seeming overreaction? Second, what motivated the startling behavior we know today as Jesus's "temple action" or the "cleansing of the temple" (11:15–17)? Third, how do we account for the apparent non sequitur between Peter's notice of the withered fig tree (11:21) and Jesus's far-ranging remarks about faith, prayer, and forgiveness (11:22–25)? Though Mark 11:12–25's oddities seem to leave readers with more questions than answers, when we understand the narrative against the background of the first-century BC Psalms of Solomon, we begin to find the clarity we need toward resolving these difficulties.

Psalms of Solomon

"AND CLOTHE HIM WITH THE STRENGTH, THAT
HE MAY SHATTER UNRIGHTEOUS RULERS,
AND PURGE JERUSALEM FROM NATIONS"

The Psalms of Solomon was likely composed only decades after Pompey's conquest of Judea (63 BC), a dark moment when the victorious Roman general profaned the inner sanctuary. For the author of the Psalms of Solomon, the calamity was ultimately a result of Israel's **covenantal** disobedience, perpetuated through the illegitimate **Hasmonean** dynasty. If the community behind the Psalms of Solomon saw the Hasmoneans and their supporters as impostors and as a cancer within Israel, it also saw itself as the righteous remnant, Israel's last great hope despite the mass apostasy. Though socially marginalized, the community "fought back" in three ways, by (1) calling out the Hasmonean priests for their sacrilege, (2) confessing their hope in a coming Davidic **messiah** who would one day purge the temple precincts of the godless pretenders, and (3) praying that God would rescue their community and issue judgment against the disobedient.

Drawing Attention to the Sacrilege. Whereas the Jewish-temple cultus depended on the purity of its worshippers, the psalmist complains that that purity has been compromised. In the first place, the priests' "transgressions went beyond those of the gentiles before them; they utterly polluted the holy things of the Lord" (Pss. Sol. 1:8).[1] According to the psalmist, the religious leaders not only consorted with prostitutes (2:1–3, 11) but also "plundered the sanctuary of God," which was to say that "they defiled the sacrifices" (8:11–12). The laity were no better: "And the children of the covenant in the midst of the mingled peoples. . . . There was not one among them that wrought in the midst of Jerusalem mercy and truth" (17:15). And so from top to bottom Israel had become corrupt: "From the chief of them to the least all were sinful; the king was a transgressor, the judge was disobedient, and the people were sinful" (17:20). Drawing God's attention to the profanations of the priests and people, which had essentially rendered the holy space inoperative, the psalmist appeals for divine intervention.

Hope in Messianic Judgment. The key figure in turning all this around would be none other than the Davidic messiah.[2] For starters, the coming messiah was expected to purge the false priests from the temple. "Look, O Lord, and raise up for them their king, the Son of David . . . that he may shatter unrighteous rulers and purge Jerusalem from gentiles that trample her down to destruction" (17:21–22). Here the term "gentiles" is used not as an ethnic but a moral label, designating Israel's officials as functional pagans. Drawing on Psalm 2, the psalmist envisions the messiah clearing God's inheritance of gentile-style sinners (17:23; cf. Ps 2:8), smashing "sinners as a potter's vessel" (17:23; cf. Ps 2:9) and "with a rod of iron, he shall entirely break them into pieces" (17:24; cf. Ps 2:9). But the goal of all this was

---

1. Translations from the Psalms of Solomon are an adaptation of the translation provided by R. H. Charles, *The Apocrypha and Pseudepigrapha of the Old Testament*, 2 vols. (Oxford: Clarendon, 1913), 2:625–52.

2. For a focused treatment on comparisons between the Davidic messiah as presented in the Psalms of Solomon and in the Gospel of Mark, see chapter 23 in this volume by Mark L. Strauss ("Psalms of Solomon and Mark 12:28–44: The Messiah's Surprising Identity and Role").

not judgment for judgment's sake but cultic purity, for the messiah would "purge Jerusalem, making it holy as of old" (17:30). Clearly the author of the Psalms of Solomon expected God's anointed, **eschatological** agent to "clean house," with a view to recovering a fully operational sacred space.

Praying in the Kingdom. Although we cannot be entirely certain how the Psalms of Solomon functioned in the original liturgical setting, the community behind it was clearly interested in lifting up prayers for protection and judgment. First, in quest for divine refuge the psalmist repeatedly draws a line from the community's beleaguered situation, prompted by its dissent, to the necessity of prayer: "When we are in distress we call on you for help" (5:5; cf. 15:1). This is consistent with what we can reconstruct from other **Second Temple** Jewish sources, which report that open challenges to the regnant priestly system would often leave the dissidents paying dearly for their opposition. Second, the psalmist's prayers also have an imprecatory character. An extended prayer directed against the community's enemies is found in 4:14–25; a similar sentiment is more succinctly stated in the plea, "Don't delay, O God, in recompensing them on their heads" (2:25). For the community behind the Psalms of Solomon, the bridge to the coming of the kingdom was to be paved with prayers for protection and prayers of judgment against the community's godless persecutors.

Mark 11:12–25

"Is It Not Written: 'My House Will Be Called a House of Prayer for All Nations'? But You Have Made It a 'Den of Robbers'"

When we look at Mark 11:12–25 through the lenses provided by the Psalms of Solomon, a handful of enigmas begin to come into focus. At the beginning of this chapter, we raised three questions regarding Mark's text:

1. Why did Jesus curse the fig tree?
2. Why did Jesus cleanse the temple?
3. What is the connection between Jesus's words in 11:22–25 and Peter's discovery of the fig tree?

By paying attention to the undergirding logic of the earlier, Second Temple Jewish text, we can begin to resolve these one at a time, though not necessarily in this order.

Drawing Attention to the Sacrilege. Mark the evangelist wastes no time: as early as Mark 1:1 Jesus is introduced as the anointed one, the royal-priestly messiah (Christ). From there Jesus undergoes a messianic baptism (1:9–11), performs numerous messianic signs (1:40–2:12; 3:1–6, 13–19; 4:35–5:43; etc.), and is climactically named messiah by his lead disciple (8:27–30). Yet throughout the Gospel Jesus is largely opposed for his messianic claims. Ironically, the most intense opposition—murderous in its depth (3:6; 11:18)—comes from the temple officials. Now if the priests' chief job was to maintain the sanctity of the temple, and that sanctity had been compromised, not least through the priests' failure to receive Jesus as the true high priest, then both the offending priesthood *and* the profaned temple itself need to be dealt with.[3] Although commentators and preachers alike will often suggest that Jesus's temple action was a protest against either the commercialization of religion or, alternatively, the principal exclusion of gentiles, it is much more likely that Mark's Jesus undertakes his dramatic temple action, much like the messiah of the Psalms of Solomon did, with the goal of declaring the temple's radical profanation.

The Imminence of Messianic Judgment. In the Psalms of Solomon we saw how the covenantal standing of the priesthood could not be entirely dissociated from the spiritual health of the people: as goes the priesthood, so goes the people who follow their lead. I think this is essentially Mark's point when he records Jesus cursing the fig tree. In Judaism the fig tree was commonly used to symbolize God's people Israel (Hos 9:10; Joel 1:7), a nation tasked with bearing spiritual fruit. Now confronting a spiritually sterile people of God, Jesus declares that the nation, like the temple itself, stands under judgment.

Such judgment is symbolized in two ways. First, Mark's Jesus is described as "driving out" the officials of the ruling priests (Mark 11:15), much as the psalmist's messiah was expected to purge the wicked priests of his day. Second, Jesus's symbolic cursing of the fig tree indicates that the nation, insofar as it was attached to the corrupt priesthood, was likewise subject to a curse. This does not mean that God intended to replace Israel with the church but rather that the God of Mark's Jesus would establish a new plantation that would produce an extraordinary crop appropriate to the people of God (4:20; 12:9). Or, as the author of the Psalms of Solomon puts it in reference to his own community: "Their planting is rooted for ever. They will not be plucked

---

3. At the same time, Mark would likely see the profanation of the temple as being also directly connected with specific behaviors on the part of the priests; see Nicholas Perrin, *Jesus the Temple* (London: SPCK; Grand Rapids: Baker Academic, 2010), 92–113.

up all the days of heaven" (14:4). The temple action and the cursing of the fig tree are interconnected as decisive acts of messianic judgment.

Praying in the Kingdom. In his temple action, Jesus insists with some help from Isaiah 56:7 that the purpose of the temple was for it to be "a house of prayer for all nations" (Mark 11:17).[4] One of the reasons for the temple's existence, at least according to Jesus, was prayer. And so it is fitting that if Jesus one day declares the imminent destruction of the temple, then the next day finds him calling his followers to prayer and forgiveness in order that they might *function as the new and better temple* (11:22–25). For Jesus, as for the author of the Psalms of Solomon (Pss. Sol. 9:6, 8), the distinguishing mark of the continuing remnant—the true temple people within Israel—was their commitment to prayer.

Of course, Jesus is aware that as soon as his followers claim to be the new locus of God's presence they would be persecuted (Mark 13:9–13), even as Jesus himself is persecuted after the temple cleansing (11:18). For Mark's Jesus, as for the psalmist, it was crucial to respond to such persecution prayerfully. This is made clear when Jesus enjoins prayerful vigilance, especially in the face of impending persecution (13:32–36). In our immediate passage, when Jesus imagines the disciples praying that "this mountain" be thrown into the sea (11:23), he is issuing a warrant to pray against the Mount-Zion-based temple elite who would—as history would confirm—soon be hounding his followers for decades to come. In contrast to the Psalms of Solomon, which calls for divine protection and retribution against the community's enemies, Mark's Jesus calls for forgiveness and the removal of the temple. But both the evangelist and the psalmist agree on this: the persecuted, righteous remnant must *pray* in order that God's eschatological purposes might be realized.

The connections between the Psalms of Solomon and Mark 11:12–25 are as multiplex as they are fascinating. Both the psalmist and Mark anticipated a Jerusalem-based, messianic judgment against the wicked. In light of the link between the apostasy of priesthood and the apostasy of the people in the Psalms of Solomon, we have added reason to suppose that the cursing of the fig tree relates to national-level disobedience, precisely as an extension of the priesthood's sin. Second, if for the psalmist the disobedience of the

---

4. The other Scripture that Jesus quotes at his temple cleansing is Jer 7:11 (a passage in which Jeremiah foretells the destruction of the sanctuary in response to national disobedience). Interestingly, Jer 7 is also one of the most oft-quoted chapters of Scripture in Pss. Sol.; cf. Kenneth Atkinson, *An Intertextual Study of the Psalms of Solomon: Pseudepigrapha*, SBEC 49 (Lewiston, NY: Mellen, 2001), 72, 89, 90, 209, 214, 271, 273, 313, 324, and 326.

priests resulted in the temple's desecration, this helps us understand the forceful intensity behind Jesus's cleansing of the temple: through his actions Jesus was intimating nothing less than the tragic profanation of Israel's sacred space. Third, given the prominence of prayer in the Psalms of Solomon, we can now begin to make sense of what otherwise seems a curious change of topics in Mark. In response to the persecution that would soon fall on their heads (partly on account of the cleansing of the temple), Jesus's followers would have to double down in maintaining their faith, persisting in prayer, and forgiving "anyone" (11:25), even their fiercest opponents. Religious dissent was no easy business in Second Temple Judaism. The authors of the Psalms of Solomon and the Gospel of Mark are both interested in helping their audiences live a God-honoring life, even while enduring fierce opposition from those outside their respective protest movements.

FOR FURTHER READING

Additional Ancient Texts

Criticism of the priesthood was not limited to either early Christianity or the Psalms of Solomon sect. In the **Dead Sea** literature, criticism of the official temple is rampant; see, e.g., CD; 1QS; 1QpHab; 4Q171. But charges of a general nature are easy enough to find in other documents too, e.g., 1 Enoch 89–90; T. Levi 14:1–6; Jub. 23:21. Both **Josephus** (*Ant.* 20.197–203) and the author of the Testament of Levi (16:1–3) speak to priests' cruel severity. Embezzlement from the temple funds was also a common charge; see 4Q390 frag. 2; Targum 1 Samuel 2:17; 29:29; b. Pesaḥ. 57a; t. Menaḥ. 13 (cf. Rom 2:21–22).

English Translations and Critical Editions

Kim, H. C. *Psalms of Solomon: A New Translation and Introduction*. Highland Park, NJ: Hermit Kingdom, 2008.

Wright, Robert B. "The Psalms of Solomon." Pages 639–70 in *The Old Testament Pseudepigrapha*. Vol. 2. Edited by James H. Charlesworth. Garden City, NY: Doubleday, 1985.

———, ed. *The Psalms of Solomon: A Critical Edition of the Greek Text*. JCT 1. New York: T&T Clark, 2007.

Secondary Literature

Atkinson, Kenneth. *I Cried to the Lord: A Study of the Psalms of Solomon's Historical Background and Social Setting*. JSJSup 84. Leiden: Brill, 2004.

Embry, B. "The *Psalms of Solomon* and the New Testament: Intertextuality and the Need for a Re-Evaluation." *JSP* 13 (2002): 99–136.

Evans, C. A. "Jesus and the 'Cave of Robbers': Toward a Jewish Context for the Temple Action." Pages 345–65 in *Jesus and His Contemporaries: Comparative Studies*. AGJU 25. Leiden: Brill, 1995 [1993].

Watts, Rikki. "The Lord's House and David's Lord: The *Psalms* and Mark's Perspective on Jesus and the Temple." *Biblical Interpretation* 15 (2007): 307–22.

Willitts, Joel. "Matthew and *Psalms of Solomon*'s Messianism: A Comparative Study in First-Century Messianology." *BBR* 22 (2012): 27–50.

CHAPTER 21

The Animal Apocalypse and Mark 11:27–12:12: The Rejection of the Prophets and the Destruction of the Temple

DAVID L. TURNER

Reading Mark 11:27–12:12 in context shows that the passage has two segments. The first (11:27–33) narrates Jesus's conflict with the Jerusalem leaders over his authority. This conflict emanated from the temple clearing (11:15–19), which is "sandwiched" between Jesus's cursing of the fig tree (11:12–14) and the subsequent discovery that the cursed tree had withered (11:20–25). The second segment (12:1–12) narrates Jesus's parable of the tenant farmers, which portrays tenants repeatedly rejecting the authority of the landowner. Jesus answers the leaders' question about his authority (11:27–28) in two ways, with a dialogical argument (11:29–33) and with a prophetic parable of judgment (12:1–11). As a result, they plan to arrest him (12:12).

Mark's teaching on Jesus's authority begins by showing how Jesus's authoritative teaching and activities differed from that of the entrenched legal teachers (1:22, 27) and led to conflict with them (2:1–12). Jesus delegated his authority to his twelve apostles (3:15; 6:7). One of Jesus's final teachings reminded his disciples that they must faithfully and alertly exercise this authority until his return (13:34).[1] And so, in its *literary* context Jesus's authority is the basis of his conflict with Israel's leaders in the temple.

---

1. The NIV's rendering of 13:34, "[he] puts his servants in charge, each with their assigned task," could be rendered "he gives *authority* to his servants, to each one a task."

Reading this passage in its *canonical* context shows its quotations, allusions, and echoes of the Old Testament.[2] The quotations of Isaiah 5:1–2 (in Mark 12:1) and Psalm 118:22–23 (in Mark 12:10–11) frame the tenant-farmer parable and help with its interpretation. Isaiah's song of the vineyard (Isa 5:1–2) describes how a vineyard was laboriously prepared by clearing the land, planting choice vines, building a tower, and cutting a winepress into the rock.[3] Ironically, the vineyard only produced bad fruit. Similarly, God faithfully cared for Israel, but Israel produced injustice and unrighteousness (5:3–7). The destroyed vineyard stands for God's judgment on Israel (5:3–7). Psalm 118 reflects on victory over enemies (Ps 118:5–18) in the setting of temple worship (118:19–20, 26–27). During Jesus's triumphal entry the crowd's "hosanna!" shout echoes 118:25–26, expressing deep longing for God to deliver Israel through Jesus the Davidic king (Mark 11:9–10). Jesus quotes Psalm 118:22–23 at the conclusion to the tenant-farmer parable, metaphorically describing how God will reverse his rejection by the leaders. Jesus likely reflected on the psalmist's struggles and ultimate vindication as anticipatory of his own.[4]

Reading the passage in its *interpretive* context involves reading how others before Jesus and Mark had reflected on these seminal OT texts. Among the Jewish texts that allude to Isaiah 5,[5] 1 Enoch's so-called Animal Apocalypse will be examined here. This text appears to allude to Isaiah 5:1–7, just as Mark does. As we shall see, its portrayal of Israel's historic resistance to God's authority resonates with Mark's narrative of the religious leaders' resistance to Jesus.

The Animal Apocalypse

"He Sent Them to the Sheep, but the Sheep Began to Slay Them"

The Animal Apocalypse, or "animal vision," spans chapters 85–90 of 1 Enoch's Book of Dream Visions (1 En. 83–90).[6]

---

2. Richard B. Hays, *Echoes of Scripture in the Gospels* (Waco, TX: Baylor University Press, 2016), 10–13. The three terms amount to a spectrum of the degree of a text's dependence on earlier texts, whether overt (quotations), implicit (allusions), or faint (echoes).

3. Similar vineyard imagery is found elsewhere in the OT (e.g., Ps 80; Jer 2:21; 6:9; 12:10–13; Ezek 19:10–14; Hos 10:1–2).

4. Additional allusions and echoes occur in the passage. For example, Mark 12:6 echoes Gen 22:2. Even Mark's narrative linkage of a fig tree and a vineyard echoes the common OT pairing of vine and fig tree to describe either the absence (Jer 8:13; Hos 2:12; Ps 105:33) or presence (1 Kgs 4:25; Mic 4:4; Zech 3:10) of *shalom*, God's covenantal blessing.

5. See also, e.g., 4Q262, 4Q500 (Benediction), t. Sukkah 3:15.

6. For more background on 1 Enoch, see chapter 2 in this volume by Kristian A. Bendoraitis.

The text allegorically envisions history from Adam to the end of time by using animals such as cows and sheep for Israel with rams and bulls standing for Israel's leaders. Israel's enemies are portrayed as predators such as dogs, lions, leopards, wolves, and raptors. These figures are used in 89:11–90:12 to survey the major events of Israel's history from patriarchal times to the days of Judah the Maccabee. The narrative concludes with the final judgment not only of Israel's enemies (90:18–19) but also of unfaithful Israel itself, along with their unfaithful shepherds (90:22–27). Finally, a new and larger "house" replaces the old one (90:28–29), and in it Israel's former enemies assemble with the Jews (90:33–36) in reverence of a horned messianic figure (90:37–38).

Israel as Sheep. Although the larger biblical use of lost-sheep imagery evokes compassion (including Mark 6:34; 14:27), in 1 Enoch there is little sympathy for the blind(ed) sheep. Nickelsburg helpfully comments, "The main part of the vision takes a dim view of Israelite history, which is portrayed as continued rebellion and apostasy (the sheep are blind and wander from the right path) that is punished by Gentile oppression."[7] Sheep become the prominent metaphor at 89:12, where twelve sheep stand for the sons of Jacob, who give one of their number (Joseph) to the donkeys (Ishmaelites), who then give him to the wolves (Egyptians). Israel's sin at the time of the giving of the law (Exodus 32) is emphasized:

> [32] And that sheep which led them [Moses] again ascended to the summit of that rock, but the sheep began to be blinded and to wander from the way which he had showed them, but that sheep did not realize it. [33] And the Lord of the sheep was wrathful exceedingly against them, and that sheep discovered it, and went down from the summit of the rock, and came to the sheep, and found the greatest part of them blinded and fallen away. (1 En. 89:32–33)[8]

Although the sheep with opened eyes soon enjoy the beauty and glory of the promised land (89:40), their eyesight dims during the period of the judges (89:41). Later they stray from God, abandon his house, and kill the sheep (the prophets) God sends to help them: "the Lord of the sheep called some from amongst the sheep and sent them to the sheep, but the sheep

---

7. George W. E. Nickelsburg, "The Temple According to 1 Enoch," *BYU Studies Quarterly* 53 (2014): 1–18, at 7. Available at: http://scholarsarchive.byu.edu/byusq/vol53/iss1/3.

8. The translation here and in following excerpts is adapted from R. H. Charles, ed., *The Apocrypha and Pseudepigrapha of the Old Testament*, 2 vols. (Oxford: Clarendon, 1913), 2:163–281.

began to slay them" (89:51; cf. 89:52–53; 90:6–7). At this point, "when they abandoned the house of the Lord and his tower, they went astray completely and their eyes became blindfolded" (89:54).

The House of the Lord and His Tower. After Israel enters the land, the tabernacle is called "a house for the Lord of the sheep" (89:36, 40). Subsequently 1 Enoch speaks of both the Lord's "house" and its "tower" (89:36, 40, 50, 54, 56, 66–67, 73). These terms are somewhat ambiguous, but most scholars take "house" as a reference to the city of Jerusalem and the "tower" as a reference to the temple. Other early Jewish texts interpret the vineyard tower of Isaiah 5:1 as Solomon's Temple.[9] The most detailed "house" text is 1 Enoch 89:50:

> And that house became great and broad, and it was built for those sheep. A great, lofty tower was built on the house of the Lord for that sheep [Solomon], and that house was low, but the tower was elevated and lofty, and the Lord of the sheep stood on the tower, and they offered a full table before him.

Unfortunately, the sheep soon abandon the house and tower, leading God to abandon them, the city, and the tower (89:56). Eventually, the "lions" (Babylonians) "burnt that tower and demolished that house" (89:66–67). Enoch views the subsequent building of the Second Temple negatively (89:72–73), but later speaks glowingly at some length about the old house being pulled down and replaced by a spacious new house where the sheep and their former predators dwell together in peace (90:28–36; 91:13). The conspicuous absence of a tower in this last passage is somewhat similar to the depiction of the New Jerusalem in Revelation 21:22: "I did not see a temple in the city, because the Lord God Almighty and the Lamb are its temple."

The Animal Apocalypse repeatedly mentions Jerusalem and its temple, covering both the building and destruction of the First Temple as well as the rebuilt Second Temple and its ultimate transformation. The Animal Apocalypse likely agrees with other Second Temple texts in viewing the tower in Isaiah 5:2 as a veiled reference to the temple. All this provides context for reading Jesus's later conflicts with the Jewish leaders in that same temple.

---

9. Such texts include Tg. Isa. 5:2, t. Meʿil. 1:16; t. Sukkah 3:15; cf. Barn. 16:5, which describes the temple as a tower, perhaps alluding to 1 En. 89:55–56.

Mark 11:27–12:12

"So They Took Him and Killed Him, and Threw Him Out of the Vineyard"

Questioning Jesus's Authority. Mark 11:27–12:12 should be understood as the sequel to Jesus's entry into Jerusalem and his clearing of the temple. These two events provoke the leaders' question about Jesus's authority, which leads to Jesus's twofold answer involving a testy dialogue (11:27–33) and a parable (12:1–12). The chiastic structure of the larger passage, in which the temple action is "nested" or "sandwiched" between the two fig-tree episodes, can be visualized as follows (see figure 21.1):

Figure 21.1: The Chiastic Structure of Mark 11:1–12:12

A. Jesus the triumphant Davidic king enters Jerusalem (Mark 11:1–11; Ps 118:25–26)

    B. The fruitless fig tree is cursed (Mark 11:12–14; Jer 8:13)

        C. Jesus clears the temple (Mark 11:15–19; Isa 56:7; Jer 7:11)

    B¹. The withered fig tree is discovered (Mark 11:20–25; Jer 8:13)

A¹. Jesus the rejected but vindicated Davidic king (Mark 11:27–12:12; Ps 118:22–23)

Jesus's bold temple action provokes the leaders' question about the source of his authority, recalling Mark 2:6–12 and 3:22–30. Although they may claim not to know the answer to Jesus's question about the source of John's authority (11:33), they know full well that they are the recalcitrant farmers of Jesus's parable (12:12). They lack the nerve to answer Jesus publicly, yet they secretly plan to do away with him (11:31–32; 12:12).

Indicting Israel's Leaders. The failure of the Jewish leaders to answer Jesus's question (11:30–33) leads him to tell a parable about the relationship between a vineyard owner and his unruly tenant farmers (12:1–9). The landowner's repeated sending of servants to the vineyard to collect fruit from the tenant farmers represents God repeatedly sending prophets to Israel, especially to Israel's leaders, who reject them. Unlike the vineyard song of Isaiah 5, Jesus's parable indicts the leaders of Israel, not the nation as a whole, and explains God's plan to dispose of Israel's existing leadership and to give oversight of his people to "others" (12:9), namely to Jesus and his apostles.[10] The landowner ultimately sending his son represents God sending Jesus as his ultimate prophet (Mark 6:4, 15; cf. Matt 23:29–36; Luke 11:47–51).[11] As the rejected stone of Psalm 118:22, Jesus is crucified, but he is vindicated by the resurrection, which installs him as the cornerstone of the people of God, pictured elsewhere in the NT as a new temple indwelt by God through the Spirit (cf. John 2:21; 4:19–24; Eph 2:11–22; 1 Pet 2:4–8).

First Enoch's symbolic narrative of OT history has several affinities with Mark 11:27–12:12. Their common referent is the rejection of the prophets. First Enoch refers to the OT teaching that rejection of the prophets led to the destruction of Solomon's Temple. Jesus's words in Mark imply that the same pattern is about to be repeated. Mark has made it clear that the majority of Israel's leaders do not respond to Jesus's authoritative prophetic call: "The time has come. . . . The kingdom of God has come near. Repent and believe the good news" (Mark 1:15). Israel's leaders refuse to accept Jesus's prophetic authority. They will arrest and crucify him (12:12; 14:1–2, 10, 43–44, 53–65; 15:9). The Second Temple will be destroyed (13:2).

Despite all this, Mark shares the ultimately positive view of 1 Enoch on the future (Mark 13:26; 14:62; 16:6–7).[12] The rejected stone will become the cornerstone (see figure 21.2 below). As Mark concludes, there is a hopeful sign. The prominent Jewish leader Joseph of Arimathea (cf. Matt 27:57–61; Luke 23:50–53; John 19:38–42) goes to Pilate, receives permission to care for Jesus's body, and buries him in his own tomb. Joseph may have previously been among those who condemned Jesus (Mark 14:64; 15:1; though see Luke 23:51), but now he is described as one who is "waiting for the kingdom of God" (Mark 15:43). Joseph, along with the centurion at the cross who said, "Surely this man was the Son of God" (15:39), shows that Jesus's vindication has begun. His rejection and crucifixion is giving way to vindication even before the resurrection. What the Lord is doing, as the psalmist put it, really is "marvelous in our eyes" (Ps 118:23; Mark 12:11).

---

10. See the argument to this effect in Robert H. Gundry, *Mark: A Commentary on His Apology for the Cross* (Grand Rapids: Eerdmans, 1993), 688–89.

11. For a broad discussion of the rejected-prophet theme in biblical theology, see David L. Turner, *Israel's Ultimate Prophet: Jesus and the Jewish Leaders in Matthew 23* (Minneapolis: Fortress, 2015). Matthew's version of the parable of the tenants (21:33–46) is discussed on pp. 225–51.

12. It must not be forgotten that Isaiah also ends well! The dismal words of judgment against Israel in Isa 1–5 are occasionally broken by oracles of hope, focusing on God's renewed presence with his people in the temple in Jerusalem (Isa 2:1–5; 4:2–5). Isa 40:1–5 provides the keynote of the Gospel of Mark (Mark 1:3). The ultimate glory of Jerusalem is portrayed in such Isaianic texts as 52:9: "Burst into songs of joy together, you ruins of Jerusalem, for the LORD has comforted his people, he has redeemed Jerusalem."

Figure 21.2

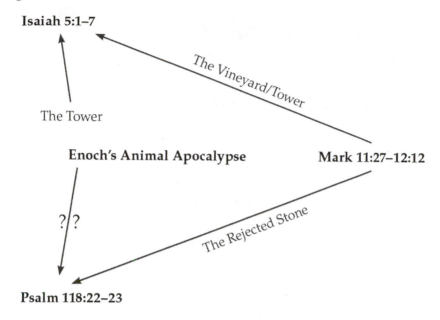

Isaiah 5:1–7

The Vineyard/Tower

The Tower

Enoch's Animal Apocalypse   **Mark 11:27–12:12**

?/?

The Rejected Stone

Psalm 118:22–23

For Further Reading

Additional Ancient Texts

Two Qumran texts, 4Q162 and 4Q500 1 [Benediction], are relevant to this study. 4Q162 alludes to Isaiah 5 and blames the "men of mockery in Jerusalem" for the coming judgment of Jerusalem and the temple. 4Q500 1 is very fragmentary, but it appears to be a benediction that interprets Isaiah 5 as referring to the Jerusalem Temple. Two texts from the Tosefta (t. Me'il. 1:16; t. Sukkah 3:15) also interpret Isaiah 5 as a reference to the temple. The Testament of Solomon (22:7; 23:1–4) alludes to Psalm 118:22. The Testament of Solomon is perhaps as late as the third-century AD and has Christian interpolations. The Psalms Targum interprets Psalm 118:22–29 as a reference to King David, apparently reading it against the narrative of 1 Samuel 16:1–13. The early Christian work Barnabas (16:5) apparently alludes to 1 Enoch 89:55–56 in its reference to the temple as a tower. Barnabas is typically dated in the first quarter of the second-century AD.

English Translations and Critical Editions

Isaac, E. "1 (Ethiopic Apocalypse of) Enoch: A New Translation and Introduction." Pages 5–89 in vol. 1 of *The Old Testament Pseudepigrapha*. Edited by James H. Charlesworth. New York: Doubleday, 1983.

Knibb, Michael A. *The Ethiopic Book of Enoch*. 2 vols. Oxford: Clarendon, 1978.

Nickelsburg, George W. E., and James C. VanderKam. *1 Enoch: The Hermeneia Translation*. Minneapolis: Fortress, 2012.

Secondary Literature

Berder, M. *"La Pierre rejetée par les bâtisseuers": Psaume 118,22–23 et son emploi dans les traditions juives et dans le Nouveau Testament*. Etudes Bibliques 31. Paris: Gabalda, 1996.

Evans, Craig A. "God's Vineyard and Its Caretakers." Pages 381–406 in *Jesus and His Contemporaries: Comparative Studies*. AGJU 25. Leiden: Brill, 1995.

Kloppenborg, John S. *The Tenants in the Vineyard: Ideology, Economics, and Agrarian Conflict in Jewish Palestine*. WUNT 195. Tübingen: Mohr Siebeck, 2006.

Nickelsburg, George W. E. *1 Enoch 1: A Commentary on the Book of 1 Enoch Chapters 1–36; 81–108*. Hermeneia. Minneapolis: Fortress, 2001.

———, and James C. VanderKam. *1 Enoch 2: A Commentary on 1 Enoch Chapters 37–82*. Hermeneia. Minneapolis: Fortress, 2011.

Olson, Daniel C. *A New Reading of the Animal Apocalypse of 1 Enoch. "All Nations Shall be Blessed."* SVTP 24. Leiden: Brill, 2013.

CHAPTER 22

Josephus and Mark 12:13–27: The Sadducees, Resurrection, and the Law

JASON MASTON

Throughout Mark's Gospel Jesus interacts with many different Jewish groups. In 11:27–12:34, Mark presents Jesus engaging with several of these groups: the temple authorities, the **Pharisees**, the **Herodians**, the **Sadducees**, and the scribes. These exchanges are important to Mark's storyline because (1) they advance an account of Jesus's relationship to the temple and the Jewish rulers, and (2) they help to explain why Jesus is rejected by the leaders. The focus of this brief essay is on the two middle exchanges in 12:13–27.

In the first pericope (12:13–17), the Pharisees and the Herodians attempt to trap Jesus by questioning him about whether one should pay taxes to Caesar. The combination of these two groups, which has already happened in 3:6, is interesting because they held differing opinions about Roman rule. The Herodians were pro-Rome. The Pharisees, while not as anti-Rome as the **Zealots**, were not friends of Rome.[1] Jesus outwits them by exposing their hypocrisy. They not only have in their possession a Roman coin with Caesar's image on it, but they have failed to understand the relationship between God and civil governments. In the second pericope (12:18–27), the Sadducees also try to trap Jesus, this time with a riddle about the resurrection, marriage, and the Mosaic Torah. The previous interchange about how

---

1. Josephus writes about the "fourth philosophy," often understood as the Zealots, that "they agree with the opinions of the Pharisees in all things, except that they have a passion for liberty that is hard to conquer, since they hold that God alone is their ruler and master" (*Ant.* 18.23). All translations of Josephus in this essay are the author's own.

197

one should interact with a pagan government is more straightforward, but when we consider Jesus's interchange with the Sadducees the question is a bit odd and can only be understood by exploring the beliefs and approach of the Sadducees further. This study, then, will focus on the beliefs of the Sadducees as described by Josephus, who provides several statements about the Sadducees' beliefs.

Josephus on the Sadducees
"THE SOUL PERISHES WITH THE BODY"

Josephus was a Jewish historian who lived in the latter half of the first century. He served as a general in the Jewish revolt against Rome (AD 66–70) before switching sides to the Romans and was granted freedom by Emperor Vespasian. Through the support of the Flavians, Josephus wrote his major works, particularly an account of the Jewish war with Rome (*Jewish War*) and a history of the Jewish people (*Antiquities*). At one point in the *Antiquities*, he describes the four main Jewish religious groups, one of which is the Sadducees. He writes about them: "The teaching of the Sadducees is that the soul perishes with the body. They do not keep any observance apart from the laws" (*Ant.* 18.16). Two features of this statement are directly relevant to Jesus's encounter with the Sadducees in Mark 12:18–27.

Rejection of Resurrection. First, Josephus remarks that the Sadducees reject resurrection when he writes "the soul perishes with the body." He writes in his account of the Jewish revolt a similar statement: "They do away with the permanence of the soul, and punishments and rewards in Hades" (*J.W.* 2.165). Josephus uses this language of immortality and the soul to put the idea of resurrection into the vernacular of his Roman and Greek readers. There was widespread discussion among non-Jews about the eternality of the soul, but the belief that dead bodies would be brought back to life made little sense to many Greeks and Romans.[2] Thus, while using language that his audience would understand, Josephus indicates that the Sadducees rejected belief in the resurrection of the body.

The Mosaic Torah as Divine Revelation. Second, unlike the Pharisees and the other Jewish groups, the Sadducees only accepted the Mosaic Torah as divine revelation. Elsewhere Josephus explains that the Sadducees rejected

---

2. Cf. Acts 17 and 1 Corinthians 15, which both indicate how resurrection struck Greeks as bizarre.

the "tradition of the fathers" passed on by the Pharisees because these were "not written in the law of Moses." The Sadducees maintain that it is only "necessary to consider the written laws and not to keep those things from the tradition of the fathers" (*Ant.* 13.297). The dispute here concerns not merely interpretations of the Torah but where authority ultimately resides. The Sadducees looked only to the Mosaic Torah for guidance in practice and belief.

These two theological claims go hand in hand. The Old Testament contains very little clear evidence for a doctrine of resurrection. Daniel 12:2–3 is probably the most overt text. Other texts, such as Job 19:26, Psalm 16:9–11, Isaiah 26:19, and Ezekiel 37:1–14, can be read, and often were, with reference to the resurrection, but it is unclear if this was the original intent. Moreover, since these texts are not in the Torah, the Sadducees probably did not give them much weight. The belief in a resurrection is, at first sight, difficult to establish from the Torah. The Sadducees' acceptance of Moses alone reinforced their denial of resurrection. It is precisely these two points that lead to the conflict with Jesus.

Mark 12:13–27

"HAVE YOU NOT READ IN THE BOOK OF MOSES"

Since the Sadducees reject resurrection, their question to Jesus in Mark 12:19–23 is not that of an eager student seeking clarity. Rather, they aim to expose the folly of belief in resurrection by highlighting the legal (and practical) problems it creates. They describe a disastrous situation in which a woman's husband dies before she bears any children. In the ancient world, this presented multiple problems, one of which was the lack of an heir. In Jewish practice the solution was for the woman to marry the next available brother. She would not only be protected within the family but through the brother could bear children who would continue the family line. But the problem, as the Sadducees' story goes, is that this second brother dies, along with the third, fourth, and so on, until the woman herself dies. They pose the question to Jesus then that if resurrection is true, whose wife will she be?

As tragic as the Sadducees' story appears, the concern is not with the ending of marriages by death or even the social pressures that arise from the lack of an heir. Rather, their real concern is with the legal code of the levirate marriage law (see Deut 25:5–10). The Sadducees' opening statement (Mark 12:19) alludes to Deuteronomy 25:5: "If brothers are living together and one of them dies without a son, his widow must not marry outside the family. Her husband's brother shall take her and marry her and fulfill the duty of a brother-in-law to her." Their question is simple: In light of the Mosaic law that required this practice, whose wife will she be in the next age? Their question assumes that the marital practices of the "supposed" resurrection age will mirror those of the present age. More importantly, their position assumes the ultimate authority of the Mosaic Torah in both the present age and the next. Their story of this unfortunate woman brings to the fore a tension between the belief in the resurrection and the validity of the Torah. If the Torah commandment of levirate marriage remains applicable, which it must, then this creates a bizarre situation that violates other laws about adultery. For the Sadducees, then, the solution is clear and obvious: resurrection is a false belief for it conflicts with the commandments given by Moses.

When compared to Josephus's portrayal of the Sadducees, several features of the Markan passage stand out. For example, Josephus and Mark agree on the nature of the Sadducees' beliefs about resurrection and the ultimate authority of the Torah. More significantly, though, it is easier to understand why Jesus responds the way he does.

Understanding the Nature of the Resurrection. In his response, Jesus begins by rejecting the problem outright because the Sadducees do not understand the nature of resurrection. In the resurrection age, marriage will not operate the same way since humans will not be married but rather will be like the angels. Jesus's response is, unfortunately, not entirely clear to us today. It should not be understood as a rejection of sexed bodies, nor as an indication that humans will become only male (all angels in Jewish tradition are male). Rather, it is probably an indication that marriage will no longer be required because procreation will be unnecessary. This initial response addresses the problem concerning which husband the woman in the story would have been given: the implicit answer is none. Jesus's response is based on the notion that the present age and the future age are not identical. There is similarity, of course, but not a one-to-one correspondence. Nevertheless, this part of Jesus's answer would not have mattered to the Sadducees since it presumes resurrection.

Reading the Torah Correctly. More to the point, then, Jesus tackles the issue head-on: "Have you not read in the book of Moses" (Mark 12:26). Knowing that the Sadducees only accept the Torah, Jesus confronts them by challenging their reading of the Torah. Whereas the Sadducees rely on the legal portions of the Torah, the commandments, Jesus draws attention to God's announcement of his own identity. Jesus calls on the experience of

Moses—the one who would receive the law—when God first made himself known. He quotes to the Sadducees Exodus 3:6: "I am the God of Abraham, the God of Isaac, and the God of Jacob." In its original context, this is God's announcement of his identity when Moses approached the burning bush.

Following his quotation of Exodus 3:6, Jesus interprets the text with relevance to the issue of resurrection: "He is not the God of the dead, but of the living" (Mark 12:27). The meaning of this statement is disputed since it seems to indicate a belief in immortality but not necessarily resurrection. That is, the statement indicates that the patriarchs are presently alive since God is the God of the living. If they are presently alive, though, this occurs without or prior to the resurrection. This reading, however, treats the statement as an abstract propositional claim about the nature of God rather than reading it in the context, which is concerned with resurrection. The statement probably means that the patriarchs are "living" in the sense that they will at some point be brought back to life. Death is not their permanent state. Because God is the God of the living, one can be certain that he will eventually give life back to his people.

The Living God of Scripture. On the surface, the dispute between Jesus and the Sadducees is about how best to interpret Scripture. For the Sadducees the legal instructions are primary, while Jesus turns to God's statements about himself. But there is more to the matter. The issue as Jesus frames it is not merely whether there will be a resurrection nor even how best to interpret Moses, but rather the very nature of God. Is Israel's God one who gives life only in the present, or is he one who also gives life in the future? If only in the present, then he "was" the God of the patriarchs. But for Jesus, binding God to the dead and the past is unsatisfactory. He "is" the God of the living. The conjunction of the double declarations of God's identity is crucial: Scripture reveals that God is "the God of Abraham, the God of Isaac, and the God of Jacob," and it is accepted truth that he is "the God of the living." Therefore, Jesus infers, the patriarchs must live again.[3] Jesus cuts through the legal questions to the core issue: Who is Israel's God?

By turning to Exodus 3:6, Jesus's tactic is not only clever but thoroughly undercuts the Sadducees' rejection of the resurrection. Jesus exposes them as hermeneutically deficient, for they had failed to grasp the full import of this text as it relates to one of their core beliefs. Moreover, their denial of resurrection is actually a denial of Israel's God. When set against Josephus's account of the Sadducees, the core issues in Mark's portrayal of the debate

---

3. Craig A. Evans, *Mark 8:27–16:20*, WBC 34B (Grand Rapids: Zondervan, 2015), 256–57.

between Jesus and the Sadducees stand out more sharply. Mark's account is not only historically accurate but centers on two issues that distinguished the Sadducees from other Jewish groups.

FOR FURTHER READING

Additional Ancient Texts

The episodes in Mark 12:13–27 are paralleled in Matthew 22:15–33; Luke 20:20–40. The Sadducees are also mentioned in Acts 23:8 with reference to their belief about the resurrection and angels. The Sadducees' tragic story about the woman's many-deceased husbands is probably based on the account in Tobit, which is a fascinating story of a Jewish family attempting to live according to the law while in exile. Some have suggested a background in 2 Maccabees 7:10–11, but the contexts are quite different. See also the account of Judah and Tamar in Genesis 38. The rabbis reflected at length on marriage and the levirate laws: see, for example, m. Yebam. 1–4 and b. Sanh. 90b–92a.

English Translations and Critical Editions

Josephus. Translated by H. St. J. Thackeray et al. 13 vols. LCL. Cambridge: Harvard University Press, 1926–65.

Mason, Steve, ed. Flavius Josephus: Translation and Commentary. 10 vols. The Brill Josephus Project. Leiden: Brill, 2001–.

Secondary Literature

Baumbach, Günther. "The Sadducees in Josephus." Pages 173–95 in Josephus, the Bible, and History. Edited by Louis H. Feldman and Gohei Hata. Leiden: Brill, 1989.

Bolt, Peter. "What Were the Sadducees Reading? An Enquiry into the Literary Background of Mark 12:18–23." TynBul 45.2 (1994): 369–94.

Janzen, J. Gerald. "Resurrection and Hermeneutics: On Exodus 3:6 in Mark 12:26." JSNT 23 (1985): 43–58.

Mason, Steve. Josephus and New Testament. 2nd ed. Peabody, MA: Hendrickson, 2003.

Stemberger, Günter. "The Sadducees—Their History and Doctrines." Pages 428–43 in The Cambridge History of Judaism: Volume 3, The Early Roman Period. Edited by William Horbury, W. D. Davies, and John Sturdy. Cambridge: Cambridge University Press, 1999.

Trick, Bradley R. "Death, Covenants, and the Proof of Resurrection in Mark 12:18–27." NovT 49.3 (2007): 232–56.

CHAPTER 23

MARK L. STRAUSS

Christology—the identity and mission of Jesus—is on center stage throughout Mark's Gospel. The first line makes this clear: This is "the good news about Jesus the Messiah" (Mark 1:1). Mark seeks to confirm for his readers that—despite Jesus's humiliating execution as a criminal—he is indeed the **Messiah**.[1] The Gospel's structure itself serves this end. The first half of the Gospel confirms Jesus's identity as the Messiah. The key thematic word here is "authority," as Jesus demonstrates messianic authority in teaching, healing, exorcism, forgiving sins, raising the dead, and controlling the forces of nature (1:1–8:30). The narrative reaches an initial climax with Peter's confession, as this representative of the disciples comes to recognize through Jesus's authoritative words and actions that "you are the Messiah" (8:29). At this point the narrative takes a dramatic turn, as Jesus predicts his suffering and death (8:31). The Messiah's role is not to conquer the Roman legions and establish Israel's independence in the land, as most Jews hoped. It was rather to suffer and die as an atoning sacrifice for sins (10:45). The rest of the Gospel describes the way of suffering, as Jesus three times predicts his coming death (8:31; 9:31; 10:33–34) and heads toward Jerusalem to accomplish the messianic task (8:31–16:8).

The narrative returns to the theme of authority when Jesus arrives in Jerusalem (11:1–11). The reader is reminded once again of Jesus's messianic identity by blind Bartimaeus's cry to Jesus as "Son of David" (10:47, 48; a messianic

---

1. R. H. Gundry describes Mark's purpose as "an apology for the cross" (*Mark: A Commentary on His Apology for the Cross* [Grand Rapids: Eerdmans, 1993], 3–4, 1026).

title) and by the shouts of the crowd entering Jerusalem, "Blessed is the coming kingdom of our father David!" (11:10). Jesus then clears the temple in an act of messianic authority. The religious leaders challenge him, "By what *authority* are you doing these things. . . . And who gave you *authority* to do this?" (11:28). A series of controversy stories follows, as the religious leaders repeatedly challenge Jesus's authority and seek to trap and humiliate him. Again and again he confounds them, confirming his messianic authority (11:27–12:37).

The last two controversies bring us to our passage. The first is a question from a teacher of the law about the greatest commandment. Surprisingly, Jesus now finds common ground with a religious leader over the issue of the two greatest commandments, loving God and loving others (12:28–34). In the last controversy story, Jesus turns the tables on the religious leaders and poses a riddle of his own based on Psalm 110:1. How can the Messiah be *both* David's son and David's lord (Mark 12:35–37)? This is then followed by Jesus's warning against the hypocrisy, pride, and greed of the teachers of the law (12:38–40) and his commendation of a poor widow who gives all she has to support the temple (12:41–44). Despite their wealth and power, the religious leaders "devour widows' houses" (12:40), while the poor widow lives a life of humility and self-sacrifice.

The question Jesus poses about the Messiah's identity as "son of David" (12:35–37) relates to traditional Jewish expectations concerning the end-time king from the line of David. Such expectations appear in a variety of Second Temple Jewish writings, but none more clearly than in the first-century BC work known as the Psalms of Solomon.

Psalms of Solomon

"RAISE UP FOR THEM THEIR KING, THE SON OF DAVID"

The consensus view of a previous generation of biblical scholars was that there was a single clear and definable expectation associated with the Jewish "messiah." The messiah was expected to be a king from the line of David who would conquer Israel's enemies, establish God's kingdom, and reign forever in justice and righteousness.[2] Today scholars recognize that there was significantly more diversity within first-century Judaism. The title of a

---

2. See, e.g., George Foot Moore, *Judaism in the First Centuries of the Christian Era*, 3 vols. (Cambridge: Harvard University Press, 1927–30), 2:323–76.

recent volume on the subject makes this clear: *Judaisms and Their Messiahs at the Turn of the Christian Era*.[3] There was not just one Judaism but multiple sects, and a range of messianic and nonmessianic expectations within these diverse groups. Some scholars go so far as to reject a messianic idea at all, claiming that the concept of "the Messiah" is a Christian invention, created by the early church to give Jesus an identity and a pedigree.[4]

This, however, is surely pushing the pendulum back too far. Although first-century Judaism had a significant diversity of beliefs and expectations, the most widespread and pervasive messianic hope was that of the Davidic Messiah. Through the prophet Nathan, God had promised King David that he would raise up one of David's descendants after him and would establish his kingdom forever (2 Sam 7:11–16). With the decline and eventual collapse of the Davidic dynasty, Israel's prophets drew on this promise to predict the coming of an end-time king from David's line, who would reign in righteousness and justice (see Isa 9:1–7; 11:1–9, Jer 23:5–6; Ezek 34:23–24; 37:24–25; Amos 9:11; cf. Pss 2; 89; 110; 132). This hope and expectation flourished in the **Second Temple period** and can be seen in such diverse writings as the **Dead Sea Scrolls**, Jewish **apocalyptic** literature (1 Enoch; 4 Ezra; 2 Baruch, etc.), later rabbinic writings, and the Psalms of Solomon.[5]

The Psalms of Solomon are a collection of psalms written pseudonymously in Solomon's name in the latter half of the first-century BC. We can identify their likely date and setting from historical allusions found in them. The psalmist cries out against certain "sinners," who have usurped the throne of David and have defiled the temple. In response, God sent a foreign conqueror, "a man alien to our race" (17:7),[6] who laid waste the land, killed or expelled many of its citizens, and defiled Jerusalem. Most scholars believe that this conqueror was the Roman general Pompey, who subjugated Judea in 63 BC, and that the Psalms of Solomon were written shortly after this time. The "sinners" who have usurped David's throne were the priest-kings of the **Hasmonean** dynasty, whose corruption and political infighting allowed Pompey to take the city without a fight.

3. J. Neusner, W. S. Green, and E. S. Frerichs, eds., *Judaisms and Their Messiahs at the Turn of the Christian Era* (Cambridge: Cambridge University Press, 1987).

4. W. S. Green, "Messiah in Judaism: Rethinking the Question," in Neusner, Green, and Frerichs, *Judaisms and Their Messiahs*, 1–14, at 2–4.

5. See John J. Collins, *The Scepter and the Star: Messianism in Light of the Dead Sea Scrolls*, 2nd ed. (Grand Rapids: Eerdmans, 2010), 1–78. Collins writes, "The concept of the Davidic messiah as the warrior king who would destroy the enemies of Israel and institute an era of unending peace constitutes the common core of Jewish messianism around the turn of the era" (78).

6. All translations of Psalms of Solomon are the author's own.

Outraged by these atrocities, the pious psalmist cries out to God to raise up the "son of David" to defeat Israel's enemies and to establish God's justice and righteousness:

> [21] Hear us, O Lord, and raise up for them their king, the son of David,
> in the time you have determined, to rule over your servant Israel, O God!
> [22] Strengthen him with the power to destroy the unrighteous rulers,
> to purge Jerusalem from Gentiles who trample and destroy her;
> [23] With wisdom and righteousness to expel the sinners from the inheritance;
> to smash the pride of sinners like a potter's jar;
> [24] to shatter all of their confidence with an iron rod;
> to destroy the lawless nations by speaking a word;
> [25] At his rebuke the nations will flee from his presence;
> and he will condemn sinners by the thoughts of their hearts.
> (Pss. Sol. 17:21–25)

The portrayal of the Messiah in the Psalms of Solomon draws from a variety of OT passages.[7] The Messiah is presented as a king from David's line, who will rule Israel with justice and righteousness. He is a warrior king after the model of Isaiah 11:1–5 and Psalm 2:9, who will "destroy the unrighteous rulers" (Pss. Sol. 17:22) and lawless nations by merely speaking a word (17:24). Though human, he exercises divine wisdom and power through God's authority (17:24–25, 35–36). He expels sinners and unrighteous rulers by his powerful word (17:36). Though he rules peoples and nations with compassion and "with wisdom and righteousness" (17:29, 34), there is no universal salvation here. Foreigners are expelled from Israel (17:28, 36) and return only to see God's glory and pay tribute to God's people (17:31). God's blessings and salvation belong to Israel. The king will gather a holy people and lead them in righteousness (17:26). He will faithfully shepherd the Lord's flock, helping the oppressed (17:40–41). He will restore the nation's borders and redistribute the land according to the original tribal divisions (17:26, 28, 44).

The Psalms of Solomon represent the earliest known use of "son of David" (17:21) as a title for the eschatological king from David's line. This is the classic presentation of the Davidic Messiah, a warrior king who will free Israel from their oppressors and make the nation great and good once

---

7. E.g., Num 24:17; Pss 2; 89; 110; 132; Isa 11:1–5; Jer 23:5–6; 33:15–17; Ezek 34:23–24; 37:24–25.

again. It is safe to assume that most Jews of Jesus's day were hoping for and expecting this kind of Messiah.

The Jesus of Mark's Gospel, however, has painted a very different picture of his messianic role. Though he will one day return to judge and to rule (Mark 8:38; 13:26; 14:62), at his first coming he is not here to conquer Rome but to offer himself as an atoning sacrifice for sins (10:45). It is in this wider narrative context that Jesus poses the riddle of Mark 12:35–37.

Mark 12:28–44

"Why Do the Teachers of the Law Say That the Messiah Is the Son of David?"

The question of David's son (Mark 12:35–37) forms the climax and conclusion to the six controversy stories between Jesus and the religious leaders in Jerusalem. In reality, the debate is over at this point. Mark informs his readers that, after the fifth controversy, "no one dared ask him any more questions" (12:34). Jesus instead goes on the offensive by raising a question about the identity of the Messiah.

In the narrative Jesus assumes two things about Psalm 110: (1) that it is a "psalm of David" so that David is the speaker, and (2) that it is messianic, meaning God is addressing the Messiah and announcing his vindication. "The Lord said to my Lord" therefore means, "The Lord God said to David's Lord, the Messiah." The riddle Jesus then poses is how the Messiah can be both David's "son" and David's "lord"—the implication being that a son is normally subordinate to a father and that the father would not call his son "lord."

Contrary to the claim of some interpreters, it seems unlikely that the passage is a refutation of Jesus's Davidic descent or his identity as the Davidic Messiah. Bartimaeus has just referred to Jesus as "Son of David" (10:47, 48), a title Mark apparently accepts as legitimate. Similarly, the crowd at the triumphal entry cries out, "Blessed is the coming kingdom of our father David" (11:10). It is also doubtful that Mark views this as a false acclamation, especially since he repeatedly refers to Jesus as the "Messiah" (*christos*), a title which, as we have seen, carries strong Davidic connotations in first-century Judaism.

Jesus does not actually answer his own riddle. He does not say *how* the Messiah can be both David's son and David's Lord. Various answers have been suggested. (1) Some claim Jesus is David's Lord because he will one day reign over all the earth, a realm far greater than David's. (2) Others say that Jesus is David's Lord because he is indeed *the* Lord God himself. Although Mark does not have an explicit divine Christology, there is a strong implicit one.[8] (3) Still others claim that Jesus is more than David's son because he is in fact *God's Son*. The title Son of God certainly plays a key role in Mark's Gospel. It is highlighted in the prologue (1:1), at the Father's acclamation at Jesus's baptism (1:11), at the transfiguration (9:7), and then climactically in the centurion's words at the cross (15:39).

While all these are possibilities, the narrative itself leaves the question open, and the passage remains enigmatic (characteristic of Mark!). Perhaps it is best to conclude that Mark's primary point is that Jesus's identity *goes beyond traditional messianic expectations*. If we look to the narrative itself to answer how this is, the answer comes at the thematic center and turning point of Mark's Gospel (8:30–31; cf. 9:31; 10:32–45). Though Jesus is indeed the promised king from David's line, his messianic role is to suffer and die as an atoning sacrifice for sins (10:45). It is at this point that Mark's narrative differs most starkly from the messianic portrait of the Psalms of Solomon. It would be unthinkable to the authors of the Psalms of Solomon that the messiah would suffer and die without achieving victory over the gentiles and the corrupt rulers of Israel. Yet from Mark's perspective, Jesus has accomplished a much greater goal than the destruction of a few Roman legions. Through his atoning death on the cross, Jesus has defeated humanity's greatest foes—the powers of Satan, sin, and death. That is the essence of Mark's "Gospel," his *good news* for the world!

FOR FURTHER READING

Additional Ancient Texts

In addition to the Psalms of Solomon, expectations for the Davidic messiah can be found in various Dead Sea Scrolls, including 4QFlorilegium (= 4Q174); 4QCommGen A (= 4Q252); 4QpIsaᵃ (= 4Q161); 4QDibHamᵃ (= 4Q504 4); and Sefer Hamilḥamah (= 4Q285); and other Second Temple literature, including Testaments of the Twelve Patriarchs (esp. T. Jud. 24); 4 Ezra 11:1–12:39; 1 Enoch 37–71. Early Christian writings also speak of Jewish expectations for the messiah (Matt 2:4; Mark 14:61; 15:32; Luke 1:69; 2:26; 3:15; John 1:20; 7:41–42). Rabbinic writings, though somewhat later, reflect a strong tradition

---

8. This is evident in many ways: Jesus's authority to forgive sins, his reconstitution of Israel through the Twelve apostles, his authority over the wind and the waves, his provision of bread in the wilderness (God sent the manna), his ability to know people's thoughts, etc.

of expectations for an end-time king from the line of David. "Son of David" is a favorite designation among the rabbis.

English Translations and Critical Editions

Kim, H. C. *Psalms of Solomon: A New Translation and Introduction*. Highland Park, NJ: Hermit Kingdom, 2008.

Wright, Robert B. "The Psalms of Solomon." Pages 639–70 in *The Old Testament Pseudepigrapha*. Vol. 2. Edited by James H. Charlesworth. Garden City, NY: Doubleday, 1985.

———, ed. *The Psalms of Solomon: A Critical Edition of the Greek Text*. JCT 1. New York: T&T Clark, 2007.

Secondary Literature

Charlesworth, James H., ed. *The Messiah: Developments in Earliest Judaism and Christianity*. Princeton Symposium on Judaism and Christian Origins. Minneapolis: Fortress, 1992.

Collins, John J. *The Scepter and the Star: Messianism in Light of the Dead Sea Scrolls*. 2nd ed. Grand Rapids: Eerdmans, 2010.

Porter, Stanley E., ed. *The Messiah in the Old and New Testaments*. Grand Rapids: Eerdmans, 2007.

Strauss, Mark L. *The Davidic Messiah in Luke-Acts: The Promise and Its Fulfillment in Lukan Christology*. JSNTSup 110. Sheffield: Sheffield Academic Press, 1995.

CHAPTER 24

The Parables of Enoch and Mark 13:1–37: Apocalyptic Eschatology and the Coming Son of Man

JONATHAN T. PENNINGTON

Mark's entire Gospel is shocking. Starting with the hairy and bold, baptizing prophet John and ending with the bloody crucifixion and startling resurrection of Jesus, Mark tells an alarming story. It is one full of demons, sharp conflicts, amazing miracles of people healed, the mysterious multiplication of food for the hungry, and Jesus's power even over nature itself. Encountering Jesus in the Gospel of Mark is a bit like reading a graphic novel—it is action packed, profound, and full of bold, black-and-white images, leaving one breathless and full of questions like, "Who in the world is this man, Jesus?"

But there is no place in Mark's Gospel more mysterious and that leaves the reader with more questions than Mark 13:1–37, what is often called the Olivet Discourse. Unlike the other Gospels, Mark doesn't give us much of Jesus's teaching because his purpose focuses primarily on revealing who Jesus is through his actions. The primary place of Jesus's teaching in Mark is found at the end of his life, when Jesus finally reaches Jerusalem. And yet this important teaching from Jesus is far from clear in its meaning. It is given in language full of mysterious metaphors and images. It was somewhat ambiguous in Jesus's day, but even more so for today's readers because we often lack the context to understand what was being communicated.

Jesus's teaching in the Olivet Discourse is both *eschatological* and *apocalyptic*. This means that it concerns the future and final state of the world that God will bring about through Jesus (eschatological), and that it is a mystery that is not comprehended by humans on their own but must be revealed by God (apocalyptic). Key to understanding this eschatological and apocalyptic teaching from Jesus is understanding who the "Son of Man" is who will bring all of this about. We are greatly helped in understanding this by some exposure to the context of apocalyptic and eschatological teachings in Second Temple Judaism, particularly the idea of the Son of Man in the Parables of Enoch (1 En. 37–71).

The Parables of Enoch

"FROM THEN ON THERE WILL BE NOTHING THAT IS CORRUPTIBLE; FOR THE SON OF MAN HAS APPEARED"

The book we call 1 Enoch is a collection of five different books that were composed over the span of five centuries and were collected together because they all connect somehow to Enoch (and his great-grandson, Noah).[1] The last-written section of 1 Enoch, and the one most directly comparable to the New Testament, is called the Parables (or Similitudes) of Enoch, covering chapters 37–71 of 1 Enoch. This section was composed sometime between the first-century BC and first-century AD, thus it is roughly contemporary with Jesus. Scholars debate how much direct influence there might have been between the Parables of Enoch and Jesus and the Gospels. We can never know for sure, but 1 Enoch 37–71 definitely provides some insights into the conceptual and literary context of Mark 13.

There are two elements of the Parables of Enoch to highlight for our purposes in this essay: its apocalyptic worldview and its depiction of the Son of Man as eschatological judge. Here is how the Parables of Enoch begin:

> [1] The second vision which he saw, the vision of wisdom—which Enoch the son of Jared, the son of Mahalalel, the son of Cainan, the son of Enos, the son of Seth, the son of Adam, saw. [2] And this is the beginning of the words of wisdom which I lifted up my voice to speak and say to those who dwell on earth: Hear, you men of old time, and see, you that come after, the words of the Holy One which I will speak before the Lord of Spirits. [3] It would have been better to declare them only to the men of old time, but even from those that come after we will not withhold the beginning of wisdom. [4] Till

---

1. For more background on 1 Enoch, see chapter 2 in this volume by Kristian A. Bendoraitis.

the present day such wisdom has never been given by the Lord of Spirits as I have received according to my insight, according to the good pleasure of the Lord of Spirits by whom the lot of eternal life has been given to me. [5] Now three Parables were imparted to me, and I lifted up my voice and recounted them to those that dwell on the earth. (1 En. 37:1–5)[2]

In this introduction, we see motifs and ideas that are classic elements of an apocalyptic worldview: a human who receives a divine vision (in this case, Enoch); this vision is a mystery of heavenly wisdom that has not been revealed before; and the seer who receives the vision recounts it to others on earth so that they might understand the true nature of things. These motifs are not unique to 1 Enoch but are a way of speaking and depicting reality that we find in a lot of literature in Second Temple Judaism as well as other, non-Jewish writings from the same time period and beyond.

We call this an apocalyptic worldview because it reflects a system of beliefs that includes the idea that what humans see and perceive as their earthly experience is in fact *not* the whole story. There is the deeper and invisible reality of a divine and heavenly realm. Moreover, the God of this heavenly realm *reveals* himself (hence "apocalyptic," from the Greek word meaning "to reveal") to his chosen people, his "elect," and he tells them how the world really is—how it is structured, what the angelic realm is like, etc. (e.g., 1 En. 59:1–3; 60:11–23; 69:17–25). This enables the elect to live rightly and with hope that despite the way things appear now, God is at work and in control.

In addition to manifesting a Jewish apocalyptic worldview, the Parables of Enoch are also eschatological, meaning they reveal not only truths about the heavenly realm now but also what God is going to do *in the future* to bring about his justice and reign on the earth. Throughout many chapters in the Parables of Enoch we are told that a time is coming when God will save the righteous and judge the unrighteous, including the current wicked kings and rulers of the earth (38:1; 46:4–8; 48:8–9; 50:1–2; 54:1–6; 55:4; 62:7–9). This is the main focus of the vision and **parables** that are revealed to Enoch.

In this final, eschatological time there are a couple of important things that will happen. God's angels will be actively involved in the final events, including revealing themselves and protecting the elect, God's chosen

---

2. Translations adapted from R. H. Charles, ed., *The Apocrypha and Pseudepigrapha of the Old Testament in English*, 2 vols. (Oxford: Clarendon, 1913), 2:163–281.

people, from all over the world (61:1–5). And most importantly, all of this will come about not just by the invisible God or through his angels but through the agency of a special and mysterious figure. This person is described with a variety of titles—the Chosen/Elect One, the Anointed One, the Righteous One, the Son of Man. For example:

> On that day my Elect One will sit on the throne of glory and will test their works, and their places of rest will be innumerable. And their souls will grow strong within them when they see my elect ones, and those who have called upon My glorious name. (45:3)

> [3] For I saw all the angels of punishment abiding (there) and preparing all the instruments of Satan. [4] And I asked the angel of peace who went with me: "For whom are they preparing these instruments?" [5] And he said to me: "They prepare these for the kings and the mighty of this earth, that they may thereby be destroyed. [6] And after this the Righteous and Elect One will cause the house of his congregation to appear: henceforth they will not be hindered in the name of the Lord of Spirits." (53:3–6)

> [27] And he sat on the throne of his glory, and the sum of judgment was given to the Son of Man, and he caused the sinners to pass away and be destroyed from off the face of the earth, and those who have led the world astray. . . . [29] And from henceforth there will be nothing corruptible, for that Son of Man has appeared, and has seated himself on the throne of his glory, and all evil will pass away before his face, and the word of the Son of Man will go forth and be strong before the Lord of Spirits. (69:27, 29)

This emphasis on a coming Son of Man who will be the eschatological judge of the world is one of the most striking and important things about the Parables of Enoch. Whoever wrote this portion of 1 Enoch certainly did not create these images out of nothing. These ideas come from several notions in the Hebrew Scriptures, most clearly and closely the night vision of Daniel 7, where the Son of Man will come from heaven to reign over the earth.

As noted, we do not know exactly when the Parables of Enoch were written and therefore we cannot know what the flow of influence is between 1 Enoch and Jesus and the Gospels, and even later Christian writers. But at least we can note that these ideas in the Parables of Enoch—an apocalyptic worldview and a mysterious, eschatological Son of Man who is coming to judge the world—are clearly part of the conceptual context of Jesus's day. With this context in mind we can now turn to Mark 13 and hear Jesus's teaching anew.

Mark 13:1–37

"AT THAT TIME PEOPLE WILL SEE THE SON OF MAN COMING IN CLOUDS WITH GREAT POWER AND GLORY"

As noted, Mark 13:1–37 is the longest portion of Jesus's teaching in this Gospel. It appears at a crucial point in Mark's story, placed between Jesus's prophetic actions against the temple (chs. 11–12) and his suffering and death (chs. 14–15). This is not an accident. Jesus's prophetic teachings about what is going to happen to Jerusalem and all the world in the future are intimately connected with his symbolic actions against the temple and how his death and resurrection are going to change the rest of history. Jesus is about to inaugurate a new order, a new **covenant**, the new way to relate to God—not in the physical temple but through himself as the new temple.

The things Jesus says in Mark 13 are filled with prophetic language and apocalyptic images. They follow the pattern of hope that we find in the OT prophets: God's people are going to return from exile, with God vanquishing his enemies, with the messiah who will reign as a new David (see especially Isa 9:5–7; 41:17–20; 43:16–19).

In overview, Mark 13:1–37 speaks about the coming destruction of the temple (vv. 1–4), other coming cataclysmic events (vv. 5–8), the persecution of God's people (vv. 9–13), culminating in a devastating desecration of God's holy temple (vv. 14–23), and finally the return of the glorious Son of Man to judge and rule (13:24–27). Therefore, Jesus instructs his disciples to be alert and prepared for these events, which will occur at an unknown time (vv. 28–37). The big mystery in this teaching is *when* these things will happen. The best answer is to understand all of this in a telescoping way—that Jesus sees all these things happening both near and far. His own death and resurrection are one fulfillment, as is the destruction of the temple in AD 70, as are the climactic events that will occur at a future and final eschatological time.

How, then, does Mark 13:1–37 connect to the Parables of Enoch? We can see that both aspects of the Parables of Enoch previously highlighted—the apocalyptic worldview and the coming Son of Man—are paralleled in Mark

13. Jesus's Olivet Discourse is not an apocalypse in terms of its genre, like the Parables and the book of Revelation. But Mark 13 clearly shares the same apocalyptic-eschatological worldview and uses many of the same images and symbols for what God is going to do in the future to vindicate his people. This is clearest in Mark 13:24–27:

> [24] But in those days, following that distress, "the sun will be darkened, and the moon will not give its light; [25] the stars will fall from the sky, and the heavenly bodies will be shaken." [26] At that time people will see the Son of Man coming in clouds with great power and glory. [27] And he will send his angels and gather his elect from the four winds, from the ends of the earth to the ends of the heavens.

Here Jesus uses stock apocalyptic and eschatological images of the sun and moon being darkened, the constellations falling, and the angels gathering up God's elect from all over the world, rescuing them from their persecution and tribulation. All of this comes from the OT prophets, who are looking forward to the day of the Lord when God will finally return and set the world right (see especially Isa 11:12; 13:9–11; 34:4; 43:6). The Parables of Enoch share this worldview and hope, speaking of the future time when God will send his angels and rescue his people (e.g., 1 En. 60:1–7).

It is not only the apocalyptic-eschatological hope that is paralleled in Mark and the Parables of Enoch, but it is also the *person* through whom all this will happen, the glorious Son of Man. Even as the Parables taught that the eschatological time would happen through the coming of the Elect One, the Anointed One, the Son of Man, so too this is true in Jesus's teaching.

Jesus regularly refers to himself somewhat mysteriously as the "Son of Man" throughout the Gospels. While this self-designation has its roots especially in Daniel 7, it is also somewhat ambiguous, allowing Jesus to fill it with his own meaning. He does so throughout Mark, showing that the Son of Man is the **Messiah** who will first suffer and die, but then will rise and later return as Judge and King (see especially Mark 8:31–38; 14:62).

The shared context with the Parables of Enoch is striking. While there is no evidence Jesus (or Mark) is borrowing directly from 1 Enoch, both documents, along with others from the same time period, reflect an expectation of a messiah who will come from heaven to earth and inaugurate the new age. Mark is using familiar language and images from his own context, but he gives a particular interpretation of Jesus as the true fulfillment of all God's prophetic promises.

FOR FURTHER READING

Additional Ancient Texts

The Parables of Enoch are part of the broader world of Second Temple Jewish apocalyptic literature. There are several other accessible texts that can be read in comparison. The first of these is the other parts of 1 Enoch, which come from different places and times but clearly share this apocalyptic worldview and language. Probably the closest Jewish apocalypse to the Parables is Daniel 7–12, especially Daniel 7, which is almost certainly the source of the Parables' emphasis on the Son of Man. The book of 4 Ezra, which comes from the end of the first-century AD, overlaps with both the Parables of Enoch and Daniel, with heavenly visions that reveal what will happen at the end of time. Closely related to 4 Ezra and the Parables of Enoch is 2 Baruch. For statements about a figure issuing judgment, see 2 Baruch 40:1–2; 72:2–3; 4 Ezra 13:10–11, 37–38. Finally, we may mention the NT book of Revelation, which also shows heavy influence from Daniel and closely parallels the Parables of Enoch in content and vision for the eschatological future.

English Translations and Critical Editions

Isaac, E. "1 (Ethiopic Apocalypse of) Enoch: A New Translation and Introduction." Pages 5–89 in vol. 1 of *The Old Testament Pseudepigrapha*. Ed. James H. Charlesworth. Garden City, NY: Doubleday, 1983.

Knibb, Michael A. *The Ethiopic Book of Enoch*. 2 vols. Oxford: Clarendon, 1978.

Nickelsburg, George W. E., and James C. VanderKam. *1 Enoch: The Hermeneia Translation*. Minneapolis: Fortress, 2012.

Secondary Literature[3]

Bock, Darrell, and James Charlesworth. *Parables of Enoch: A Paradigm Shift*. JCT 11. London: T&T Clark, 2014.

Collins, John J. *The Apocalyptic Imagination: An Introduction to Jewish Apocalyptic Literature*. 3rd ed. Grand Rapids: Eerdmans, 2016.

Healy, Mary. *The Gospel of Mark*. Grand Rapids: Baker Academic, 2008.

Nickelsburg, George W. E., and James C. VanderKam. *1 Enoch 2: A Commentary on the Book of 1 Enoch, Chapters 37–82*. Minneapolis: Fortress, 2011.

---

3. See also the secondary literature recommended in chapter 2.

CHAPTER 25

Mishnah Pesaḥim and Mark 14:1–25: The Passover Tradition

Amy Peeler

The fourteenth chapter of Mark ushers readers into the time of the Passover, which will become the time of Jesus's passion. The first sections of this chapter form a Markan "sandwich," in which the scheming high priests and scribes (14:1–2) find a willing accomplice in Judas Iscariot (14:10–11), both of which serve as the ominous foil to the anointing woman who, rather than planning for Jesus's death, prepares him for it (14:3–9).

The following set of stories in Mark 14 that tell of the Passover celebration of Jesus with his disciples and his institution of the Lord's Supper is the focus of this essay. Mishnah tractate Pesaḥim provides the comparator text illuminating the backdrop and foreground of this seminal evening.

Pesaḥim

"Why Is This Night Different from Other Nights?"

Pesaḥim is one of the tractates of the Mishnah, a compilation of Jewish law.[1] Organized into its present form in the late second-century AD, the Mishnah seeks to extol, explain, and apply the law of Israel. This focus on law includes the written law of the Torah, the five books of Moses, and the oral law, or the

---

1. For more on the history of the Mishnah and its relation to other rabbinic literature, see chapter 16 in this volume by David Instone-Brewer.

tradition of the fathers that developed for centuries in response to the written law. Pesaḥim is part of the second of six divisions in the Mishnah, called Mo'ed, a section that focuses on the feasts in the Jewish calendar. Its ten chapters give guidance for the practice of the Passover festival.

Readers should exercise caution when appealing to any section of the Mishnah for a better understanding of the time of the New Testament writings. There is no guarantee that the texts describe the actual situation of the first century; they might reflect practices of the second century or a purely academic discussion of an ideal situation.[2] Nevertheless, many scholars have looked to the Mishnah as a possible conversation partner for the New Testament because the Mishnah asserts that it contains ancient tradition (m. ʾAbot 1:1) and, instead of seeking to change that tradition, venerates it. Moreover, its assertions often find corroborations in other first-century Jewish literature, such as **Josephus**, **Philo**, or the **Pseudepigrapha**. Therefore, it can be used responsibly to serve as a possible illumination of Jewish thinking in the first century. This is especially so for a practice like Passover, for which Pesaḥim remains one of the only possible parallel texts for illuminating the ritual's timing, preparation, and meal.

Timing. In Exodus 12 when God gives Moses the instructions for the Passover remembrance, he asserts that this event recalibrates time for the Israelites: "This month is to be for you the first month, the first month of your year" (Exod 12:2). On the tenth day of the month, families are to select an unblemished lamb or goat for sacrifice (12:3, 9–10), and to slaughter that animal on the fourteenth of the month at twilight (12:6). Jewish days run from nightfall to nightfall, so on the night which begins the fifteenth, the animal would be roasted and the Passover meal would occur. During the day of the fifteenth, the Jews observe a solemn assembly where they do not work and do not consume any leaven (12:15–16). This feast of unleavened bread then lasts for seven days (12:16). The same instructions for Passover appear in other texts of the Torah (Exod 34:25; Lev 23:5; Num 9:2–14; 28:16; Deut 16:1–6).

The Mishnah builds upon these instructions and specifies when things should take place; put simply, Passover is a nighttime observation. Since the Jewish calendar moves to the next calendar day at nightfall rather than at midnight, a visual chart might help to clarify the timing of these events.

---

2. Herbert Danby, *The Mishnah: Translated from the Hebrew with Introduction and Brief Explanatory Notes* (Oxford: Oxford University Press, 1974), xiv–xv. All citations are from Danby.

	13th of Nisan[3]			14th of Nisan Day of Preperation			15th of Nisan First Day of Feast		
Jewish Calendar	Night-fall	Day	Twilight Can search for leaven (m. Pesaḥ 1)	Nightfall Can search for leaven (m. Pesaḥ 1)	Day Can search for leaven (m. Pesaḥ 1)	Twilight Slaughter of animal (m. Pesaḥ 5)	Nightfall Passover meal (m. Pesaḥ 10)	Day Solemn assembly	Twilight
Present Day	12th / Midnight		13th	Midnight	14th		Midnight	15th	

Preparation. Those celebrating the Passover would need to carry out several different actions in order to prepare for the meal. Pesaḥim opens with instructions for the removal of yeast from the house (m. Pesaḥ. 1). The searching for yeast must be serious but not obsessive. For example, people need not worry if a weasel has dragged yeast from one place to another because once that question is opened, "there is no end to the matter" (m. Pesaḥ. 1:2).

In addition, they would have needed to ensure that the meal was prepared. Representatives of a family unit would make a trip to the temple to offer their Passover sacrifice. In its fifth chapter, tractate Pesaḥim gives a description:

> The Passover-offering was slaughtered [by the people] in three groups. . . . When the first group entered in and the Temple Court was filled, the gates of the Temple Court were closed. . . . The priests stood in rows and in their hands were basins of silver and basins of gold. (5:5)

> An Israelite slaughtered his [own] offering and the priest caught the blood. The priest passed the basin to his fellow, and he to his fellow, each receiving a full basin and giving back an empty one. The priest nearest to the Altar tossed the blood in one action against the base [of the Altar]. (5:6)

> In the meantime the Levites] sang the *Hallel.* (5:7)[4]

---

3. The first month of the Jewish calendar is called Abib in Deut 16:1, but comes to be known as Nisan after the Babylonian exile (Esth 3:7; Neh 2:1).

4. The *Hallel* consists of Psalms 113–118.

Representatives of the family would have been witness to a blood sacrifice on their behalf, thereby providing a tangible remembrance of the first Passover. They would retrieve the animal slaughtered for them and take its roasted meat for the meal.

The Meal. In its tenth chapter, Pesaḥim gives the structure for how the meal should be conducted and what should be said. During that day participants should fast before this meal (10:1). When they sit down to it, the table is spread with unleavened bread, lettuce, bitter herbs, a chutney made of fruit, nuts, and vinegar called *haroseth*,[5] and the roasted lamb (10:3). The meal begins with a good word, a blessing, over the day and the first cup of wine. Then the bread is broken.

Pesaḥim instructs that a liturgy of remembrance begins with the second cup. According to the Mishnah, it should be a child who voices the questions: "Why is this meal different?" (10:4). The presider over the meal would then recount the story of God's redemption from Deuteronomy 26:5–10. It includes God's election of Abraham, slavery in Egypt, the powerful redemption of God, and the gift of the land. Then the presider returns thanks to God in recognition of his provision.

After this there must be two more cups of wine at this meal, each of which includes a blessing. The tractate makes this explicit: "Even the poorest in Israel must not [have] less than four cups of wine to drink" (m. Pesaḥ. 10:1).

Along with the benedictions, the Mishnah encourages participants to recite the *Hallel* psalms just as had been sung by the Levites at the Passover sacrifice (5:7). Some rabbis urged the recitation of only Psalm 113, others the inclusion of 114 as well. Both songs praise God for his goodness: lifting up of the lowly (Ps 113), and deliverance of the nation of Israel (Ps 114). They may doze or sleep after the meal, but they should not "disperse to join in revelry" (m. Pesaḥ. 10:8). Pesaḥim gives a sense of the great power of this meal of remembrance in the life of Israel as it recounts the numerous details of how it can and should be practiced.

Mark

"TAKE IT; THIS IS MY BODY"

Timing. The Gospel of Mark refers often to the timing of this meal. Chapter 14 opens with the Passover two days in the future (14:1),[6] and by the time Mark

---

5. This could be the bowl Jesus mentions into which both he and his betrayer dip their bread. Danby's commentary on the Mishnah suggests that participants would dip their food into this mixture to mitigate the bitterness of the herbs (Danby, *Mishnah*, 150n6).

6. It is unclear if Mark means to include the day he is about to narrate or not. But the point stands that the events of the story are nearing the time of the festival.

has narrated the anointing of the woman (14:3–9) and the plot against Jesus (14:10–11), it is the first day of the unleavened-bread festival when they were sacrificing the Passover (14:12). To assert that this is the first day of the festival *and* the day of sacrifice creates a bit of difficulty, because according to the Old Testament and the Mishnah, the sacrifice should happen at the very end of the fourteenth of Nisan (at twilight) and be consumed after nightfall, once it becomes the next day, the fifteenth, which is the first day of the feast of unleavened bread. It could be the case that Mark is slipping into a pattern evidenced by other first-century Jews who call the day of preparation the beginning of the feast (cf. Josephus, *J.W.* 6.9.3). Conversely, he could be thinking in Roman time whereby the sacrificing of the lambs on the afternoon of the fourteenth of Nisan would precede the evening meal, also on the fourteenth to the Romans. Hence, the difficulty here is in no way insurmountable. According to Mark, then, as informed by Pesaḥim, the events of Mark 14:12–25 must take place on 14–15 Nisan.

Preparation. On that Thursday, the disciples ask Jesus where they should prepare the Passover. He directs them to go into the city, meet a man carrying water, follow him into a house, and ask the steward of that house for a guest room. Jesus promises that they will find a furnished upper room and commands that they should get ready for the group (14:12–15).

Everything happens as Jesus had instructed (14:16). It is quite possible that these disciples would have themselves participated in a blood sacrifice to remember God's redemption of Israel that day. And as night was falling, they would have gathered the roasted lamb and returned it to the others (m. Pesaḥ. 5:10).[7] When these disciples entered the upper room, they would have needed to check and ensure that no yeast was in the room. Then, they would have brought in the lamb and prepared the unleavened bread and bitter herbs.

The Meal. The preparations having been made, Mark says that Jesus and the *Twelve* arrive at this upper room (Mark 14:17). This indicates that the disciples who made preparations were part of a larger group following Jesus. If they had participated in these rituals, they would have been fasting before this meal and would have greatly looked forward to the meal.

Mark recounts two interchanges that take place during the meal. In the first (14:17–21), Jesus voices the fact that he will be betrayed, which has already happened earlier in the chapter (14:10–11). While the whole group of disciples seems dismayed by this proclamation, and each seeks out

---

7. The Mishnah allows people to offer the Passover sacrifice on behalf of others (m. Pesaḥ. 6:6; 8:4). So, these disciples could have made the sacrifice for the rest of their group.

confirmation that he is not the culprit, Jesus specifies that it will be one of the Twelve (14:20).

In the second recorded dinner speech, Jesus takes bread, prays over it, breaks it, and gives it to those with him (14:22). Here Jesus adds an aspect of the liturgy not present in the Mishnah. As he distributes the unleavened bread that he has broken into pieces, he makes an association between that bread and his body, saying, "Take it; this is my body" (14:22). If there is roasted lamb present at their meal, flesh—particularly the flesh of the lamb—might make for a more natural association. Jesus, however, chooses to make an association between his body and the bread rather than the meat.

Then Jesus takes a cup of wine and gives thanks for it (14:23). This could be the moment at which a child would ask about the special meaning of this night. If the disciples had families of their own, it would have been expected for them to celebrate the Passover together, so it could have been one of their children who asked this question. After recounting the story and giving thanks, Jesus gives the cup to them and reinterprets this element of the meal by declaring it to be the "blood of the covenant, which is poured out for many" (14:24). His reference recalls the blood of the **covenant** sprinkled upon the people when they agreed to God's law (Exod 24:8). The disciples eating with Jesus are familiar with recounting God's deliverance of their people at this meal, but now Jesus invites them to associate him with God's redemption of Israel in the exodus.

He declares that this will be his last partaking of wine (Mark 14:25), which indicates that Jesus's reassociation of the wine with his blood may have taken place on the fourth cup. After this statement of finality, they all sang a hymn. Psalms 113 and 114 would surely have been transformed in light of what Jesus had said.

Conclusion. The study of rabbinic instructions for the Passover celebration sets into sharp relief the unexpected words of Jesus—words that, coming in the midst of an ancient liturgy, were so new that believers adopted them and repeated them as their central celebration of God's redemption.

This remembrance of Israel's slavery and God's redemption segues into Jesus's foretelling of a different kind of suffering and redemption. Once they arrive at the Mount of Olives, Jesus warns that his disciples will all be scandalized by the upcoming events but that he will be raised and will go before them to Galilee. Peter and the other disciples fixate on Jesus's assertion of their failure and vigorously deny it. They continue to have trouble seeing the new breaking into the old. They still have little idea that the events of the next few hours will bring the new Passover.

For Further Reading

Additional Ancient Texts

The Last Supper is also recorded in Matthew 26:17–29; Luke 22:7–20; and John 13:1–26 (cf. 6:51–58). For other Jewish accounts of the Passover, compare Jubilees 49; Philo, *On the Special Laws* 2.144–73; and Josephus, *Jewish Antiquities* 2.311–17; 3.248–51; 5.20; 9.260–73; 10.68–73; 11.109–13; 14.21–28; 17.213.

English Translations and Critical Editions

Danby, Herbert. *The Mishnah: Translated from the Hebrew with Introduction and Brief Explanatory Notes*. Oxford: Oxford University Press, 1933.

Instone-Brewer, David. *Feasts and Sabbaths: Passover and Atonement*. Volume 2A of *Traditions of the Rabbis from the Era of the New Testament*. Grand Rapids: Eerdmans, 2011.

Secondary Literature

Bokser, Baruch M. *The Origins of the Seder: The Passover Rite and Early Rabbinic Judaism*. Berkeley: University of California Press, 1984.

Pitre, Brad. *Jesus and the Last Supper*. Grand Rapids: Eerdmans, 2015.

Scotland, Nigel. "A Passover-Style Meal." Pages 1–19 in *The New Passover: Rethinking the Lord's Supper for Today*. Eugene, OR: Cascade, 2016.

Streett, R. Alan. *Subversive Meals: An Analysis of the Lord's Supper under Roman Domination during the First Century*. Eugene, OR: Pickwick, 2013.

CHAPTER 26

The Babylonian Talmud and Mark 14:26–52: *Abba*, Father!

NIJAY K. GUPTA

The proverbial "calm" before the storm of Jesus's arrest and execution in Mark happens in the garden of Gethsemane—all four Gospels mention this preparation time for Jesus (see Mark 14:26–42). First, Jesus tells his disciples that they will lose heart and abandon him. When Peter speaks up about his unfaltering faith, Jesus predicts his denial (14:26–31). After that, we learn that Jesus is deeply troubled and overwhelmed, as if he is already dying from grief (14:32–34). Jesus knows a great test lies ahead for him, and he offers this prayer: "*Abba*, Father, . . . everything is possible for you. Take this cup from me. Yet not what I will, but what you will" (14:36). There are several remarkable features of this garden scene. What does the "cup" language mean? How could Jesus and his Father have divided wills? Why does he pray this multiple times (14:39–41)? Our main focus in this chapter will remain on Mark's distinctive use of the Aramaic word *abba* here.[1] Mark's Gospel was written in Greek, but sometimes he transliterates Aramaic words or phrases into Greek (see figure 26.1).

It would appear that certain elements of Jesus's work and words left an indelible mark on the memory of his life—that Jesus prayed to God as *abba* appears to be an example of this.[2]

---

1. *Abba* literally means "the father." In Jewish expression, *abba* can carry the meaning of "*my* father" or "*our* father."

2. Most scholars believe that Jesus would have been able to speak and understand three languages (though with varying degrees of skill). Aramaic would have been the language that Jesus used with other Jews in conversation. Greek would have been employed in interactions with gentiles. Hebrew would have been used in worship, at least in part; see Gerhard Lohfink, *Jesus of Nazareth: What He Wanted, Who He Was* (Collegeville, MN: Liturgical Press, 2012), 100.

Chart 1: Aramaic Words in Mark

3:17	*Boanerges* ("sons of thunder")
5:41	*Talitha koum* ("Little girl, get up!")
7:11	*Corban* ("gift," "devoted to God")
7:34	*Ephphatha* ("Be opened!")
10:51	*Rabbouni* ("Rabbi")
14:36	*Abba* ("Father")
15:22	*Golgotha* ("the place of the skull")
15:34	*Eloi, Eloi, lema sabachthani* ("My God, my God, why have you forsaken me?")

Mark is the only Gospel that explicitly uses the Aramaic word *abba*, though many scholars assume that the "our Father" of the Lord's Prayer would have been *abba* in Aramaic (Matt 6:9; Luke 11:2). But the apostle Paul also uses the Aramaic word *abba* in his letters (see Rom 8:15; Gal 4:6).

In the past, scholars have sometimes assumed or argued that Jesus was the first Jew to pray to God with the mind-set of a son appealing to a father. More specifically, some have urged that Jesus was the first Jew to pray to God as *abba*. Therefore, we will investigate these matters regarding Jewish practice of prayer and use of *abba*, and then turn to Mark's use of *abba* in 14:36.

The Babylonian Talmud
"Father, Father, Give Us Rain"

The idea sometimes passed on, that before Jesus Jews did not worship God as "father," is simply wrong. As we read in Exodus 4:22–23, Jewish tradition recognized that when Israel was delivered out of Egypt, the message Moses gave to Pharaoh was "Israel is my firstborn son, and I told you, 'Let my son go, so he may worship me.'" While it is true that the Old Testament rarely offers occasions where Israelites invoke God as "father," we see glimpses of this in places like Psalm 68, where the worshipper proclaims that God is the one who gives a home to the forsaken as "father to the fatherless, a defender of widows" (68:4–5).

Once we enlarge our study to include Jewish texts like Sirach, we see the prayer, "O Lord, Father and Master of my life, do not abandon me to their designs, and do not let me fall because of them!" (23:1; cf. 23:4). And in

Wisdom of Solomon, God is addressed as "Father," the one who steers life on a set path, a safe course through stormy waves (Wis 14:3; cf. 2:16). These early Jewish texts are in Greek, so it is more difficult to find examples of the Aramaic *abba* in reference to God. Perhaps one of the closest examples we have comes from the Targum of Psalms. The Targums are Aramaic paraphrases of the Old Testament. Our English Psalm 89:26 (based on the Hebrew text) reads, "You are my Father, my God, the Rock my Savior." The English translation of the Aramaic Targum text reads, "You are my Father [*abba*], my God, and the strength of my redemption" (89:27).

Some of the most interesting and illuminating comparisons for Jesus's use of *abba* involve the rabbinic literature. The most extensive and significant rabbinic text that relates the word *abba* to the fatherhood of God comes from the Babylonian Talmud. In the tract called Ta'anit, we read about a teacher named Ḥanan ha-Neḥba. During a drought, the rabbis would tell the school children to go to Ḥanan ha-Neḥba and they would say, "Father, father, give us rain." And he would pray, "Master of the Universe, do it for the sake of these who are unable to distinguish between the Father [*abba*] who gives rain and the father [*abba*] who does not" (b. Ta'an. 23b). Here we have a Jewish text that clearly recognizes that the God whom Israel worships is *abba*, the Father who provides for and protects his people. Ḥanan ha-Neḥba recognizes not only that God is a powerful and gracious father but also that, while others come to him for a rain miracle, he has no such power in and of himself.

Does this demonstrate that Jews already prayed to God *as father* during the time of Jesus? Some think not. First, we have the problem of dating the rabbinic literature—we cannot be sure these ideas precede the time of Jesus. Second, even with Ḥanan ha-Neḥba's prayer, while he *acknowledges* God as *abba*, his address is directed to the "Master of the Universe." Still, we must recognize that when Jesus emphasizes the fatherhood of God, he would have been developing or intensifying an existing Jewish tradition, rather than creating it *ex nihilo*.

Mark 14:26–52

"ABBA, FATHER. . . . TAKE THIS CUP FROM ME"

Kenneth Bailey observes that in the Middle East today the word *abba* is employed by young children for their fathers. In the Arabic use of *abba*,

Bailey explains, we see retained the Aramaic idiomatic usage of this word, which carries "both respect in addressing a superior and a profound personal relationship between the one who uses it and the one addressed."[3] This understanding of *abba* is helpful as we consider its use in Mark 14:36.

The Vulnerable Jesus. One interesting feature of Mark's account of Jesus's prayer in Gethsemane is how he mentions both *abba* and *patēr*, often translated "*Abba*, Father," but a literal English translation might be, "Papa, Father." Mark tells us that Jesus was overwhelmed with sorrow (Mark 14:34). When he prays, then, he is in a state of intense vulnerability, openness, and weakness. His petition is one of the most honest prayers in Scripture: "Remove this cup from me" (14:36).

This can be contrasted with the confidence and resolve that Jesus has shown up to this point in Mark. He boldly warns his disciples of persecution, betrayal, and societal rejection, and he calls them to perseverance (13:11–13). As for Jesus's "cup," some associate this image with the symbolic use of the cup at the Last Supper—Jesus solemnly drank from the cup that symbolized his bloodshed (14:23). Yet, at this moment—as Martin Luther says—"no one feared death so much as this man."[4] John Reumann cleverly mentions that in this garden scene Jesus is presented with the bill for the world's redemption, and he is forced to count the cost.[5] In this moment, Jesus is the scared child who appeals to his *abba*, knowing his Father's compassion and power ("all things are possible for you," 14:36b). We are reminded here that just because the church has affirmed Jesus as "God from God" and "true God from true God" (Nicene Creed) does not mean that he did not experience human emotions and even human doubts. While that moment gave way to trust, it is a crucial reminder that Mark portrays Jesus as committed to obedience *despite* grief, weariness, and doubt.

The Trusting and Obedient Jesus. According to Mark, just as soon as Jesus petitions for his cup to be taken away, he introduces a contrast: "Yet not what I will, but what you will" (14:36c). Jesus makes this qualification or condition not to a distant lord or domineering deity but to the same *abba* he invoked to begin with. While Mark himself does not include a version of the Lord's Prayer in his Gospel, most scholars note a parallel between the Lord's Prayer (Matt 6:9–13) and the prayer(s) in Gethsemane.

---

3. Kenneth Bailey, *Jesus through Middle Eastern Eyes* (Downers Grove, IL: InterVarsity Press, 2008), 98.

4. Martin Luther, *Luther's Works*, ed. R. H. Fischer (Philadelphia: Fortress, 1961), 37:326.

5. John Reumann, *Jesus in the Church's Gospels* (Minneapolis: Fortress, 2006), 107.

Matthew 6:9–13	Mark 14:36
Our Father	*Abba*, Father
Lead us not into temptation	Take this cup from me
Your kingdom come, your will be done	Yet not what I will, but what you will

The Lord's Prayer in both Matthew 6:9–13 and Luke 11:2–4 model the dual notions of (1) the gracious fatherhood of God, and (2) the dependent relationship that the child has toward the father. Children need grace (and forgiveness). Children need daily bread. Parents are responsible for taking care of their own sons and daughters as a primary obligation.

Parents also carry the responsibility of ensuring that their children grow up in a mature way and face tests and trials with courage and hope.[6] In the garden Jesus faces the problem of two wills—his own desire to bypass the cup of suffering, and the divine will of his Father that has set out this difficult path for redemption. Jesus models for his disciples what it means to have faith and to trust God the Father. In Mark 7 Jesus affirms the Torah teaching that a child (presumably of any age) ought to honor mother and father (Mark 7:10; cf. 10:19), and so Jesus honors his *abba*.

We may also detect here an allusion to the parable of the wicked tenants (Mark 12:1–12). When the landowner sent a slave to collect the profit from his vineyard, the tenant farmers beat this messenger and sent them away (12:3), and later killed other messengers (12:5). The landowner thought then to send his one and only beloved son. Surely this son would have known the situation. There is no signal of his defiance or refusal. He did as he was told and was murdered because he was the sole heir (12:8).

While Jesus's prayer for relief is to the reader both troubling (*how else could the story end?*) and reassuring (*he shares the human struggle*), it is obvious how Jesus's focused prayers are contrasted with the utter failure of the disciples. Three times Jesus went to pray alone, and each time he came back to his disciples and found them unsupportive and asleep (14:35–41). "Enough!" he cries out to them. "The hour has come. Look, the Son of Man is delivered into the hands of sinners" (14:41). Jesus faces his betrayers with resolve, while his disciples abandon him (14:50).

The Cacophonic Cry of Dereliction. We jump ahead now to the cry of dereliction, that horrific moment of Jesus's crucifixion on the cross when

---

6. See Eph 6:4; Heb 12:5–10; Sir 6:18.

he utters, "My God, my God, why have you forsaken me?" (Mark 15:34). Throughout Mark's Gospel, Jesus is in full control and anticipates the hour of his sacrifice (10:38–45). Only two moments in Mark find Jesus in the darkness of despair. The climactic moment is the cry of dereliction, and the prayer in the garden serves as an ominous foreshadowing. Just as with the garden prayer, so here too we have Aramaic transliterated into Greek for the original reader: "*Eloi, Eloi, lema sabachthani.*" As is well known, Jesus here repeats the words of the first verse of Psalm 22, a psalm of David. David laments that God seems distant; he cries out all day, but there is no answer. David feels alone as he is mocked and shamed by others (Ps 22:2–18). So it was with Jesus.

Some scholars believe that Jesus's words imply the hopeful tone of the end of the psalm (vv. 19–31), while others think that those difficult words of v. 1 simply came to mind for Jesus without remainder. Augustine seems to have the most compelling reading. He argues that in the cry of dereliction "Jesus appropriated the psalmist's voice to himself, the voice of human weakness."[7] That is, in that moment Jesus embodied the position of God's people in sin and spiritual exile. In that instance, Jesus was distanced from his intimacy with his *abba* and took on himself the full punishment due to Israel. As R. T. France observes, this is the first and only time in Jesus's recorded prayers that he does not call out to his Father, but to "my God."[8]

So troubling was this text to early Christians that they often tried to explain it away. Some patristic writers claimed that it was Jesus in his *humanity* that said this, and that it did not come from his *divine* nature.[9] We also know that at least one early Greek manuscript of the Markan text softened Jesus's words to "My God, my God, why have you *dishonored* me?"[10]

If the Gospel of Mark ends at 16:8 as most scholars are prone to believe, then Mark does not narrate resurrection appearances or an apostolic commission for his disciples. Still, the reader is not left with the impression that Jesus failed or that the darkness won the day. The angels announce the empty tomb and the resurrection (16:6). But more importantly for the turn from Jesus's "*abba*" prayer to his "my God, my God" prayer, Mark narrates the profound confession of the Roman centurion in view of Jesus's holy

---

7. Letter 140, to Honoratus 6, as cited in Thomas C. Oden and Christopher A. Hall, eds., *Mark*, ACCS (Downers Grove, IL: InterVarsity Press, 1998), 222.

8. R. T. France, *The Gospel of Mark*, NIGTC (Grand Rapids: Eerdmans, 2002), 652.

9. See Ambrose, *On the Christian Faith* 2.7.56. Ambrose speculates, "As God he was not distressed, but as a human he was capable of being distressed" (*NPNF*[2] 10:230).

10. See Joel B. Green, *The Way of the Cross: Following Jesus in the Gospel of Mark* (Eugene, OR: Wipf & Stock, 2009), 3–4.

self-offering: "Surely this man was the Son of God!" (15:39). This affirmation of the unique sonship of Jesus (whether or not the centurion himself fully understood any of this, we are not told) is related to earlier pronouncements, such as in 1:11. Jesus is associated with his Father, and the relationship is not ultimately severed but renewed (or at least anticipated).

FOR FURTHER READING

Additional Ancient Texts

In the New Testament, Paul's texts that employ the word *abba* are worthy of close examination (Rom 8:15; Gal 4:6). For better understanding of the uses and meaning of *abba*, see Job 38:28 in the **Dead Sea Scroll**'s 11Q10 31:5 ("Does the rain have a father?"). In the rabbinic literature, we find the phrase "Father in heaven" (in Hebrew, *ab*). These can be instructive for the study of the Aramaic *abba*. Important texts include m. Soṭah 9:15, m. Yoma 8:9, m. Roš Haš. 3:8, and t. Ber. 3:14.

English Translations and Critical Editions

Neusner, Jacob, trans. *The Babylonian Talmud*. 22 vols. Peabody, MA: Hendrickson, 2011.

———. *The Mishnah: A New Translation*. New Haven: Yale University Press, 1997.

Stec, David. *The Targum of Psalms: Translated, with a Critical Introduction, Apparatus and Notes*. The Aramaic Bible 16. Collegeville, MN: Liturgical Press, 2004.

Secondary Literature

Barr, James. "*Abba* Isn't Daddy." *JTS* 39 (1988): 28–47.

Jeremias, Joachim. *New Testament Theology: The Proclamation of Jesus*. New York: Charles Scribner's Sons, 1971.

Neusner, J. *Rabbinic Literature: An Essential Guide*. Nashville: Abingdon, 2005.

Sandnes, Karl Olav. *Early Christian Discourses on Jesus's Prayer at Gethsemane: Courageous, Committed, Cowardly?* NovTSup 166. Leiden: Brill, 2015.

Thompson, M. M. "Joachim Jeremias and the Debate about *Abba*." Pages 21–24 in *The Promise of the Father: Jesus and God in the New Testament*. Louisville: Westminster John Knox, 2000.

CHAPTER 27

The Parables of Enoch and Mark 14:53–73: Blasphemy and Exaltation

DARRELL L. BOCK

Jesus was crucified as "the King of the Jews." This is confirmed for us in two ways. First, the Gospels all report this as the point of the charge on the placard (known as the *titulus*) that accompanied Jesus to the cross (Matt 27:37; Mark 15:26; Luke 23:38; John 19:19). Second, **Josephus**'s remarks place the responsibility for Jesus's rejection at the hands of the Jewish leadership and Pilate (*Ant.* 18:63–64).[1] What this shows is that there was enough in Jesus's ministry to lead others to see him making regal claims. Jesus died as more than a prophetic figure. So what exactly got him into trouble?

What the Gospels show in their portrayal of the action leading into Jesus's death is primarily a twofold movement in the Jewish and Roman examinations of Jesus. The key events involve an examination before the Jewish leadership, followed by Pilate's questioning. The examination by Pilate leads to the crucifixion based on charges that are largely political (Luke 23:2–3), since only Pilate had the authority to crucify, and a religious charge would not have been of interest to him. This is in part why the charge shows up in regal form. A competing ruler to Caesar without being appointed by the emperor was something Pilate was responsible to stop. Rome appointed her own rulers and reacted to anyone claiming to be a king. Pilate was also to defend Caesar's interests, keep the peace, and ensure that Rome received

---

1. For a defense of the authenticity of the core of Josephus's remarks, making clear that Jesus was crucified by a combination of Jewish leadership and Roman involvement, see John P. Meier, *A Marginal Jew: Rethinking the Historical Jesus, Volume 1: The Roots of the Problem and the Person*, ABRL (New York: Doubleday, 1991), 59–69.

her taxes. According to Luke 23:1, the Jewish leadership presents charges to Pilate that touch on all these points, putting pressure on him to meet his responsibilities to Rome.

The Jewish examination is therefore the key, because without it Jesus would not have been brought to Pilate in the first place. Here the discussion is both political and religious. Mark 14:53–64 covers this event. An initial effort to focus on a claim that Jesus would destroy the temple fails to get a collection of credible witnesses (vv. 56–59). So the discussion turns to the question about whether Jesus is the **Messiah**, specifically "the Son of the Blessed One," as Mark puts it (v. 61). Jesus's reply gives them far more. He responds saying, "I am. . . . And you will see the Son of Man sitting at the right hand of the Mighty One [Ps 110:1] and coming on the clouds of heaven [Dan 7:13–14]" (Mark 14:62). We have noted the two allusions to the Scriptures the Jews recognized in the reply. Through these allusions Jesus affirms the question and says more,[2] provoking the high priest to tear his clothes, accuse Jesus of blaspheming, and condemn him (vv. 63–64). But what exactly was Jesus saying and claiming? And why was it problematic, indeed blasphemous and "worthy of death" (v. 64)?

It is here the debate attested in the Jewish sources helps us to sense what Jesus was evoking. The claim to sit in heaven with God was controversial. There were two approaches to this question in Jewish literature. Some thought it possible for very special, high luminaries to sit with God; others saw it as a direct affront to God that made it an impossibility. In this essay we will examine the Parables of Enoch, as well as some related rabbinic literature, to help us see what ultimately led to Jesus's condemnation by the Jewish leadership.

The Parables of Enoch

"THE ELECT ONE SHALL IN THOSE DAYS SIT ON MY THRONE"

Sitting with God as Non-Blasphemous. A few ancient Jewish texts suggest the possibility of someone being able to sit with God in heaven. Perhaps the

---

2. The more indirect responses in Matthew and Luke to this question—Matthew's "you have said so" (26:64), and Luke's "you say that I am" (22:70)—represent qualified affirmations as well. Those Gospels are using an idiom that means, "It is as you ask, but not quite with the sense that you mean." Jesus's reply and use of Scripture in Mark explains why the other two Gospels go the way they do.

most important one is part of the portrait in the Parables of Enoch (1 En. 37–71).[3] Here a figure called "the Son of Man" or "the Elect One" sits with God in heaven. For example, in 1 Enoch 51:3 the Elect One shall sit on the throne uttering wisdom, and the creation shall rejoice at his presence. The text says, "the Elect One shall in those days sit on *My* throne," so it is clearly God's throne that is in view. In 55:4, the Elect One is seated on the throne and exercises judgment over evil spirits, demonstrating his judicial authority. Again, in 61:8 the Elect One is placed on "the throne of glory" where "he shall judge all the works of the holy above in the heaven."

This figure has a similar role in 62:2–3 as the Elect One, but then in 62:7 he is described as the "Son of Man" who "from the beginning . . . was hidden." In 62:9, kings, governors, and high officials even worship the Son of Man. The linking in chapter 62 shows the Elect One and Son of Man are the same figure. This is significant, because the title "Son of Man" was Jesus's favorite way to refer to himself. The title comes from Daniel 7:13–14 (alluded to by Jesus in Mark 14:62), but 1 Enoch not only shows how some Jews thought about the title but also develops the function of the Son of Man in detail. In addition, it is quite possible this text emerged out of the Galilean region in the period Jesus ministered, likely being written in the late first-century BC or early first-century AD. What these two texts show, therefore, is how some Jews writing around the time and provenance of Jesus anticipated God giving the Son of Man a great deal of divine authority and honor to be shared in heaven. The parallels to the Markan Jesus are striking indeed.

It is also worth noting the contribution of the Babylonian Talmud (fifth-to-sixth century AD) to this debate. The text records the claim of Rabbi Akiba that David could sit with God in heaven. This view, expressed in two passages (b. Ḥag. 14a; b. Sanh. 38b), arises from Akiba's explanation of Psalm 110:1, one of the scriptural texts alluded to by Jesus in reply to the high priest (Mark 14:62). The text also shows the seriousness of the debate, because Rabbi Jose the Galilean responds critically to Akiba's explanation with, "How long will you treat the divine presence as profane?"[4] Here Jose is accusing Akiba of risking blasphemy because of his explanation, and so he warns him. The fact that Jose's remark closes the dialogue shows his is

---

3. All 1 Enoch translations are from R. H. Charles, ed., *The Apocrypha and Pseudepigrapha of the Old Testament in English,* 2 vols. (Oxford: Clarendon, 1913), 2:163–281. For more on the background of 1 Enoch, see chapter 2 by Kristian A. Bendoraitis and chapter 24 by Jonathan T. Pennington in this present volume.

4. Translation is from Isidore Epstein, ed., *The Soncino Talmud,* Soncino Classics Collection (New York: Judaica, 1973), digital edition.

the official position. It also shows that the idea of such shared authority was debated and controversial.

Sitting with God as Blasphemous. There are texts that speak against this view as well. The rabbi's response to Akiba is one such negative text. Another comes from the fifth-sixth century AD work known as 3 Enoch.[5] In this text, an angel called Metatron, who is giving a tour of heaven, refers to himself as the "lesser YHWH" and is said to sit on a throne at the entrance to God's palace, executing judgment (12:5). His throne is said to be "at the door of my palace, on the outside, so that he might sit and execute judgment over all my household" (48C:8). This scene is tied to the remark in 16:1–2 about having a seat "at the door of the seventh palace," where he would sit "upon a throne like a king, with ministering angels standing beside [him]." This is a negative scene, for the vision shows how Metatron's stature results in there being "two powers in heaven!" (16:4). The result is divine discipline for Metatron for acting in a way equal to God. The angel receives lashes and is made to stand to his feet (16:5).

It is important to see what is at stake here. Metatron is seen as dishonoring God by his sitting on "a great throne" (16:1). The same is said for Akiba's suggestion of David. God's honor is unique. To allow someone to sit with God suggests a kind of equality that was an offense to those who saw God's honor as unique.

Mark 14:53–72

"AND YOU WILL SEE THE SON OF MAN SITTING AT THE RIGHT HAND OF THE MIGHTY ONE AND COMING ON THE CLOUDS OF HEAVEN"

Jesus's Claims of Exaltation and Vindication. As we have seen, the belief in Judaism was that God's glory was unique. So a claim like that of Jesus to sit with God in heaven (Mark 14:62), although theoretically discussed by some Jews with a figure like the Son of Man in 1 Enoch 37–71, would have been heard by others as an affront to the unique glory of God. This would have been all the more troubling coming from a humble teacher of Judaism from the Galilean backwoods.

---

5. Translation is from P. Alexander, "3 (Hebrew Apocalypse of) Enoch," in vol. 1 of *The Old Testament Pseudepigrapha*, ed. James H. Charlesworth (Garden City, NY: Doubleday, 1983–85), 255–315. This is a later text, but it shows the attitude.

The fact that the Jewish judges in Mark were made up primarily of Sadducees who did not like tradition and additions to the Pentateuch makes their reaction to Jesus's claim unsurprising. When the high priest tears his robe in Mark 14:63, his judgment was that Jesus had made more than a regal claim; he saw Jesus as blaspheming (14:64). In the view of the Jewish leadership, Jesus's answer made him worthy of facing judgment before Pilate for sedition because he was making two problematic claims simultaneously.

In claiming a seat at God's right hand from Psalm 110:1, Jesus was appealing to a Davidic psalm that stressed kingship. In appealing to the imagery of Daniel 7:13–14 about riding the clouds, Jesus appealed to the picture of a transcendent ruler-judge who receives authority from God. In combining the two Jesus was saying, *I am the king, and more than that, regardless of what happens now, God will give me a place at his side and I will rule and judge, even over you.* Jesus was saying in effect, *I am not really on trial here; one day you will be subject to me. More than that, God will bring me to a place as Son of Man that means I am ruling from his side.* Here Jesus claims that regardless of what is done, God will vindicate him. Indeed, this vindication will result in a rule from the same throne as God's.

Yet the leaders did not accept Jesus's claim of exaltation and vindication and saw the remark as an ultimate dishonoring of God. The claim was worse than someone saying, "I will go and live in the holy of holies in the temple," because Jesus had in mind God's very presence above, not the sacred locale where that presence was represented on earth. Jews had fought a war, the **Maccabean Revolt**, to reclaim the honor of a desecrated temple. Jesus's claims were more radical still.

Jesus's Complex Portrait. The relevance of this claim is that we get an affirmation from Jesus that he is an exalted Messiah, this time in public. But once again, we see this affirmation combined with other portraits, here with a transcendent Son of Man. What Jesus is doing here is showing once again that his messianic identity is at the heart of who he is in his mission. However, there are other images that must be grasped to truly understand who Jesus is and what he is doing in his messianic role. Whereas after the confession by the disciples at Caesarea Philippi there was a need to appreciate that Messiah must suffer (Mark 8:27–31), here Jesus gives an open affirmation of total authority and vindication from God. What Jesus is doing with these scenes is saying, *I am the Messiah, but that Messiah is also the Servant who suffers and the Coming Son of Man who will rule and judge.*

Thus, this Jewish scene is in many senses a climactic one. Jesus goes fully public here as he faces rejection and death. He proclaims the certainty of his vindication and authority, even as the Jewish leadership tries to bring his ministry to a halt by obtaining evidence for a political charge they can take to Pilate. Jesus's confession ironically leads to Peter's denial (14:66–72), and then to his crucifixion (14:20–37). In a real sense, Jesus chose the cross simply by revealing who God would show him to be.

Crucifixion for a political charge is what resulted, but it was not the end of the story as the Jewish leadership had hoped it would be. The empty tomb followed and demonstrated the divine vindication Jesus had anticipated for the Messiah. In fact, his response in answer to the high priest's question about being the Messiah was also a prediction of divine vindication that indicated his status with God. This vindication Jesus had announced to them. This claim led to Jesus's death. The resultant resurrection was something God had done to set things straight and to show who Jesus was. The proof was that God had brought Jesus to sit at his side. In this, God revealed Jesus to be more than a prophet and more than Messiah, at least as Messiah had been conceived of in Second Temple expectation. The synthesis showed Jesus to be Messiah, Servant, and exalted Son of Man in one unifying package that older revelation had set forth in distinct pieces. A look at the background helps us to see the cultural script Jesus invoked to reveal who he was at one of the most climactic moments in the Gospel of Mark.

FOR FURTHER READING

Additional Ancient Texts

Ezekiel the Tragedian (second-century BC) has a dream attributed to Moses where God invites him to sit with him on his throne (chs. 68–89). For various understandings of blasphemy, see Josephus, *Antiquities* 4.202; 13.293–95; Philo, *Moses* 2.38; and m. Sanhedrin 7:5. Jesus's Jewish trial scene is paralleled in Matthew 26:57–68 and Luke 22:66–71.

English Editions and Critical Texts

Isaac, E. "1 (Ethiopic Apocalypse of) Enoch: A New Translation and Introduction." Pages 5–89 in vol. 1 of *The Old Testament Pseudepigrapha*. Edited by James H. Charlesworth. Garden City, NY: Doubleday, 1983.

Knibb, Michael A. *The Ethiopic Book of Enoch*. 2 vols. Oxford: Clarendon, 1978.

Nickelsburg, George W. E., and James C. VanderKam. *1 Enoch: The Hermeneia Translation*. Minneapolis: Fortress, 2012.

Secondary Literature

Bock, Darrell L. *Blasphemy and Exaltation in Judaism and the Final Examination of Jesus*. WUNT 2/106. Tübingen: Mohr Siebeck, 1998; reprinted, Grand Rapids: Baker Academic, 2000.

Bock, Darrell L., and James H. Charlesworth, eds. *Parables of Enoch: A Paradigm Shift*. JCT 11. London: T&T Clark, 2013.

Collins, Adela Yarbro. "The Charge of Blasphemy in Mark 14.64." *JSNT* 26 (2004): 379–401.

Nickelsburg, George W. E., and James C. VanderKam, *1 Enoch 2: A Commentary on the Book of 1 Enoch, Chapters 37–82*. Hermeneia. Minneapolis: Fortress, 2012.

Van Oyen, Geert, and Tom Shepherd, eds. *The Trial and Death of Jesus: Essays on the Passion Narrative in Mark*. Leuven: Peeters, 2006.

CHAPTER 28

Philo of Alexandria and Mark 15:1–15a: Pontius Pilate, a Spineless Governor?

HELEN K. BOND

At the start of Mark 15, Jesus is transferred into Roman custody. Without any preamble, Pilate asks Jesus if he is "king of the Jews," presumably a Roman version of the Jewish title "Christ" (v. 2a). Jesus answers enigmatically, "You have said so," a guarded acceptance of the charge, but with the implication that he might have put things differently himself (v. 2b). Faced with a barrage of accusations from the Jewish priests, however, Jesus chooses to remain silent (and will not speak again now until he is on the cross).

When this first interrogation fails to come to any conclusion, the scene changes into a much more public gathering (vv. 6–15). A crowd appears, asking Pilate to honor his annual Passover custom of releasing a prisoner of their choosing (vv. 6–8). Pilate offers to release the "king of the Jews" (that is, Jesus), but the chief priests persuade the crowd to shout instead for Barabbas, a man who was in prison alongside those who had committed murder in a recent insurrection (vv. 9–11). When Pilate asks what he should do with Jesus (now referred to as "the one you call the king of the Jews"), the crowd demands that he be crucified (vv. 12–13). "Why? What crime has he committed?" Pilate asks, but the crowd continues to shout for crucifixion (v. 14). Wishing to please the assembled throng, Pilate sends Jesus to the cross (v. 15).

This passage raises many fascinating questions. On a basic level, why does Jesus need to go before Pilate at all? He has just been sentenced by a Jewish court (14:64), but now proceedings appear to start all over again before a Roman governor. Scholars usually assume that Jewish courts no longer possessed the power of capital jurisdiction and so were obliged to pass prisoners over to Rome. This may have been the case, though the evidence for the claim is much less certain than scholars often acknowledge.[1] Still, it remains curious that Mark gives no explanation for the handover.

On a historical level, there is no evidence for a regular Passover amnesty, and the idea that a Roman governor would allow a Passover crowd to demand the release of *any* prisoner does seem politically perilous.[2] Moreover, on a literary level there are intriguing parallels between the Jewish and Roman trial scenes as Mark presents them. In both, Jesus answers questions regarding his identity ("the Messiah, the son of the Blessed One" in 14:61; "king of the Jews" in 15:2), but remains silent in the face of other charges (14:61; 15:5). And in both Jesus is contrasted with another person: the cowardly Peter in the Jewish trial and the rebellious Barabbas before Rome. These contrasts allow the audience both to appreciate Jesus's courage in the face of extreme adversity, but also to understand that although Jesus is indeed a king, he will exercise his authority in a different way than the violent bandits and rebels who have been such a prominent feature of the Jewish nation's recent relations with Rome.

Perhaps one of the strangest features of our passage, however, is the character of Pontius Pilate. Mark introduces him abruptly as "Pilate," with no indication of his official title (15:1). Clearly his identity and role in the execution of Jesus were well known to the audience already. But what are we to make of Pilate's odd behavior in the central scene (15:6–15)? Is he really trying to secure Jesus's release? Does he not realize that his use of the term "king" seems only to inflame the situation? Or should we interpret him as a rather more shrewd operator? After all, he does in the end rid himself of a **messianic** claimant with the full approval of the people.

Luckily, a number of contemporary texts shed some light on the figure of Pilate and his ten-year governorship of Judea (roughly 26 to early 37 AD). One story from the time of Pilate is found in **Philo** of Alexandria's *Embassy to Gaius*. Not only does Philo describe an otherwise unknown incident, but he includes a detailed—and damning—character description of the Roman prefect.

---

1. For discussion, see Helen K. Bond, *Pontius Pilate in History and Interpretation*, SNTSMS 100 (Cambridge: Cambridge University Press, 1998), 15–16.
2. Again, see Bond, *Pontius Pilate*, 199–200.

Philo

"With All His Vindictiveness and Furious Temper, He Was in a Difficult Position"

Philo was a Jewish philosopher from the Egyptian city of Alexandria. His dates are roughly 20 BC–AD 50, making him an exact contemporary of Jesus. A member of the wealthy, highly educated elite, Philo had the leisure to devote himself to literary pursuits. His extensive writings include commentaries on the Jewish law and philosophical treatises; many of these show a preoccupation with **allegorical** readings, in which he sought to integrate the Scriptures with Hellenistic philosophy. Two of his works, however, treat historical themes. *Against Flaccus* and *Embassy to Gaius* are part of a longer book (the rest of which is now lost) that described events in Philo's home city. It is the *Embassy to Gaius* that contains a description of Pilate.

The *Embassy to Gaius* is an autobiographical account of Philo's involvement in a deputation of Alexandrian Jews to the emperor in AD 38/39.[3] The Jewish delegation went to Gaius (Caligula) to complain about the treatment of their own community by the Alexandrian Greeks. While in Rome, however, they learned some even more distressing news: the emperor was planning to set up a statue of himself in the Jerusalem Temple! The passage concerning Pilate occurs within a letter to the emperor, supposedly written by Agrippa, attempting to dissuade him from this course of action (§§276–329). It is quite possible that Agrippa did intervene in the affair in some way,[4] but the letter as we have it now is clearly the work of Philo himself: the language, style, and vocabulary match the rest of Philo's writings, and the letter's rhetoric fits perfectly with Philo's own.

The letter tells of an incident in the time of Tiberius, in which Pilate set up golden shields in his headquarters in Jerusalem (the *praetorium*).[5] Philo admits that they contained no image or anything else that was forbidden by the Jewish law, but they did contain this title for the emperor: *Tiberius Caesar, son of the divine Augustus.* When the crowds learned that Pilate had set up references to a pagan god (Augustus) within the holy city

---

3. The work itself was probably written soon after Claudius's succession in AD 41.

4. Agrippa was the grandson of Herod the Great, had grown up at the imperial court in Rome, and was on friendly terms with Caligula. He would go on to be king of Judea from AD 41–44.

5. It is difficult to date the incident, though some time around AD 31 would make good sense; see Bond, *Pontius Pilate*, 45–46.

of Jerusalem, they petitioned four Herodian princes to put their grievances before the "governor":

When he [Pilate], naturally inflexible, a blend of self-will and relentlessness, stubbornly refused they clamoured, "Do not arouse sedition, do not make war, do not destroy the peace; you do not honour the emperor by dishonouring ancient laws. Do not take Tiberius as your pretext for outraging the nation [Israel]; he does not wish any of our customs to be overthrown. If you say that he does, produce yourself an order or a letter or something of the kind so that we may cease to pester you and having chosen our envoys may petition our lord."

It was this final point which particularly exasperated him, for he feared that if they actually sent an embassy they would also expose the rest of his conduct as governor by stating in full the briberies, the insults, the robberies, the outrages and wanton injuries, the executions without trial constantly repeated, the ceaseless and supremely grievous cruelty. So with all his vindictiveness and furious temper, he was in a difficult position. He had not the courage to take down what had been dedicated nor did he wish to do anything which would please his subjects. At the same time he knew full well the constant policy of Tiberius in these matters.

The magnates saw this and understanding that he had repented of his action but did not wish to appear penitent sent letters of very earnest supplication to Tiberius. When he had read them through what language he used about Pilate, what threats he made! The violence of his anger, though he was not easily roused to anger, it is needless to describe since the facts speak for themselves. For at once without even postponing it to the morrow he wrote to Pilate with a host of reproaches and rebukes for his audacious violation of precedent and bade him at once take down the shields and have them transferred from the capital to Caesarea on the coast surnamed Augusta after your great-grandfather, to be set up in the temple of Augustus, and so they were. So both objects were safeguarded, the honour paid to the emperor and the policy observed from of old in dealing with the city. (§§301–5)[6]

---

6. Translation from Philo, *On the Embassy to Gaius (and General Indexes)*, trans. F. H. Colson, LCL (Cambridge: Harvard University Press, 1962).

Although broadly historical in nature, Philo's work evinces a strong theological outlook in which the enemies of Israel are the enemies of God. Through stereotypical characterization and strongly emotional language, Roman emperors and officials are judged according to their attitude toward Jews and their law. In this passage, Tiberius is a patron of the Jews, an upholder of Jewish rights and privileges, and so receives extravagant praise (as does Emperor Augustus elsewhere in the *Embassy to Gaius*). Pilate, however, shows no respect for the law and so is characterized with unrelenting negativity (as elsewhere are Gaius, other Roman officials, and the Alexandrian mob). Pilate's character perfectly conforms to the common picture of a Roman official bent on undermining the Jewish law. In fact, every single adjective used to describe him in the above account is elsewhere thrown at other "enemies" of the Jews.

What, then, are we to make of Philo's account of Pilate? On a purely historical level, it is clear that Pilate's "crime" was only a small one. The use of Tiberius's official title within the Roman headquarters in Jerusalem was hardly unexpected, and the building must have contained many other similar references to the emperor. If Pilate had set up the shields in order to honor Tiberius, his reluctance to remove them is understandable and may have had nothing to do with fear that a bad report of his administration might make its way to Rome. Within the rhetoric of the letter, however, the whole point of the story is to focus on a comparatively small issue in order to highlight Tiberius's virtuous concern to have it immediately rectified. Tiberius's behavior contrasts markedly with Gaius's planned desecration of the temple and provides a model for a truly noble emperor.

Mark 15:1–15

"WANTING TO SATISFY THE CROWD, PILATE RELEASED BARABBAS"

How does Philo help us to understand Mark's account of Jesus's trial before Pilate? Philo's account shows just how free ancient writers often were with their material. Although there is undoubtedly a historical event behind his story and we can still reconstruct it with some confidence, Philo's accounts of characters and conversations are heavily colored by his rhetorical concerns. His portrait of a pro-Jewish Tiberius, for example, is at odds with other contemporary sources that chart a growing animosity toward Jews in his reign, resulting in their expulsion from Rome in AD 19.

In a similar manner, Mark allows his own concerns to color the way he recounts Jesus's trial before Pilate, particularly in the way in which Pilate and the Jewish leadership are portrayed. By the time that Mark wrote his Gospel in the late first century, most converts to the new faith were from the Roman world. The fact that Jesus had been crucified by a Roman governor was a real problem: Did that mean Jesus was nothing better than a criminal, an outlaw against Rome? Mark's strategy (which is picked up and developed by the other evangelists) is to insist that Pilate was reluctant to send him to the cross, and to lay the "blame" for Jesus's crucifixion as forcefully as possible on the Jewish leaders.

Philo's account also offers a fascinating window onto the world of first-century diplomacy, with its face-to-face negotiations, concern for male honor, and subtle intimidation. In order to air their grievances, the people enlist the support of four Herodian princes, men of means and status, whose eminence and connections in Rome might sway the prefect. In the case of the shields, Pilate chooses to remain firm and allow the matter to be referred to the emperor rather than back down.

In the trial of Jesus, Mark similarly imagines that the first round of negotiations take place before elite males, this time between Pilate on one side and the high priest and his entourage on the other. However, when the people appear, the Markan Pilate is anxious to save face; he cannot too quickly accept their choice of prisoner, particularly as he knows they have been manipulated by the chief priests (Mark 15:11). Instead, he continues to push them with his questions until they themselves demand Jesus's execution. And Pilate is all too ready to capitulate: "Wanting to satisfy the crowd, Pilate released Barabbas to them. He had Jesus flogged, and handed him over to be crucified" (15:15).

Whatever the Markan Pilate thought of Jesus (and we are told only that he was amazed by him, 15:5), the crucifixion of a popular messianic leader with the full support of the people could only have been a welcome outcome in the court of a provincial governor. Thus Mark achieved his aim of pinning primary responsibility for Jesus's death on the Jewish leaders, while at the same time presenting a manipulative and self-serving prefect.

FOR FURTHER READING

Additional Ancient Texts

Josephus reports three incidents that occurred in the time of Pilate: a demonstration following his introduction of troops into Jerusalem with unlawful images of the emperor on their standards (*J.W.* 2.169–77); a riot that broke out in connection with the building of an aqueduct (*Ant.* 18.55–62); and his dismissal from the province by the legate of Syria after he brutally put down a movement connected with a Samaritan messiah (*Ant.* 18.85–89). An inscription found in Caesarea Maritima in 1961 gives his title as "prefect," a military title which reminds us that the province had only been under direct Roman rule for around twenty-five years by the time of the execution of Jesus (see Jerry Vardaman, "A New Inscription Which Mentions Pilate as 'Prefect,'" *JBL* 81 [1962]: 70–71).

English Translations and Critical Editions

Philo. Translated by F. H. Colson et al. 12 vols. LCL. Cambridge: Harvard University Press, 1929–62.

Secondary Literature

Bond, Helen K. *Pontius Pilate in History and Interpretation*. SNTSMS 100. Cambridge: Cambridge University Press, 1998.

Kamesar, Adam, ed. *The Cambridge Companion to Philo*. Cambridge: Cambridge University Press, 2009.

Smallwood, E. Mary. *Philonis Alexandrini Legatio ad Gaium: Edited with an Introduction, Translation and Commentary*. 2nd ed. Leiden: Brill, 1970.

Thatcher, Tom. "Philo on Pilate: Rhetoric or Reality?" *ResQ* 37 (1995): 215–18.

CHAPTER 29

11QTempleᵃ and Mark 15:15b–47: Burying the Crucified

CRAIG A. EVANS

After interrogating Jesus and hearing the clamor of the crowd, the Roman governor Pontius Pilate condemns Jesus to execution by crucifixion (Mark 15:15). A man assists Jesus in carrying his cross (v. 21). Jesus is crucified and mocked. He cries out to God and then dies (vv. 24–37). The centurion overseeing the crucifixion refers to Jesus as "Son of God" (v. 39). Joseph of Arimathea, a member of the Jewish council, arranges to have the body of Jesus placed in a rock-cut tomb (v. 46). Two women, Mary Magdalene and Mary the mother of Joseph, observe where Jesus is buried (v. 47).

These events have a significant function in Mark's narrative, serving to create suspense leading into the story's climax in chapter 16. Yet some scholars have questioned Mark's account of the crucifixion and burial of Jesus, claiming that in all probability Jesus was not buried, or if he was he was not buried in a tomb known to his followers. Accordingly, the Markan narrative of the burial of Jesus by Joseph of Arimathea and the discovery of the empty tomb early Sunday morning may well be unhistorical.

There is in fact little grounds for such skepticism, for there is a significant amount of relevant evidence that not only supports the Markan narrative but also clarifies a number of details. The evidence shows that Mark's account of the crucifixion and burial of Jesus closely corresponds with everything we know about capital punishment in Roman-controlled lands in late antiquity and with Jewish burial practices as well.

Numerous sources cast helpful light on Jesus's crucifixion and burial, as we will see below. A key piece of literary evidence is found in the so-called Temple Scroll. This scroll clarifies important aspects of the Markan narrative, especially the Jewish expectations of burying a crucified criminal.

11QTemple

"YOU MUST NOT LET THEIR BODIES REMAIN ON THE TREE OVERNIGHT"

The longest scroll recovered from **Qumran** is the Temple Scroll recovered from Cave 11, known as 11QTemple[a] (11Q19). 11QTemple[a], a text probably written sometime around 150 BC, is in a sense a rewriting of Deuteronomy. As such, it modifies some of the Old Testament precepts on the burial of criminals.

Burial of a Hung Body before Nightfall. According to Deuteronomy 21:22–23, "If someone guilty of a capital offense is put to death and their body is exposed on a pole, you must not leave the body hanging on the pole overnight. Be sure to bury it that same day, because anyone who is hung on a pole is under God's curse. You must not desecrate the land the LORD your God is giving you as an inheritance." This passage from Deuteronomy does not prescribe or assume a particular form of execution (such as stoning); it simply assumes that execution *precedes* hanging. The concern of the passage is that the corpse of the executed person be taken down and buried before nightfall. The corpse is not to remain hanging overnight.

Burial of a Crucified Man before Nightfall. This passage from Deuteronomy is paraphrased in 11QTemple[a] 64:7–13. The concern with burial before nightfall remains, but there is a significant alteration in sequence. The text reads as follows:

> [7] If a man is a traitor against his people and gives them up to a foreign nation, so doing evil to his people, [8] you are to hang him on a tree until dead. On the testimony of two or three witnesses [9] he will be put to death, and they themselves shall hang him on the tree. If a man is convicted of a capital crime and flees [10] to the nations, cursing his people and the children of Israel, you are to hang him, also, upon a tree [11] until dead. But you must not let their bodies remain on the tree overnight; you shall most certainly bury them that very day. Indeed, [12] anyone hung on a tree is accursed of God and men, but you are not to defile the land that I am [13] about to give you as an inheritance. (11QTemple[a] 64:7–13)[1]

---

1. Translation of all DSS in this essay are based on M. O. Wise, M. G. Abegg Jr., and E. M. Cook, *The Dead Sea Scrolls: A New Translation* (San Francisco: HarperCollins, 1996).

11QTemple[a] seems to reflect the realities of crucifixion, in which the victim, yet alive, is hung on the cross until he dies. 11QTemple[a] has reversed the sequence from death-then-hanging to hanging-then-death. When did this change take place?

The mid second-century BC 11QTemple[a] presupposes the change, which suggests that it had been in place for some time. The practice may have been adopted in the aftermath of Alexander's fourth-century BC conquest of the Middle East. Alexander the Great, who swept through Israel in the 330s BC, is said to have crucified thousands (cf. Curtius Rufus, *Hist. Alex.* 4.4.17). His successors, including the Jewish **Hasmonean** rulers, continued the practice. One horrifying example of crucifixion under Jewish rule was when Alexander Jannaeus (ruled 103–76 BC) exacted revenge against the **Pharisees**, who had plotted against him, by having eight hundred of these men crucified and their wives and children slaughtered "before the eyes of the still living wretches" (*Ant.* 13.380).[2] This gruesome event is alluded to in the **Dead Sea Scrolls**: "This refers to the Lion of Wrath [7] [. . . ven]geance against the Flattery-Seekers, because he used to hang men alive, [8] [as it was done] in Israel in former times, for to anyone hanging alive on the tree [Deut 21:23] . . ." (4Q169 frags. 3–4, col. i, lines 6–8; see also 4Q282i). Most interpreters agree that the "Lion of Wrath" is Alexander Jannaeus, while the "Flattery-Seekers" are the Pharisees, a group the men of Qumran despise.

11QTemple[a] has changed the sequence of death and hanging, but it retains the command to bury the corpse on the day of execution: "You are to hang him, also, upon a tree until dead. But you must not let their bodies remain on the tree overnight" (lines 10–11). This understanding of Deuteronomy 21:22–23 is witnessed in the time of Jesus and the early church in **Josephus**. He remarks that in peacetime all must be buried, even the crucified: "Even malefactors who have been sentenced to crucifixion are taken down and buried before sunset" (*J.W.* 4.317). Josephus states this for the benefit of his Roman readers, who may not have known about Jewish concerns that all be buried, even executed malefactors. His "taken down and buried before sunset" is an unmistakable reference to Deuteronomy 21:22–23. That the passage is alluded to in discussion of crucifixion clearly reflects the understanding of Deuteronomy that is attested in 11QTemple[a], that is, hanging preceding death. We can know therefore that the expectation of 11QTemple[a] concerning the burial of a crucified man by nightfall

---

2. Translations of Josephus are from H. St. J. Thackeray et al., *Josephus*, 13 vols., LCL (Cambridge: Harvard University Press, 1926–65).

was shared beyond the bounds of the Qumran community. All this literary evidence has significant implications for the plausibility of Mark's narrative.

Mark 15:15b–47

"As Evening Approached, Joseph of Arimathea . . . Asked for Jesus' Body"

Despite the skepticism of some, Jesus's scouring, crucifixion, and burial in Mark 15:15b–47 cohere quite closely with what is learned about Roman executions from ancient literature.

Jesus's Scourging and Crucifixion. In Mark 15:15, the evangelist reports that Pilate had Jesus scourged and then led away to be crucified. This was standard Roman practice: scourging, then crucifixion. Josephus, for example, reports that Governor Florus had a number of citizens of Jerusalem "first scourged and then crucified" (*J.W.* 2.306; cf. P.Flor. 61, line 59). Scourging, which resulted in severe injuries and blood loss, was the principal cause of death in execution by crucifixion. The scourge or whip was made up of leather straps, to which were attached sharp, abrasive items, such as nails. Scourging resulted in severe lacerations of the skin and damage to the underlying flesh. Josephus describes one man in the first century who was "flayed to the bone with scourges" (*J.W.* 6.304). The beating itself was not supposed to cause death, but it often did (Justinian, *Dig.* 48.19.8.3).

Crucifixion was probably the cruelest form of execution in antiquity (Cicero, *Verr.* 2.5.168; cf. Josephus, *J.W.* 7.203).[3] It was primarily reserved for murderous or rebellious slaves, its primary purpose being to deter rebellion and keep slaves in line. It is to deterrence that one Latin writer refers: "Whenever we crucify the condemned, the most crowded roads are chosen, where the most people can see and be moved by this terror. For penalties relate not so much to retribution as to their exemplary effect" (Ps.-Quintilian, *Decl.* 274).[4] This is the very reason given in Deuteronomy 21 for hanging the malefactor on the tree until sundown: "All Israel will hear of it and be afraid" (Deut 21:21).

After describing the mockery of Jesus (Mark 15:16–20a) the evangelist resumes his account of the crucifixion (15:20b–39). Like other criminals,

---

3. A few writers provide gruesome descriptions (Juvenal, *Sat.* 14.77–78; Suetonius, *Aug.* 13.1–2; Horace, *Ep.* 1.16.48; Seneca, *Dial.* 3.2.2; 6.20.3).

4. C. Ritter, ed., *Quintilian Declamationes Minores* (Leipzig: Teubner, 1884), 124; cited by M. Hengel, *Crucifixion* (Philadelphia: Fortress, 1977), 50.

Jesus is expected to carry his "cross," by which is meant the cross-beam or *patibulum*, to the place of crucifixion: "Every criminal who is executed carries his own cross on his back" (Plutarch, *Mor.* 554ʙ).[5] However, Jesus is so weakened from the scourging that his executioners "forced" a bystander to carry it (Mark 15:21). To force someone to assist was part of Roman law, a practice attested in inscriptions and papyri from late antiquity (*SEG* XXVI 1392; P.Lond. III 1171; *PSI* V 446).

Jesus is brought to a place called Golgotha, or "the place of the skull" (Mark 15:22). There he is offered "wine mixed with myrrh" (v. 23). This may have been part of the ongoing mockery, in that Jesus is offered spiced wine, something normally enjoyed by kings: "The finest wines in early days were spiced with scent of myrrh" (Pliny the Elder, *Nat.* 14.15 §92; cf. Luke 23:36–37).[6] Mark goes on to say that the soldiers who crucified Jesus divided his garments among themselves (Mark 15:24). This, too, is consistent with Roman practice: "A man legally condemned forfeited his estate" (Tacitus, *Ann.* 6.29; cf. Justinian, *Dig.* 48.20.1).[7]

Mark tells us that an inscription read, "The King of the Jews" (Mark 15:26). The *titulus* was usually inscribed on a shingle or placard. It might be placed around the neck of the victim, declaring his name and punishment, and might also be affixed to the upright cross: "[Caepio's father led the slave] through the center of the forum with an inscription that made known the reason why he was to be put to death, and then he crucified him" (Dio Cassius, *Roman History* 54.3.6–7; cf. Suetonius, *Cal.* 32.2).[8]

The inscription, "the King of the Jews," alludes to the grounds for punishment, namely, that Jesus had claimed to be the Jewish king. The language of this inscription is hardly confessional. Early Christians did not refer to Jesus as "the King of the Jews" but rather spoke of him as **Messiah** (or Christ), Son of God, Lord, and Savior. Nor was this the language of the Jewish people, who spoke of "this Messiah, this king of Israel" (as in Mark 15:32). "King of the Jews" is Roman, and the language may have originated when Rome installed Herod the Great (Josephus, *J.W.* 1.282–85; *Ant.* 15.409).

Jesus's Burial. After Jesus dies on the cross, Mark tells us that "as evening approached, Joseph of Arimathea . . . went boldly to Pilate and asked for

---

5. D. W. Chapman and E. J. Schnabel, *The Trial and Crucifixion of Jesus: Texts and Commentary*, WUNT 344 (Tübingen: Mohr Siebeck, 2015), 289.

6. H. Rackham, *Pliny: Natural History IV, Books XII–XVI*, LCL (London: Heinemann; Cambridge: Harvard University Press, 1945), 249.

7. J. Jackson, *Tacitus IV: Annals Books 4–6, 11–12*, LCL (Cambridge: Harvard University Press, 1937), 203.

8. Chapman and Schnabel, *Trial and Crucifixion of Jesus*, 297.

Jesus' body" (Mark 15:42–43). After learning from the centurion that Jesus had in fact already died, Pilate has Jesus's body given to Joseph (vv. 44–45), who then wraps the body in linen and places it in a tomb (v. 46). How plausible is it that Jesus's body would have been delivered to Joseph in the way Mark describes? The historical evidence suggests that this could very well have happened.

As we saw earlier in 11QTemple[a], the precept in Deuteronomy 21:22–23 not to leave the body of an executed man "hanging on the pole overnight" was applied by the Qumran community to the victims of crucifixion. The reader of the Temple Scroll, who is instructed "to hang him on a tree until dead," is further instructed "not [to] let their bodies remain on the tree overnight; you shall most certainly bury them that very day" (lines 8–11).

As observed earlier, the theoretical observance of this custom by the Dead Sea Scroll community is complemented by Josephus's testimony that such was both practiced by Jews and permitted by the Romans in first-century Palestine. What is important in what Josephus says is that during the time of Roman rule, which includes the time of Jesus's public activities and death, no one could be executed except by Roman authority (as underscored in John 18:31–32; cf. Josephus, *J.W.* 2.117). Therefore, those "malefactors who have been sentenced to crucifixion" have been crucified by Roman authority. Yet, continues Josephus, they "are taken down and buried before sunset" (*J.W.* 4.317). This clearly implies that Roman authority permitted burial of the crucified, which in Israel means burial before sundown.

Philo also testifies to Rome permitting crucified men to receive burial, at least on special occasions in Alexandria, Egypt:

I have known instances before now of men who had been crucified when this festival and holiday was at hand, being taken down and given up to their relations, in order to receive the honours of sepulture, and to enjoy such observances as are due to the dead; for it used to be considered, that even the dead ought to derive some enjoyment from the natal festival of a good emperor, and also that the sacred character of the festival ought to be regarded. (*Flacc.* 83)[9]

Philo, writing in response to a pogrom against the Jewish people in AD 38, then complains that Flaccus, the Roman governor of Egypt, "did not

---

9. Translations of Philo in this essay are from C. D. Yonge, *The Works of Philo Judaeus, the Contemporary of Josephus: Translated from the Greek* (London: H. G. Bohn, 1854–90).

order men who had already perished on crosses to be taken down" (*Flacc.* 84). Philo clearly believes that burial of the crucified men should take place, especially on occasions such as the one he mentions here, a holiday celebrating the Roman emperor's birthday. That Governor Flaccus refused this mercy is cited as evidence of his prejudice and cruelty against the Jewish people. Philo's expectation is evidence that Roman law in fact did not categorically disallow burial of the executed.

In fact, according to the *Digesta*, compiled in the early sixth century by Emperor Justinian, the executed were often buried (*Dig.* 48.24.1–3), though it was permitted only "when this has been requested and permission granted."[10] Josephus himself made this request of Titus, commander of the Roman army during the Jewish rebellion (AD 66–70), and it was granted (*Life* 420–21). And this is precisely what we see in Mark's account of the crucifixion and burial of Jesus. Joseph requests the body of Jesus from Pilate, who then grants permission for Jesus's burial "as evening approached" (Mark 15:42).

Mark's account of the crucifixion and burial of Jesus is concise and exhibits little, perhaps no embellishment. At every point we find verisimilitude, as his narrative closely matches what we know of first-century Jewish Palestine through written sources.

For Further Reading

Additional Ancient Texts

There are several texts from late antiquity that discuss or refer to crucifixion and burial. These include Justinian's *Digesta*, book 48, as well as a number of passages in Josephus (e.g., *Ant.* 13.371–81; 17.295) and in Greco-Roman authors (e.g., Plutarch, *Mor.* 554B; Dio Cassius, *Roman History* 54.3.6–7), of which some are discussed above. All the relevant texts are discussed in Chapman and Schnabel (see Secondary Literature below).

English Translations and Critical Editions

García Martínez, Florentino, and Eibert J. C. Tigchelaar, eds. *The Dead Sea Scrolls: Study Edition.* 2 vols. Leiden: Brill, 1997–98.

Wise, M. O. *A Critical Study of the Temple Scroll from Qumran Cave 11.* Studies in Ancient Oriental Civilization 49. Chicago: The Oriental Institute of the University of Chicago, 1990.

---

10. Translation from O. Robinson, "Book Forty-Eight," in *The Digest of Justinian*, ed. T. Mommsen, P. Krueger, and A. Watson, 4 vols. (Philadelphia: University of Pennsylvania Press, 1985; repr. 1998), 4:863.

Secondary Literature

Chapman, D. W., and E. J. Schnabel. *The Trial and Crucifixion of Jesus: Texts and Commentary*. WUNT 344. Tübingen: Mohr Siebeck, 2015.

Evans, C. A. "'He Laid Him in a Tomb' (Mark 15.46): Roman Law and the Burial of Jesus." Pages 52–66 in *Matthew and Mark across Perspectives: Essays in Honour of Stephen C. Barton and William R. Telford*. LNTS 538. Edited by K. A. Bendoraitis and N. Gupta. London: Bloomsbury T&T Clark, 2016.

———. *Jesus and the Ossuaries: What Jewish Burial Practices Reveal about the Beginning of Christianity*. Waco, TX: Baylor University Press, 2003.

Hachlili, R. *Jewish Funerary Customs, Practices, and Rites in the Second Temple Period*. JSJSup 94. Leiden: Brill, 2005.

CHAPTER 30

2 Maccabees and Mark 16:1–8: Resurrection as Hope for the Present

BEN C. BLACKWELL

As the account of Jesus's resurrection, Mark 16 stands as the climax of Mark's narration of "the good news about Jesus the **Messiah**, the Son of God" (1:1). Jesus's ministry proclaimed and demonstrated God's kingdom, and he foretold that his death and resurrection were central to his messianic identity as king (8:27–9:1; 9:31–37; 10:32–45; cf. 12:18–27). Now that Mark has narrated Jesus's trial and brutal crucifixion in chapter 15, he ends with Jesus's victory over death through resurrection. And yet, in Mark 16 Jesus himself does not make an appearance, and neither do his male disciples who have been with him throughout the narrative. Rather, it is his female disciples present at his crucifixion (15:40–41, 47) who receive from an angel the message of Jesus's resurrection from the dead. It is not that women have been absent from Mark's narrative, but they have played less prominent roles until this point. Even more odd is that the text appears to end quite abruptly: "Trembling and bewildered, the women went out and fled from the tomb. They said nothing to anyone, because they were afraid" (16:8). They eventually told others (cf. Matt 28:8; Luke 24:9), but how do we make sense of this juxtaposition of the victorious climax in Jesus's resurrection and the abrupt ending marked by continued fear?

If a reader is looking at his or her Bible, they may be wondering why the ending is so abrupt. Doesn't Mark run to 16:20, not just to 16:8? In 16:9–20 Jesus does appear, the women do tell their story, and Jesus commands the disciples to preach and live out the gospel of the kingdom. All of that seems to be an ending we would expect, and it is much more like the endings of Matthew and Luke. So why are there two separate endings to Mark's Gospel?

The reason has to do with the fact that we do not have the original manuscripts penned by the NT authors, just hand-written copies that were made in the subsequent centuries. Most modern translations show two different endings, one short (only 16:8) and one long (16:9–20), because each appears in some of these ancient copies. The earliest and most reliable copies, however, do not have 16:9–20, and the longer ending has some stylistic differences that point to it being from a different hand. The shorter ending of Mark, therefore, is probably original. While it may be disconcerting to some that verses have been "added" to the Bible, this actually shows the reliability that we can achieve through the process of textual criticism (the science of analyzing manuscripts to determine what is most likely the original).[1] Because our text-critical methods so clearly show in this instance what is original and what is an addition, we can be quite confident of the text we have received.

If this is the case, it still leaves us with the odd combination of Jesus's victorious resurrection and the fearful women. It helps if we consider Mark's account of Jesus's foretelling of his death and resurrection (8:27–9:1; 9:31–37; 10:32–45). In each one of those passion predictions, Jesus explains his messianic identity in **eschatological** terms: he will suffer but later will be raised. Each time the disciples fail to understand this path of suffering (seeking rather the path of power), and so Jesus explains how true discipleship will involve their following him in suffering. This is *eschatological* suffering because they will be vindicated in the end, just as Jesus is. Therefore, they should live differently now, rejecting the values of this current age in light of the life of the age to come. These eschatological values are similarly expressed in other Second Temple Jewish texts, particularly those that focus on resurrection. Perhaps the most well-known among these is 2 Maccabees 7, which we will examine below.

2 Maccabees

"THE KING OF THE UNIVERSE WILL RAISE US UP TO LIVE AGAIN FOREVER"

Oppression and Eschatological Restoration. From the time of the Babylonian exile through to the end of the Second Temple period, various gentile groups

---

1. Cf. Bruce M. Metzger and Bart D. Ehrman, *The Text of the New Testament: Its Transmission, Corruption, and Restoration,* 4th ed. (Oxford: Oxford University Press, 2005).

controlled Palestine. Many Second Temple texts therefore focus on Jewish attempts to remain faithful to the **covenant** in the midst of gentile influence. At times this negative influence was more passive, as societal pressures encouraged many Jews to assimilate to foreign ways of life. But at other times, the pressure was quite active and oppressive, particularly when sponsored by ruling authorities.

One such time of intense oppression by the ruling Greek leadership is recounted in the Maccabean literature. These texts recount how **Antiochus IV (Epiphanes)** went to great lengths to force covenant-observant Jews into **Hellenistic** assimilation and how there arose Jewish opposition to the oppression of this **Seleucid** monarch. Like much of the literature during this time, questions of justice abound: How will God's justice prevail when injustice at the hands of pagan rulers seems so prevalent? As with the OT material addressing these same questions (especially the prophets, like Daniel), there was an expectation that God would return and redeem his covenant people, bringing restoration to the land of Israel. This expectation that God would restore justice and peace is bound up with what we call eschatology: things are broken now, but God will act to fix them in the future. In the OT, this eschatological restoration was mostly focused on the broader community, but in the **Second Temple period** an additional focus on individual restoration in the afterlife became more widespread—though some, namely the **Sadducees**, rejected this idea.[2]

Resurrection as Individual Restoration. Although variations existed, individual restoration during the Second Temple period came to focus on postmortem immortality (life after death), especially when death came at the hands of oppressive enemies. Building primarily from a couple of OT texts that contain resurrection imagery (Ezekiel 37; Daniel 12:1–3), Jewish communities developed distinct beliefs about postmortem immortality, such as immortality through communal commemoration, immortality through the eternal bliss of the soul, and immortality through the resurrection of the body. In some texts that speak of ontological immortality (that which is based in reality, not just in memory), it is unclear whether the afterlife in view relates to the soul alone or to the soul and body together.[3] (While some use the term "resurrection" ambiguously, usually it is reserved for the raising of the soul together *with the body*.) The main purpose of this individual

---

2. See the discussion of the Sadducees by Jason Maston in chapter 22.

3. Not all Jews would even speak of a soul as distinct from the body, so I am using heuristic language to help capture some basic positions.

eschatology relates to ethics: if I know that I will have a blessed afterlife later, then I can and should live in obedience and sacrifice now.

Eschatology and Ethics. We see this exact relationship between eschatology and ethics at play in 2 Maccabees. Second Maccabees is found in the **Apocrypha** and dates to about 125–100 BC. Rather than a sequel to 1 Maccabees (originally written in Hebrew), 2 Maccabees (originally written in Greek) recounts similar events to 1 Maccabees 1–7 and is based on a non-extant five-volume work by Jason of Cyrene (cf. 2 Macc 2:23–28).

As it recounts Jewish rejection of pagan oppression, 2 Maccabees 7 shows how the hope of resurrection motivates a Jewish family to endure extreme torture and eventual martyrdom rather than forsake God's covenant stipulations for Israel. The account begins:

> ¹ It also happened that seven brothers with their mother were arrested and tortured with whips and scourges by the king to force them to eat pork in violation of God's law. . . . ⁵ [And] the brothers and their mother encouraged one another to die nobly. (2 Macc 7:1, 5 NAB)

One by one the brothers, and then the mother, are put to death. Before they are martyred, however, most of the family members explain their willingness to remain faithful to God in the midst of their suffering. For example, regarding the second brother the text reads:

> With his last breath he said: "You accursed fiend, you are depriving us of this present life, but the King of the universe will raise us up to live again forever, because we are dying for his laws." (7:9 NAB)

The mother is especially encouraging, giving her final living son a wider view of creation and eschatology:

> Therefore, since it is the Creator of the universe who shaped the beginning of humankind and brought about the origin of everything, he, in his mercy, will give you back both breath and life, because you now disregard yourselves for the sake of his law. (7:23 NAB)

Based on her encouragement, the final son also commits to obey Moses over the king and explains:

³² We, indeed, are suffering because of our sins. ³³ Though for a little while our living Lord has been angry, correcting and chastising us, he will again be reconciled with his servants. ³⁴ But you, wretch, most vile of mortals, do not, in your insolence, buoy yourself up with unfounded hopes, as you raise your hand against the children of heaven. ³⁵ You have not yet escaped the judgment of the almighty and all-seeing God. ³⁶ Our brothers, after enduring brief pain, have drunk of never-failing life, under God's covenant. But you, by the judgment of God, shall receive just punishments for your arrogance. ³⁷ Like my brothers, I offer up my body and my life for our ancestral laws, imploring God to show mercy soon to our nation, and by afflictions and blows to make you confess that he alone is God. (7:33–37 NAB)

In each of these statements, the family member testifies to how "the almighty and all-seeing God," "the King" and "Creator of the universe," will resurrect their physical bodies from the dead. God will "raise [them] up to live again forever," "give [them] back both breath and life," and allow them to "[drink] of never-failing life."

The family did not claim to be sinless, but nevertheless their righteousness and faithfulness were the basis of their hope for future resurrection. At the same time, this *eschatological* hope provides the motivation for their *ethical* steadfastness: because of their postmortem beliefs, they can and will remain faithful, not only in times of most horrific torture and martyrdom but also in the midst of their daily challenges to assimilate to pagan values. This eschatological ethic similarly undergirds Mark's narrative about Jesus and his disciples.

Mark 16:1–8

"HE HAS RISEN! HE IS NOT HERE"

Resurrection and Restoration. Jesus's bodily resurrection is central to Mark's narrative, yet it takes the women by surprise. The young man dressed in white (an angel) tells them that "He has risen! He is not here. See the place where they laid him" (Mark 16:6). Since the tomb is empty, this gives a clear indication of Jesus's postmortem immortality. Jesus is not just perpetually remembered in the community, nor is his soul merely experiencing eternal bliss. Rather, the focus here is on his body: his crucified body has been raised from the dead; he has been resurrected, just as he had predicted (8:31; 9:9, 31; 10:34; 14:28).

Though 2 Maccabees and Mark introduce the notion of resurrection, the great difference between these two accounts is that in Mark resurrection has already occurred. Most Jews anticipated a general resurrection in the eschatological future (and this is evidenced in other NT texts), but Jesus has broken the mold by being resurrected prior to this. Moreover, he was resurrected individually and not with the community of the righteous. While only Jesus has been raised to immortality, his resurrection gives eschatological hope to his followers and is thus the climax of his preaching of the good news of the kingdom of God (cf. 1:15). His healings and exorcisms point to God's deliverance of the world from the power of death and the agents of Satan, and his resurrection demonstrates the reality of that hope as an embodiment of the kingdom. This is surely good news for his disciples as they search for him at the tomb.

The Absence of Jesus. And yet his disciples appear to have little faith.[4] The apostles are nowhere in sight, and the women who are present are "alarmed" by the angel (Mark 16:5), so they flee from the tomb "trembling and bewildered" (16:8). In fact, the whole narrative ends with them too "afraid" to say anything to anyone. Encountering an angel is surely a fantastic scene; they of course would have never seen any CGI movies. Why does Mark end the narrative this way?

Richard Hays argues that Mark is attempting to draw the reader into the narrative as real-life participants of God's theological drama. Just as Jesus is absent from the scene in Mark 16, so he is seemingly offstage today. Yet, as Hays writes, "The community of Jesus's followers is called to live out their vocation of suffering discipleship without the immediate presence of the Lord."[5] In other words, the pending return of Jesus does not exempt believers from living faithful and cruciform lives in the present. This is especially so in light of Jesus's resurrection.

How, then, will we as readers respond to this message of the risen but departed Jesus? Will we go through life "trembling and bewildered" (16:8) whenever challenges present themselves, or will we answer our call not to be "alarmed" (16:6) as we faithfully bear witness to "the good news about Jesus the Messiah, the Son of God" (1:1)? The Maccabean martyrs had the

---

4. Faith is a key discipleship theme throughout Mark. See the discussion by Jeanette Hagen Pifer in chapter 14.

5. Richard B. Hays, *The Moral Vision of the New Testament: A Contemporary Introduction to New Testament Ethics* (New York: HarperOne, 1996), 88.

hope of resurrection, but this hope is even more assured for those who follow the already-risen Christ. With the onset of Jesus's resurrection, ancient and modern disciples alike can follow him in faith rather than in fear. They are to embody an eschatological ethic, living differently now in light of their future hope assured by Jesus's resurrection.

For Further Reading

Additional Ancient Texts

For other Jewish texts discussing resurrection and the afterlife, see 1QS 11.5–8; 4Q385; 4Q386; 1QHᵃ 19.13–17; 2 Baruch 49–51; Jubilees 23.31; Wisdom of Solomon 1–3; and Josephus (*Ag. Ap.* 2.217–18; *J.W.* 2.163–65; *Ant.* 18.14–16). Fourth Maccabees 8:3–13:1 recounts the experience of the seven brothers but removes all references to resurrection. Other texts discuss the hope of glory: Targum Pseudo-Jonathan Genesis 2:25; 3:7; 4 Ezra 7:116–31; 2 Baruch 15.1–19.8; 54.13–21; 1QS 4.22–23; CD 3.19–20; 1QHᵃ 4.14–15. Key NT texts include Matthew 28; Luke 24; John 20; Acts 23:6–8; 1 Corinthians 15; 1 Thessalonians 4–5; and Revelation 2–3, 20–22.

English Translations and Critical Editions

NAB

NETS

NRSV

Hanhart R. *Maccabaeorum Liber II*. Septuaginta 9.2. Göttingen: Vandenhoeck & Ruprecht, 1976.

Secondary Literature

Avery-Peck, Alan J., and Jacob Neusner, eds. *Death, Life-after-Death, Resurrection and the World-to-Come in the Judaisms of Antiquity*. SJLA 4. Leiden: Brill, 2000.

Chester, Andrew. "Resurrection and Transformation." Pages 47–77 in *Auferstehung-Resurrection*. Edited by Friedrich Avemarie and Hermann Lichtenberger. WUNT 135. Tübingen: Mohr Siebeck, 2001.

Doran, Robert. *2 Maccabees: A Critical Commentary*. Hermeneia. Minneapolis: Fortress, 2012.

Elledge, C. D. *Resurrection of the Dead in Early Judaism, 200 BCE–CE 200*. Oxford: Oxford University Press, 2017.

Levenson, Jon D. *Resurrection and the Restoration of Israel: The Ultimate Victory of the God of Life*. New Haven: Yale University Press, 2006.

Nickelsburg, George W. E. *Resurrection, Immortality, and Eternal Life in Inter-testamental Judaism and Early Christianity*. 2nd ed. HTS 56. Cambridge: Harvard University Press, 2006.

Schwartz, Daniel R. *2 Maccabees*. CEJL. Berlin: de Gruyter, 2008.

Wright, N. T. *The Resurrection of the Son of God*. Minneapolis: Fortress, 2003.

Glossary[1]

allegory, allegorical: An interpretive method that goes beyond the literal meaning of a text by highlighting connections to other ideas or events.

ancient Near East, ANE: The phrase describes the peoples who lived in Egypt, Palestine, Syria, Mesopotamia, Persia, and Arabia from the beginning of recorded history up until the conquest of Alexander the Great, though some also informally use this to refer all the way up to the first-century AD.

Antiochus IV Epiphanes: Lived ca. 215–164 BC. A ruler of the Seleucid Kingdom, the Hellenistic state in Syria partitioned from Alexander the Great's vast empire. Antiochus provoked the Maccabean conflict by trying to Hellenize Jews.

apocalyptic, apocalyptic tradition: An apocalypse is literally a "revelation" of previously hidden things. These terms are normally associated with the revelation of God and of heavenly realities through visions and dreams, including the revelation of divine actions that will establish God's (future) rule among his covenant people and the whole world. Thus, there is often focus on spatial (heaven/earth) and temporal (present/future) dualisms.

Apocrypha, apocryphal: Also known as the deuterocanonical books. A collection of Jewish texts written after the OT period that are included in the Septuagint. These were considered authoritative by patristic Christians and therefore accepted by Roman Catholic and Orthodox Christians as canonical, but they are rejected by Protestants as Scripture. In nonacademic settings, "apocryphal" is often used as a description of stories that sound true but are not.

canonical: Texts are considered canonical when they are included in a collection of texts considered to be inspired and authoritative Scripture. The OT and NT are indisputably part of the Christian canon, whereas different Christian traditions dispute the inclusion of the Apocrypha. See Apocrypha.

---

1. Some definitions are adapted from Mark L. Strauss, *Four Portraits, One Jesus: A Survey of Jesus and the Gospels* (Grand Rapids: Zondervan, 2007).

Christology, christological: This term describes the person and work of Jesus in general. Specifically, the term relates to Jesus's role as the Christ. "Christ" (*christos*) is Greek for "anointed one," and it often served as the direct translation of the Hebrew term for "messiah." See Messiah.

covenant, covenantal: An agreement between two parties that places obligations on each party. Important covenants in the Bible include the Abrahamic covenant (Gen 15; 17), the Mosaic covenant (Exodus; Leviticus; Deuteronomy), the Davidic covenant (2 Sam 7), and the New covenant (Jer 31:31–34; Ezek 34–37).

Dead Sea Scrolls: An ancient library discovered in caves near the Dead Sea in 1947 and likely associated with the first-century Jewish community at Qumran. (Strauss, p.528). The scrolls include copies of biblical and other Jewish literature, as well as sectarian texts arising from the Qumran community. See sectarian.

deuterocanonical: See Apocrypha.

eschaton: The final state after God brings resolution to history.

Essenes: One of the Jewish sects referred to by Josephus and Philo. Many scholars associate this group with the Qumran community and those responsible for authoring the Dead Sea Scrolls.

Hasmoneans, Hasmonean Period: The Jewish family who ruled a semi-autonomous and later fully autonomous kingdom as the Jews secured independence from the Seleucids (167–63 BC). As a result of infighting among the family, the Jews lost their independence to the Romans in 63 BC. See Maccabean Revolt, Seleucids.

Hellenism, Hellenize, Hellenization: The spread and influence of Greek language and culture in the ancient world, particularly after the military conquest of Alexander the Great (ca. 333 BC).

Herodians: A group who supported the Herodian dynasty begun by Herod the Great and continued through his sons. They are mentioned three times in the New Testament: Matthew 22:16; Mark 3:6; 12:13.

intercalation: A "sandwiching" technique whereby one episode is inserted ("intercalated") into the middle of another. Examples in Mark include Jesus's conflict with scribes and his family (3:20–35), as well as Herod's beheading John the Baptist within the context of the disciples' mission (6:6b–31).

Josephus: A Jewish Pharisee and military leader who lived AD 37–ca. 100, Josephus was taken captive during the Jerusalem War against Rome and eventually made a Roman citizen and dependent of Emperor Vespasian. His four extant works are important for our understanding of the history and culture of Second Temple Judaism. They include a history of the Jewish people (*Antiquities of the Jews*), an account of the Jerusalem War (*Jewish War*), a work in defense of Judaism and the Jewish way of life (*Against Apion*), and an autobiography (*Life*).

LXX: An abbreviation for the Septuagint. See Septuagint.

Maccabean Revolt (or Crisis/Conflict): The Jewish rebellion against Seleucid rule in 175–164 BC. The conflict is titled after "the Maccabees" (Hebrew for "hammer"), which was a name given to Judas and his brothers who led Israel during this period.

Messiah, messianic: A transliteration of a Hebrew word meaning "anointed one" and which is translated into Greek as *christos* ("Christ"). There was no single Jewish view about the Messiah, though most views envision this person as God's agent who will deliver his people.

parable: A short fictional story or vignette illustrating a moral or spiritual lesson.

pericope: A short, self-contained Gospel episode such as a miracle story, a parable, or a pronouncement story, which may have originally circulated as an independent unit of oral tradition.

Pharisees: One of the Jewish sects mentioned by Josephus and throughout the Gospels. They were widely known for their skill in interpreting the law.

Philo: A diaspora Jew influenced by Platonism from Alexandria, Egypt (ca. 20 BC–AD 50). He authored numerous philosophical treatises and exegetical studies on the Pentateuch.

Pseudepigrapha, pseudepigraphic: Literally, "falsely ascribed writings." A pseudepigraphic text is a text written under the name of another person, often one who lived centuries earlier. The Pseudepigrapha specifically refers to Jewish pseudepigraphic texts not included in the Apocrypha, but since this was a common practice for Second Temple Jews, the term pseudepigrapha has generally become a catchall for all Jewish texts not included in another specific category, such as the Apocrypha or Dead Sea Scrolls, or authored by specific writers, like Josephus and Philo.

Qumran: A site located near the Dead Sea and the caves in which the Dead Sea Scrolls were found. The common view is that the community who lived there during the Second Temple Period were Essenes and were responsible for producing the Dead Sea Scrolls.

Sadducees: One of the leading Jewish sects of the Second Temple Period. They were formed mostly of the priestly leadership and elite.

Second Temple Period, Second Temple Judaism: The period in Jewish history that begins roughly from the return from exile (about 516 BC) until the destruction of the temple by the Romans in AD 70. Other phrases used for all or part of this time period include early Judaism, middle Judaism, and the intertestamental period.

Seleucids, Seleucid Kingdom: A kingdom in the region of Syria that was formed after Alexander the Great's kingdom was subdivided after his death and which lasted from 312–115 BC. Judea was eventually ruled by the Seleucids, who attempted to force the Jews to assimilate to Hellenism. See Hellenism; Maccabean Revolt.

sectarian: That which pertains to a particular religious group, notably the texts composed by and for the Dead Sea Scroll community. See Dead Sea Scrolls.

Septuagint (LXX): A collection of authoritative Jewish texts in Greek that includes the Greek translation of the Hebrew Bible as well as other Jewish writings. The abbreviation LXX is the Roman numeral for 70 and is based on the tradition that 70 (or 72) Jewish men translated the Hebrew Pentateuch into Greek.

Zealots, zeal: Jews during the Second Temple Period who sought freedom through military means to free Judea from foreign domination. They were not only looking for political independence but also Torah purity not attainable with a pagan presence in the land.

Contributors

Jeffrey W. Aernie (PhD, University of Aberdeen) is lecturer in New Testament studies at United Theological College, Charles Sturt University, Australia.

Holly Beers (PhD, London School of Theology) is assistant professor of religious studies at Westmont College.

Kristian A. Bendoraitis (PhD, University of Durham) is adjunct lecturer at Spring Arbor University.

Michael F. Bird (PhD, University of Queensland) is lecturer in theology at Ridley College, Australia.

Ben C. Blackwell (PhD, University of Durham) is associate professor of early Christianity at Houston Baptist University.

Darrell L. Bock (PhD, University of Aberdeen) is executive director of cultural engagement and senior research professor of New Testament studies at Dallas Theological Seminary.

Helen K. Bond (PhD, University of Durham) is professor of Christian origins at the University of Edinburgh.

Craig A. Evans (PhD, Claremont Graduate University) is the John Bisagno Distinguished Professor of Christian Origins at Houston Baptist University.

David E. Garland (PhD, Southern Baptist Theological Seminary) is professor of Christian Scriptures at George W. Truett Theological Seminary.

Timothy Gombis (PhD, University of St. Andrews) is professor of New Testament at Grand Rapids Theological Seminary.

John K. Goodrich (PhD, University of Durham) is associate professor of Bible at Moody Bible Institute.

Sigurd Grindheim (PhD, Trinity Evangelical Divinity School) is professor of New Testament at Fjellhaug International University College, Oslo, Norway.

Nijay K. Gupta (PhD, University of Durham) is associate professor of New Testament at Portland Seminary.

Jeanette Hagen Pifer (PhD, University of Durham) is assistant professor of biblical and theological studies at Talbot School of Theology, Biola University.

Suzanne Watts Henderson (PhD, Duke University) is associate professor of religion at Queens University of Charlotte.

David Instone-Brewer (PhD, University of Cambridge) is senior research fellow in rabbinics and the New Testament at Tyndale House, Cambridge.

Kelly R. Iverson (PhD, The Catholic University of America) is associate professor of religion at Baylor University.

Morten Hørning Jensen (PhD, University of Aarhus) is associate professor of New Testament at the Lutheran School of Theology in Aarhus, Denmark, adjunct professor at MF Norwegian School of Theology, Oslo, and research fellow at the University of South Africa.

Mary Marshall (DPhil, University of Oxford) is departmental lecturer in New Testament studies at the University of Oxford, and fellow and tutor in theology at St. Benet's College.

Jason Maston (PhD, University of Durham) is assistant professor of theology at Houston Baptist University.

Mark D. Mathews (PhD, University of Durham) is senior pastor of Bethany Presbyterian Church, Oxford, Pennsylvania.

Amy Peeler (PhD, Princeton Theological Seminary) is associate professor of New Testament at Wheaton College.

Jonathan T. Pennington (PhD, University of St. Andrews) is associate professor of New Testament interpretation at Southern Baptist Theological Seminary.

Nicholas Perrin (PhD, Marquette University) is Franklin S. Dyrness Professor of Biblical Studies and dean of the graduate school at Wheaton College.

Elizabeth E. Shively (PhD, Emory University) is lecturer in New Testament studies at the University of St. Andrews.

Klyne Snodgrass (PhD, University of St. Andrews) is Paul W. Brandel Chair of New Testament Studies at North Park Theological Seminary.

Mark L. Strauss (PhD, University of Aberdeen) is university professor of New Testament at Bethel Seminary, San Diego.

David L. Turner (PhD, Hebrew Union College) is professor of New Testament at Grand Rapids Theological Seminary.

Rikk Watts (PhD, University of Cambridge) is dean of theology at Alphacrucis College, Australia, and research professor of New Testament at Regent College, Vancouver.

Sarah Whittle (PhD, University of Manchester) is postgraduate support advisor at the University of St. Andrews, and research fellow in biblical studies at Nazarene Theological College, Manchester.

Passage Index

New Testament
Matthew

Author Index

Reading Romans in Context

Paul and Second Temple Judaism

Ben C. Blackwell, John K. Goodrich &
Jason Maston, Editors

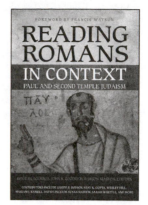

Readers of Paul today are more than ever aware
of the importance of interpreting Paul's letters
in their Jewish context. In *Reading Romans in
Context* a team of Pauline scholars go beyond
a general introduction that surveys historical events and theological
themes and explore Paul's letter to the Romans in light of Second Temple
Jewish literature.

In this nontechnical collection of short essays, beginning and intermediate students are given a chance to see firsthand what makes Paul
a distinctive thinker in relation to his Jewish contemporaries. Following
the narrative progression of Romans, each chapter pairs a major unit of
the letter with one or more sections of a thematically related Jewish
text, introduces and explores the theological nuances of the comparative text, and shows how these ideas illuminate our understanding of the
book of Romans.

Available in stores and online!

ZONDERVAN®
.com